Günter Hefler

Taking Steps

Studies in Lifelong Learning

edited by

Wolfgang Jütte, Jörg Markowitsch
and Ada Pellert

Volume 5

The books of this series enrich both the empirical and conceptual-theoretical discussions around lifelong learning and the reorganisation of learning in different life stages. In a time of strong social change, this series contributes insights from research and scholarly debates on important social conditions and developments.

LIT

Günter Hefler

TAKING STEPS

Formal Adult Education in Private and Organisational Life

LIT

Gefördert durch die Europäische Kommission
im Rahmen des 6. Forschungsrahmenprogramms

Eine Vorfassung wurde an der Universität Klagenfurt
als Dissertation angenommen.

∞

Gedruckt auf alterungsbeständigem Werkdruckpapier entsprechend
ANSI Z3948 DIN ISO 9706

Bibliographic information published by the Deutsche Nationalbibliothek
The Deutsche Nationalbibliothek lists this publication in the Deutsche Nationalbibliografie; detailed bibliographic data are available in the Internet at http://dnb.d-nb.de.

ISBN 978-3-643-90096-8
Zugl.: Klagenfurt, Univ., Diss., 2012

A catalogue record for this book is available from the British Library

Klosbachstr. 107
CH-8032 Zürich
Tel. +41 (0) 44-251 75 05
Fax +41 (0) 44-251 75 06
E-Mail: zuerich@lit-verlag.ch
http://www.lit-verlag.ch

LIT VERLAG Dr. W. Hopf
Berlin 2013
Fresnostr. 2
D-48159 Münster
Tel. +49 (0) 2 51-62 03 20
Fax +49 (0) 2 51-23 19 72
E-Mail: lit@lit-verlag.de
http://www.lit-verlag.de

Distribution:
In Germany: LIT Verlag Fresnostr. 2, D-48159 Münster
Tel. +49 (0) 2 51-620 32 22, Fax +49 (0) 2 51-922 60 99, E-mail: vertrieb@lit-verlag.de
In Austria: Medienlogistik Pichler-ÖBZ, e-mail: mlo@medien-logistik.at
In Switzerland: B + M Buch- und Medienvertrieb, e-mail: order@buch-medien.ch
In the UK: Global Book Marketing, e-mail: mo@centralbooks.com
In North America: International Specialized Book Services, e-mail: orders@isbs.com

Dedication

To my parents, who fell in love while
attending Vienna's oldest evening school,
and to my family: Jakob, Karin and Susie.

Content

Diagrams & Overviews

1. Introduction

1.1 How this study has come into life

What does formal adult education actually mean? I haphazardly came to this question when I started in 2005 – as one of more than 80 researchers – to work on a large-scale, European comparative research project. Revealing the significance, social reality and meaning of formal adult education in a comparative way was the aim of the project 'Lifelong Learning 2010: Towards a Lifelong Learning Society in Europe: The contribution of the education system', funded by the European Commission within the Sixth Framework Programme and bringing together research teams of thirteen European societies.[1] For me and other researchers involved in the partnership, the focus on formal adult education came somewhat as surprise. Why should we focus on what we expected to be a small aspect of lifelong learning? The partnership had applied for a project on lifelong learning in Europe. However, during the contract negotiations, the European Commission asked us to focus 'only' on *formal* adult education and to concentrate on the questions: *What are the contributions of formal education to lifelong learning and the achievement of the Lisbon Goals?* By sharpening the focus of the multilevel project, its aims became more demanding not less: nobody in the partnership was fully aware of the implications of shifting to a comparably small, yet, widely unexplored research topic. The partnership needed most of the project's lifetime to compensate for the surprising consequences of this shift. The foundation of the project was assumed to be competing, yet similar reasonable understandings of formal adult education. The team members needed a surprisingly long time to figure out what other researchers actually have in mind when thinking about formal adult education. Although the partnership managed quickly to establish some shared definitions, most of the researchers were very unsatisfied with the compromises and found it difficult to make its consequences explicit for their own work and for the work of the whole project. I will quickly describe the two main camps and, for the sake of clarity, over-exaggerate their conflicting views.

---

1 For details on the project, refer to Annex 8.1.

Opposing meanings of formal adult education

One camp takes 'formal' as the composite of 'informal': 'formal' learning or education stands for any 'taught course', while informal learning refers to learning outside a classroom. The education system comes in twice: firstly, initial education provides the foundations for any continuing, post-compulsory education. Secondly, although educational organisations vary widely, schools and universities rank high among the providers of 'courses'. Higher education for adults that offers degree and non-degree courses forms a particular topic in its own right; this should not be unconditionally subsumed to formal adult education. Formal adult education does not need a complex definition, because the components of the concept – 'taught courses' and 'adults' – seem self-explanatory or a matter of somewhat arbitrary specifications – as when defining adult as 'being 25 or older'. Some programmes lead straightforwardly to particular qualifications, others not. Many 'taught courses', at least, issue a certificate, which participants could use for gaining credit-based qualifications. Therefore, in one way or another, 'taught course' and qualification will likely be linked, but this provides no reasonable basis for clearly distinguishing between types of adult education. This understanding of 'formal' education of adults dominates the English-language, research literature on adult education and training, no matter if prepared by native or second-language speakers. Finally, it resonates well with the most frequent use of 'formal' education in various societies. Adherents of this camp think that any other, more complex, understanding of 'formal adult education' is at best somewhat artificial, at worst somewhat 'imperialistic'. In any case, they do not consider 'formal' adult education as a coherent subject of research, because by definition it consists of uncountable variants of 'taught courses' in adult education.

The opposing camp distinguishes 'taught courses' into 'formal' and 'nonformal' varieties. 'Formal' refers to courses provided under public authority and leading to officially recognised qualifications and consequently to a particular part of the education system – open to or reserved for adults. However, 'nonformal' refers to the courses offered within liberal adult education, the educational work of churches, political parties, trade unions or other social movements and – as a world of its own – corporate training. 'Formal' covers a bundle of divergent, yet, identifiable educational activities, regulated by law in one way or other, so that an exhaustive list could possibly identify what is 'formal' education – everything else is not. 'Adult' refers partly to established definitions for beneficiaries of particular programmes. In other cases, 'adult' merely signifies participating after the most typical age for attendance or someone who left school and returns later. By definition, any 'formal' adult education leads to a particular qualification. Thus, 'formal' adult education refers to a highly country-specific set of educational activities that depend on the qualifications available. Consequently, a lot must be explained, country-by-country, and the overall picture becomes highly complex. Each country's language has various ways to address types of 'formal' adult education. Although not many people may know about all details, many commonly speak of 'formal' adult education in various societies. Blurring the border between 'formal' and all the other – nonformal – activities seems, at best, a 'loss of clarity' and, at worst, a 'violation of facts'. Altogether, the most visible branches of formal adult education form particular subjects within the extended research on the educational system (but not so much within adult education and lifelong learning).

The partnership's two camps do not only reflect the project member's country of origin; they mark two views on 'formal' education of adults within the European Union and the global discourse on adult and further education. An ambitious project on the languages of education in European discourse defines 'formal' learning as: *'Learning that occurs in an organised and structured environment (for example, in an education or training institution or on the job) and is explicitly designated as learning (in terms of objectives, time or resources). Formal learning is intentional from the learner's point of view. It typically leads to validation and certification.'* (CEDEFOP 2004, 70). However, the European manual for educational statistics provides as a 'conceptual definition' for formal adult education "*... education provided in the system of schools, colleges, universities and other formal educational institutions that normally constitutes a continuous 'ladder' of full-time education*" (EUROSTAT 2006, 13) and then refined in an operational definition as "*formal education refers to institutionalised learning activities that are designed to lead to a learning achievement (qualification or award) that can be positioned in a National Framework of Qualifications.*" (EUROSTAT 2006, 15). When adults (anyone 25 years or older) use this system, formal adult education takes place.

Researchers frequently face concepts with more than one possible meaning. Usually, they take a pragmatic approach and simply define exactly how one will use the concept. However, simplifying by resorting to the power to define has unexpected consequences, particularly in comparative research. Any chosen definition requires indicating the consequences of comparing its results across surveys, studies and countries. Clear and appropriate definitions for analysing a particular slice of reality *in one society* can result in a mess, hardly manageable, when applied *to various societies*, even when everybody earnestly tries to follow the commonly agreed framework. Where definitions differ from the implicit assumptions of the populations studied, reinterpreting their implicit components alters the common definitions. Research reports become overloaded by digressions and footnotes that explain what is and is not in the data, the significant data as opposed to mere artefacts and how different definitions in various societies might undermine research results.

Comparative research considers widely divergent social phenomena and has difficulty weighing the differences between societies and different 'objects' within the societies. Pragmatists in comparative research accept the ambiguities involved in any comparison: following common definitions seems the best choice with the hope that inconsistencies could be refined by further research based on improved concepts and methods. However, other traditions in comparative research take the issue more seriously and ask what the difficulties of comparison can reveal about both the object of research – in this book, formal adult education – and possible significant differences between societies.

1.2 Towards a new research framework on formal adult education

For a fresh start, while taking seriously the competing perceptions of formal adult education, I propose and develop an institutional approach towards formal adult education. I ground my line of argument mainly on organisational institutionalism (Greenwood et al. 2008, Scott 2008a, Schoonhoven & Dobbin 2010) and the study of education as an institution and – consequently – the institutionalised effects of education. This research field has been among the early preferred subjects of this variant of 'new institutionalism' in the 1970s, pursued by Aaron Benavot, John W. Meyer, Brian Rowan, Richard Rubinson, Richard W. Scott and many others. It has remained a vibrant field of research until today.

What does formal adult education promise?

Between the early 1970s and the turn of the millennium, lifelong learning has become institutionalised as a global norm for educational policy (Jakobi 2009) because of its potential to support both economic progress and social equity. Securing opportunity for earning formal qualification later in life has become a keystone of various lifelong learning policies, from early statements by the OECD (OECD et al. 1973) to the latest European Union policy documents (European Council 2009). 'Second chance education' or the opportunity to return to education at any time throughout the life course are thought to counteract inequalities produced by the initial education system and the consequences of ever-changing skill requirements in the 'knowledge society'.

'Formal adult education', leading to (vocational) qualifications that allow for upwards mobility, forms a core strategy of lifelong learning; this education should be powerful enough to overcome social marginalisation for various disadvantaged groups such as ethnic minorities, migrants or anybody with few formal qualifications. Various policy documents and large-scale lifelong learning programmes throughout Europe refer to the central function of 'allowing for steps upwards on the educational ladder'. However, the undeniable importance of 'formal adult education' has not led to broad research and policy discussions on how formal adult education can actually achieve these expectations for lifelong learning.

I argue that formal adult education – as initial education and contrary to nonformal adult education – has an institutionalised *'social charter'* (Meyer 1970), which promises that 'taking steps' on the educational ladder results in eligibility to move up on established career ladders. By completing a programme of formal adult education, the participant belongs to a different, more esteemed category of personnel – a 'skilled worker', a 'craft master', an academic – perceived as able and worthy to enter or make progress in a chosen occupational path. The credential allows recognition of a qualification before any proof of individual skills or competences. Therefore, the focal issue becomes how to achieve the social charter of educational programmes provided to adults.

Because 'taking steps' lies at the core of formal adult education, the latter is necessarily interwoven with 'social mobility'. This type of education involves transitions, not only from 'work to school' and back to work, but also between institutionalised categories of personnel. The transition can certainly imply, provoke or require a change in personal identity. Consequently, involvement in formal adult education *potentially* matters much more than nonformal education. One lesson per week in a foreign language or a refresher course in bookkeeping has little in common with a several-years-long project of attaining university entrance permission through evening school and then completing higher education. However, some formal adult education programmes differ greatly from the most common nonformal activities in adult education, but others do not. We therefore need a framework that allows for differing expectations for various types of formal adult education.

What levels of analysis are required to study formal adult educations' promise (not) becoming a reality?

To understand how formal adult education allows for 'taking steps', we have to consider the interrelations between the micro (individual), meso (educational organisations, enterprises and their organisational fields) and macro level (the education system, industrial relations, global norms for educational policy and so forth). Beyond any gain of competences or socialisation effects, we must explore the relevant institutions and how various parties come to share beliefs in formal adult education and its credentials.

Diagram 1 outlines the dimensions of 'formal adult education' understood as a *total social fact* (in Marcel Mauss' sense, as understood by Berger & Luckmann, 1967, 187), which I will address in the present book.

Diagram 1: The social charter: linking the institutional worlds of education and work

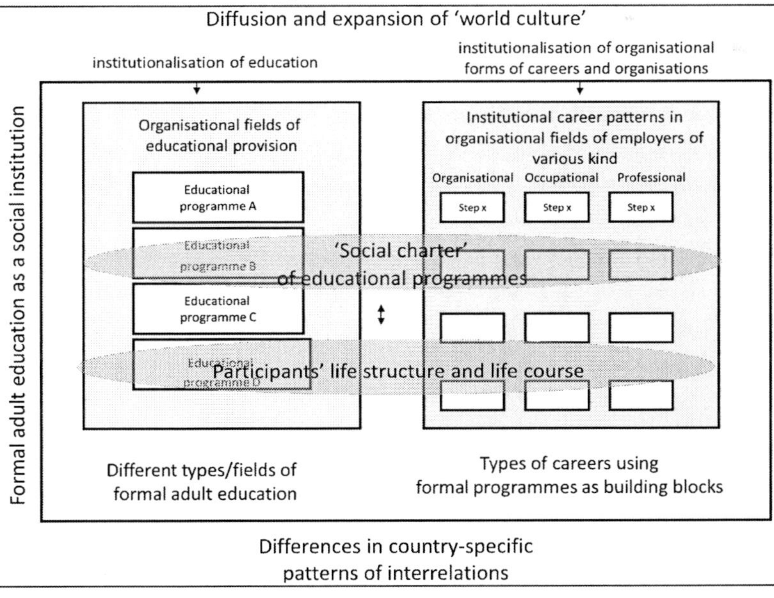

Source: Own description

At the core, we find on the one side the 'educational programmes' and on the other side the types of social trajectories or 'careers'. Programmes link to careers in various ways, yet two links are the most important. First, the individual forms a bridge by 'returning' to education, combining education with other adult commitments and 'exploring' what can be earned in further career progression. I will address this by applying the concept of 'life structure' and referring to life-course research frameworks in Chapter 4. Moreover, the life course itself relates to processes of institutionalisation and de-institutionalisation, which adds to the complexities. Second, the 'social charter' as an institutionalised definition of the 'formal' status of educational programmes signifies a particular link between 'education' and occupational 'careers'. I address the nature of this link in Chapter 3. However, the two bridges between education and work interfere with each other; for example, an institutional charter may fail to hold its promises for particular life courses. The single most important difference between initial education and formal adult education emerges from the complex interface of social charter and an adult's life course.

The 'charter' results from educational programmes and organisations institutionalising their particular *organisational fields* (DiMaggio & Powell 1983). Only by addressing the institutional processes and its social contexts can we fully understand the emergence, strength and decline of a programme's ability to make a difference. A programme owes its charter not to its innate properties, but to its relations to competing programmes. I give an outline for the study of organisational fields of formal adult education in Sections 3.3 and 3.4 and show that highly different types of formal adult education emerge in different organisational fields. Moreover, understanding adult education must include reflecting on education's social institutionalisation: participants depend on, yet also expand, institutional processes that shape society's faith in education.

We have to understand the particular situation of adult participants, who have already entered a social trajectory and have to balance returning to school with other elements of their adult life structure, notably their gainful work and their family responsibilities. As we will learn, formal adult education typically implies a constant high workload over several years and substantial changes of individual life structures, so that participation becomes a distinct life event. Moreover, formal adult education could involve transforming individual identity to reflect the changing social perception of oneself after graduation, a change which could put much strain on the individual. However, the institutionalised pattern of the life course, prescribing a strict time order for education – work – family transitions, could effectively limit individual choices and additionally burden participants who have to deal with their 'anomic' pathways. I will discuss in Chapter 6 how societies provide highly different frameworks conducive (or not) for participation in formal adult education.

Programmes receive their 'charter' by becoming institutionalised within career patterns. After completing a programme, individuals can take particular steps in careers. The programmes may differ in degrees and type of institutionalisation. Formal adult education may be used differently as 'building blocks' for particular career goals. To a certain degree, the institutionalisation of career patterns and the institutional weight of formal education within careers become indispensable; career boundaries may change as formal adult education allows entry for previously ineligible groups. The formation, change, and dissolution of career patterns, therefore, interact and co-emerge with the institutionalisation of formal education. One can not decide what comes first, the career pattern built on a particular programme or the formal programme delivering for a career. Societies develop quite different patterns for institutionalising careers and formal adult education. While it makes sense to discern – as types for governing work and the employment relationship – 'organisational', 'occupational' and 'professional' careers, any institutionalisation of careers occurs with employers who construct a particular labour market. Organisational behaviour shapes available career patterns, while institutionalised patterns become building blocks for the organisations that provide stability and meaning to its members and constituencies. I broadly outline types of careers in Section 3.2 and turn in Chapter 5 to the questions of why employers may or may not support training and formal adult education. In Chapter 6, I use a cross country comparative framework to consider the interrelation between organisations, type of careers and formal adult education.

The institutional worlds of programmes and careers patterns interplay and define the 'social charters' for particular types of formal adult education. These two worlds make up *formal adult education as a social institution* and it becomes a social fact in its own right. We need to understand the interplay of all components to understand what formal adult education means in a particular society.

Societies clearly differ in how they institutionalise formal adult education. However, transnational institutional processes may also drive the overall expansion of formal schooling, including formal adult education. These transnational processes may propel institutional change within career patterns and their legitimising ideological underpinning. Without the world-wide diffusion of particular 'models' for formal adult education – the second-chance evening gymnasium, the MBA degree and so forth – we probably could not even do a cross-country comparison. Transnational processes could influence some types of formal adult education (for example, higher secondary education) and careers (for example, in various professions). However, societal level institutions would remain decisive for other types of education (for example, vocational tracks) or careers (for example, crafts and trades). Consequently, formal adult education evolves as a social institution because of both country-specific traditions and transnational processes and actors that press for change. While I explore societal differences in institutionalising formal adult education throughout the book and in particular in Chapter 6, I address transnational processes only occasionally. The latter should clearly become a topic of future research and should not be considered as less important than the processes emerging on more local level. We know little about how formal adult education as a social institution will be challenged and transformed by global trends and policies in education and lifelong learning such as crafting qualification frameworks, implementing output-oriented and standard-based approaches, decentralising educational authority, acknowledging prior learning and spreading credit-based provision. In the outlook (Chapter 7), I will come back to transnational trends in education and lifelong learning and their impact on the framework for formal adult education.

Who are the adult learners in formal education?

When European societies constructed childhood and, much later, adolescence (Ariès 1962; Kamens 1985), 'being in school' became the defining criteria for 'childhood' and 'youth,' and adulthood began with the end of 'initial education' and the beginning of paid work. Supported by their parents, students in higher secondary and tertiary education enjoy a prolonged adolescence. Adults returning to 'school' lose their 'adult' status, becoming 'students among students'. This holds true, as we will see, only for a fraction of adults. However, formal adult education could be considered somewhat as an oxymoron, because one remains responsible for all other adult activities while in school.

Finishing initial education yet returning to education later becomes the core of most definitions of adult participants in formal education. However, due to a lack of information, adult learners are usually identified with age breakdowns. In Europe – following a convention of labour market research – adult learners are understood as being 25 years and older.

Returning to education involves a particular decision and a *work-to-school,* transition. Societies greatly differ in the extent that they institutionally support or limit work-to-school transitions or the combination of formal education and work. Work-to-school transitions could be both institutions of adult life in industrialised societies and an unpredictable personal decision to dare to change one's path of life (see Chapter 6)

Studies of formal adult education generally have underexplored adulthood. Institutional and psychological factors can help determine the phase of adulthood in which participation takes place. Participation in formal adult education – defined by having previously left initial education – most likely occurs in late adolescence shortly after finishing initial education. Defining adult education as something offered to those 25 years and older excludes this important part of formal adult education. 'Returning to school' commonly occurs in an extended 'transition period' that spans the larger part of 'young adulthood'. In many industrialised societies, participating in formal adult education is a quite common, *institutionalised* event up to the age of 35 years. Those older than 35 years rarely engage in institutionally supported formal adult education.

What is covered under the 'umbrella' of formal adult education?

'Formal adult education' emerged worldwide mainly as a statistical concept and a counterpart of newly introduced 'nonformal education' in the late 1960s and early

1970s. (In Chapter 2, I extensively track the history of the concept and explain much of its ambiguities). Traditionally, 'formal adult education' has covered only adult participation in 'second-chance education' and in 'higher education'. However, more and more educational activities of adults have been classified as formal adult education following reforms of the education system, the expansion of labour market and welfare policies, the rise of training programmes in firms and the ever-increasing importance of professions, para-professions and occupations. Moreover, the line between 'formal' and 'nonformal' education has become increasingly blurred in various ways in different countries. For example, countries with a strongly developed framework of credit-based qualifications typically label as 'formal activities' those regarded as 'nonformal' in other countries. (I discuss the predicaments involved in interpreting statistics on formal adult education in Chapter 2). The statistical representations of formal adult education regularly provided by EUROSTAT do not clearly indicate what types of educational activities are actually covered by the unit and what makes up for their 'formal' status or their 'social charter'.

Today, activities counted as 'formal adult education' typically go beyond 'second-chance education' and 'higher education' to also include 'formal' variants of 'adult basic education', 'retraining', 'customised formal programmes' for enterprises, 'continuing higher education' and 'continuing professional education'. Obviously, these types of formal adult education have little in common, cater for highly different populations and represent distinct 'areas of institutional life'. They make not only different promises; they also apply different institutional strategies for serving their causes. Based on the reasoning of organisational institutionalism, I have developed, in Chapter 3, a typology for seven types of formal adult education and their particular ways to achieve their 'social charter'.

How significant is formal adult education in today's industrialised societies?

Formal adult education has expanded as the culmination of the initial education system and is far from being a minor social phenomenon in most industrialised societies. However, any attempt for quantification involves the previously mentioned conceptual and methodological difficulties that will be discussed in detail in Chapter 2.

Using the statistical reports as a proxy for adult education, we can make the following observations.

- Between 8 and 12 million adults (25–64 years old) participated in formal adult education in 2003 in the European Union (EU25); this represents between 3 and 5 percent of the corresponding adult population. We will see, that participation differ considerably between countries, even when controlling for differences in applied understandings.
- In 2007, within the EU27, among all individuals within the officially represented education systems (ISECD 1–6) about 12 percent consisted of adults (25 years and older). Country figures range between approximately 5 and approxi-

mately 20 percent in this respect. Formal adult education considerably contributes to the expansion of the education system.
- Consequently, although not documented in many countries, public spending for formal adult education likely exceeds public resources used for any other form of adult education.
- We have no comparable information on lifetime participation in formal adult education. However, based on available studies and on estimates, we could expect between 20 and 40 percent of the population to return to education at any time of their life and in some countries even more.
- Given the inconsistencies in data available, we know little about short-term growth rates of formal adult education. However, as the educational system expands, formal adult education certainly also rises constantly.

Programmes and participants in formal adult education form an 'inverted educational pyramid'. Formal adult education programmes can typically state the level of education and very often a kind of curricula. Consequently, we could position participation cases on an educational pyramid, leading from elementary to advanced level. However, throughout all the studied societies, many more individuals participate in more advanced educational levels than on lower levels. Speaking of mere numbers, 'mature' students in higher education represent the majority of all participants in formal adult education. However, more students in one field must not lead to neglecting fields with clearly lower number of participants. Moreover, the 'inverted pyramid' clearly indicates that adults with few formal qualifications, who lack the prerequisites and the right to enter higher education, have more restricted opportunities for formal adult education than adults with more qualifications.

Who does research on formal adult education?

Ironically, before the LLL2010 project started in 2005, many publications – monographs, collections and articles – analysed 'nonformal' adult education, yet hardly any publication considered 'formal adult education'. To my knowledge, the two edited collections summarising the results of the LLL2010 partnership (Saar et al. 2012 forthcoming; Riddell et al. 2012) and my own monograph are the first books explicitly devoted to this broad area, which was only introduced as a 'by-product' for 'nonformal' education. Interestingly, EURYDICE – the Education, Audiovisual and Culture Executive Agency of the European Community – delivered a report on 'adults in formal education' in 2011 that represented the first cross-country, comparative overview on formal adult education published by a European Community institution.

However, formal adult education covers various topics previously explored by well-established streams of research. Consequently, my analysis of formal adult education intersects with these lines.

Firstly, the 'formal' education of adults has been seen as part of the 'sociology of (initial) education'. Formal adult education builds on institutionalised structures, created by initial education. Various types of formal adult education are often seen as a natural part of the 'initial education system', despite only adult students being eligible for access. 'Multiple training episodes' also become a topic within the study of education (Hillmert & Jacob 2003).

Secondly, 'formal' adult education forms an aspect in any study on adult education and lifelong education. 'Formal' adult education has often been studied as part of lifelong learning, its access routes, its inclusiveness, its desirableness or its outcomes – although by using alternate heading such as 'degree-programmes'[2]. Surprisingly often, researchers inadvertently study formal adult education; for example, when researching 'motives' for participation in adult education yet only considering the participants of formal programmes (for example, colleges).

Thirdly, and most importantly, any particular field of formal adult education represents a field of research in its own right. 'Second-chance education' (Inbar 1990) and 'non-traditional' students in higher education (Bourgeois et al. 1999) have attracted much scrutiny for decades. The study of 'continuing higher education' forms also a branch of the sociology of higher education. With the outstanding expansion of 'supply-side' market policy since the late 1980s, vocational retraining programmes have become a field of study, dominated by labour market economists. Basic education has been studied within evaluation studies of welfare policies. 'Customisation' of formal programmes and 'formalisation' of firm-provided, 'nonformal' programmes has been studied as more marginal topics within research on HRD and company training. The sociology of professions has identified continuing professional education as an important mechanism for social closure.

Fourthly, formal adult education arises as a 'particularity' in the more far-reaching research frameworks that examine social stratification, the economic returns on education, workplace learning or organisational learning. When educational attainment predicts the social status achieved, will this also be true for credentials gained in formal adult education? How do advantages or disadvantages of resources available in the family of origin accumulate over the life-course? (More precisely, does formal adult education add to or break with the pattern of (dis)advantage of initial education?) Do the economic returns on education differ for 'normal' (youth) and 'delayed'

2 In the literature in English, formal adult education in the sense of my study is often addressed by different notions. One strategy uses a difference within programmes open for adults, differing for example between 'degree' and 'non-degree' programmes as well 'credit-awarding' and 'non-awarding' courses and many further variations. Another strategy uses the timing of participation in formal education, using 'belated entry' (Taniguchi & Kaufman 2007), 'off-the-time' entry or 'delayed participation'. (Loewenstein & Spletzer 1997). A third strategy uses the implicit fact, that a particular type of education of adults involves a 'transition'; consequently applying notions such as 'returning' to education or 'work-to-school' transitions. Finally, adults could be marked among 'traditional' participants in formal education, as in 'mature' students, 'returners' or even 'non-traditional' students. Together, all these expressions address populations of learners and programmes, typically belonging to 'formal adult education', with far from perfect overlapping between the concept and the broad statistical category.

(adult) education? How does the informal workplace learning of employees interact with their formal adult education? How do organisations support formal adult education of their employees and incorporate their individual learning into organisational processes?

To sum up, while we lack research that focuses only on 'formal adult education', the 'umbrella' concept covers vast contributions to the various single topics.

1.3 The outline of the book

In the following section, I present the guiding research questions, introduce the empirical work, give an overview on the chapters of the book and note briefly the important aspects of the developed framework I do not discuss in any further detail.

The research questions

My main intention in this book is to outline a new research framework on formal adult education, understood as a particular social institution. I apply and further develop ideas of organisational institutionalism in the field of (initial) education for the study of formal adult education. The guiding research questions in this study include:

1. *How does formal adult education achieve its 'social charter', allowing the transformation of steps on the educational ladder into eligibility for steps on established career ladders?*
2. *How are 'social charters' of different types of formal adult education achieved?*

Research questions on the level of individual participants include:

3. *What constitutes the particularities of formal adult education as a life event – compared to nonformal adult education?*
4. *How does participation in formal adult education interact with the prior educational and occupational careers of employed participants?*

On the meso-level, I restrict myself to the behaviour of enterprises as employing organisations (while not discussing, for example, the behaviour of organisations providing education) and ask the following questions:

5. *Do organisations support formal adult education of their employees?*
6. *Does support for formal adult education represent an independent dimension within HRD and training policies?*
7. *How could we explain the support or non-support for formal adult education?*

I use a comparative approach for developing my research framework. Moreover, I address the following research questions on a comparative level:

8. *How can we interpret statistically represented differences in participation levels in formal adult education between European states?*
9. *How can we explain the competing meanings of formal adult education in European societies and research communities?*
10. *How do different employment and skill-formation systems shape the status and provision of formal adult education?*

The empirical studies used

This book deals with formal adult education in contemporary European societies. Empirical work was mainly done in 2008 and 2009 and primarily used statistical data stem from between 2003 and 2007. My empirical analysis does not closely examine the historical dimensions of formal adult education.

My conceptual work emerges primarily from the comparative empirical studies conducted by members of the LLL2010 project. Within the project, I was particularly responsible for a subproject on the cross-country significance of formal adult education for small and medium enterprises and their employees. Therefore, in the empirical results presented in this book, I focus on the 'meso' level of the enterprise and the relations spanned by the employed participants between formal adult education, educational organisations, established career patterns and the organisation.

In Chapters 4, 5 and 6, I build on results of this subproject and its 89 case studies on the use of formal adult education in small and medium enterprises. Based on my development of a common framework, case studies were provided by teams from twelve countries (Austria, the Flanders region of Belgium, Bulgaria, England, Estonia, Hungary, Ireland, Lithuania, Norway, Russia, Scotland and Slovenia). For the Austrian case studies, I also served as the lead researcher. My analysis builds on my experience with the overall preparation of the subproject, on the research on the Austrian situation and my case studies conducted together with my colleague Daniel Bacher, as well as the case studies and national reports prepared by the various national teams.

Furthermore, throughout the book, I draw extensively on another part of the project for which I was responsible and that explores two major microdata sources on formal adult education in Europe, namely the Ad-hoc module on Lifelong Learning (LFS-LLL2003) and the Adult Education Survey (AES 2005–2007) (Hefler et al. 2011).

A guide to the six chapters

In Chapter 2, I reconstruct four layers of the concept of formal adult education, which together shape its present use and cause its ambivalence. Firstly, I track the introduction of the 'formal/nonformal/informal' triad by UNESCO's chief researcher Philip H. Coombs and colleagues between 1968 and 1974. The triad is at the heart of today's statistical measurement of lifelong learning. However, while the newly introduced concept of 'nonformal' education attracted much scrutiny, the concept of formal adult education hardly received attention. Secondly, I show that there has been a long tradition of measuring formal adult education within the register-based educational statistics. Thirdly, I study the use of formal (adult) education in English because it has become dominant for the lifelong learning research and policy development in Europe. Finally, I discuss the consequences of the layers of meaning for interpreting competing data sources on formal adult education for the selected countries. I end with the conclusion that we urgently need a new approach for defining and analysing formal adult education.

In Chapter 3, I spell out my theoretical framework for analysing formal adult education as a social institution. I argue that particular institutional dimensions have always served as the basis for distinguishing formal from nonformal adult education. I show that an appropriate starting point for studying formal adult education considers a 'social charter' of educational programmes and the ways a programme offers (or does not offer) eligibility for a particular career path. Formal adult education could even be classified by how it secures its particular social charter for addressing predefined social issues. Consequently, I propose a new typology of formal adult education that focuses on different 'areas of institutional life' and gives programmes in formal adult education their particular charter. In the outlook, I discuss how the new theoretical foundation for formal adult education could be developed into an independent reference for defining and measuring formal adult education.

In Chapter 4, after reviewing theories that explain adults' participation in education, I further develop the idea that participating in formal adult education constitutes a particular life event that must be studied in its own right. I use the frameworks of Daniel Levinson to discuss the adult-developmental view on the participation in formal adult education. Based on the previously mentioned case studies, I present a typology for participation patterns in formal adult education. In the outlook, I discuss opportunities for 'cross-tabulating' further dimensions with the typology to construct a framework that explains participation in formal adult education.

In Chapter 5, I explore the significance of formal adult education within more general training and development policies of small and mediums enterprises. I start with an overview on existing theoretical frameworks for explaining companies' engagement in training and discuss the consequences for formal adult education. I argue that to understand organisations' training behaviour, we might have to introduce 'training cultures' as a new unit for analysis. Based on the SMEs' case studies, I outline seven types of enterprise training cultures. In the remaining sections of the chapter, I explore the relative dependence or independence of the support for formal adult education from the established training cultures of a company and demonstrate that formal adult education is certainly an issue for an organisation. Finally, I review patterns of support for formal adult education against the backdrop of established training cultures.

In Chapter 6, I refer to the 'societal effects approach' and use its most significant contribution – *The Social Foundations of Industrial Power – A comparison of France and Germany* (Maurice et al. 1986) – to establish a comparative framework of the relations between employment systems and formal adult education. I show that we cannot understand the position of formal adult education without referring to how work is organised and how formal education and institutionalised career pathways are interwoven. The social charter of any formal adult education depends on control over organisation of work and, on a country level, shaping the industrial relations between the organised employers and the organised employees. However, I further emphasise that countries do not have a universal system of skill formation but specific systems at the local or organisational field level. Using Japan and the United States as extreme cases at ends of a spectrum, and France and Germany as further points of orientation, I will analyse my collected case study evidence for Austria and Scotland. In the conclusion, I explore further opportunities for comparative research on formal adult education.

In Chapter 7, I take my research questions as a guideline to explain how my conclusions could shape both research and policy development in the field of lifelong learning.

Outside the scope of my book

In this book, I focus on developing a theoretical framework and on interpreting my case studies of SMEs and hardly touch many other important fields of empirical research. I do not analyse the participants in formal adult education in any further detail. This type of research could focus on motivational patterns, social inequalities and the question of inclusion or exclusion. Various studies explore why some social groups are represented among students and others not; the studies seek differences in, for example, motivations or opportunities and investigate barriers for participation. The LLL2010 project considered these issues and the results can be found in Saar et al. 2012 forthcoming and Riddell et al. 2012 forthcoming. I reflect on the consequences of my theoretical proposals for redirecting research on participation in formal adult education, which I also summarise in Chapter 7.

Reflecting the clear restriction of my empirical material, I do not explore *empirically* the biographies of the participants and the very position of the formal adult education in their lives. However, biographies and theories of the human life course and life cycle development lie at the core of my work in Chapter 4 and of my general approach to lifelong learning. In my view, biographical research on 'non-traditional' learners form the single most important source for exploring the very meaning of formal adult education for the individual and thereby for the society; this is something considerable different than exploring the institutional qualities of formal (adult) education. However, within this book, I do not contribute to the empirical body of evidence.

I hardly address the issue of educational provision of formal adult education beyond my assumptions in Chapter 3, when I develop a typology of formal adult education. As previously mentioned, I do not explore the historical development of formal adult education or the 'history of its institutionalisation' as a particular topic, although I draw on historical arguments for developing my conceptual work.

I do not provide an account of policies in place, fostering or governing formal adult education on national, European or global level. Clearly, policies concerning formal adult education emerge within broad educational policies and within the much more narrowly defined field of lifelong learning policies. A growing body of literature informs about the worldwide institutionalisation of a norm of 'lifelong learning' and 'higher secondary/tertiary education for all', although formal adult education hardly forms a particular object of study. My research does not particularly examine policy beyond occasional references to existing research literature and to core documents on European or global level. However, in the outlook, I will draw conclusions of particular relevance for lifelong learning policy on formal adult education.

Acknowledgements

The book builds on my synthesis report on Subproject 4, which has been published as a working paper within the project's framework (Hefler 2010a) and which contains an overview on all organisational case studies and country reports. These are also available on the LLL2010 project webpage (http://lll2010.tlu.ee/). Also, I use some of my contributions to Subproject 2 (Hefler et al. 2011). I occasionally used (as noted in the reference) other insights and results emerging from the project (summarised in Saar & Roosalu 2011). However, many of the project results (for example, the two final books) were not available when I wrote the current text. Earlier or shorter versions of sections of chapters have already appeared: (Hefler & Markowitsch 2010) covers broadly Section 4.4, (Hefler & Markowitsch 2012c forthcoming) presents material now in Sections 5.4 to 5.7, (Hefler & Markowitsch 2012b forthcoming) brings together Sections 2.5 and 3.4, finally, (Hefler & Markowitsch 2012a) presents Sections 6.3 and 6.4.

My work is based on the 6th European Research Framework project LLL2010 and I would not have been able to write my book without all the support and contributions of the participating countries' project teams, the stimulating atmosphere, critical exchange at the partnership meetings, and the constant flow of communication over the entire project. I would like to thank the members of the Austrian project team Daniel Bacher, Silvia Benda-Kahri, Regina Gottwald, Stephanie Rammel and Paul Ringer. As representatives for all the international colleagues, my special thanks go to Ellu Saar, who initiated and coordinated the project and remained constantly interested in the progress of my work; Pepka Boyadjieva, who gave me the decisive hints to engage more extensively with organisational institutionalism and to Odd-Bjön Ure for invaluable support, in particular on cross-country comparison. I would also like to thank Dragana Avramov, Philipp Grollmann and Hanne Shapiro of the international reviewer team for their valuable feedback and Marc Goffart, project officer on behalf of the European Commission, for his encouragement and his patience.

The book has profited greatly from my membership in the *DoktorandInnenkolleg Lifelong Learning* – a doctorate programme oriented towards part-time students with a professional background in the field of lifelong learning, set up by the universities of Klagenfurt, Graz and Krems and initiated and led by Werner Lenz and Wilhelm Berger. I would like to thank the professors as well as the participants of the *Kolleg* for their encouragement and feedback provided on various occasions. My special thanks go to Wilhelm Berger, who has been my reviser and who has encouraged and supported the work.

This book has profited in many ways by the constant exchange with my – in various changing and overlapping roles – project leader, superior, collaborator and regular co-author, colleague and friend Jörg Markowitsch. He invited me nearly a decade ago not only to work for his organisation but also to consider research on lifelong learning as my future main field of activity. After collaborating in more than a dozen projects, we share a common pool of experiences and reflections, without which I could not imagine more fruitful work. While leaving me alone when I delve into all the subjects and theories that so easily attracted me, he helped me to 'come to an end' and urged me to come up with 'a product', clear and commensurable enough to build future work on. Only one year my senior, he has taken the role as my mentor, providing as much space as I like to have, as much restraint as I needed and enough guidance to come finally to the point. I am very grateful to Jörg for all I have received. He could not have done more in 'taming my wild thoughts'. What has remained simply wrong, unclear and sketchy is all my responsibility.

My current employer and my colleagues at 3s have supported the work on the current book, allowing me to focus on its finalisation. My special thanks go to Stefan Humpl and Michael Juricek for arranging the flexible framework required.

I would like to express my gratitude to my proofreader Harold Otto, who has accompanied this book project from the very beginning and has revised and edited various provisional reports and earlier versions of each chapter since 2006. Moreover, over the years, he has understood how to strengthen my confidence as a writer in English. His accurate and patient work provided a safety net and set me free to experiment with English phraseology far above my level of skill and allow me to feel at home in a foreign language.

When I started to work on the subproject, which became the base for this book, I lived alone. Yet early in the process, I met Susie, who answered my love and became my partner, sharing – a researcher herself of much creativity, insight and rigor – the ups and downs of a long writing process in its fruitful and crippling interaction with all my other professional obligations. I owe her more than I could say – nonetheless intellectually, because I could participate in the clarity of her reasoning, the broadness of her knowledge and her readiness to provide me access to the rich traditions of her highly developed field of research. Finally, our two children Karin and Jakob (who arrived just before the book was drafted) have helped me to put my work into perspective and expanded my view on learning as becoming – as receiving – more than any text could ever do. I am very grateful for their support and patience and am glad for all four of us that I finally stopped writing.

Chapter 2: Formal *adult* education – The ambivalence of a global category

2.0 Introduction – The rise of the educational ladder and the place of formal adult education

The global use of 'formal adult education' appeared as a minor phrase when lifelong learning became for a first short period an important part of economic, educational and developmental policy in the early 1970s. The concept of lifelong learning was in troduced for breaking up the 'learning = school' equation. The triad 'formal/nonformal/informal' education was proposed as a way to express the components of lifelong learning. While formal education seemed well-established, nonformal and informal education remained to be discovered.

The expression 'formal adult education' can be analysed in two equally reasonable ways.

Firstly, it could be rephrased as 'formal education' of and for 'adults'. This implies starting with the formal 'education system' and then investigating the peculiar position of adult learners in it. 'Formal adult education' would appear as a 'by-product' of the rise and expansion of modern 'formal' education, starting in the second half of the 19th century. To understand 'formal adult education', we would have to follow the creation and constant change of 'formal education' as a particular social institution of the modern nation-state, while 'nation-states' and their 'education systems' may express a rising 'world culture' (Meyer 1992).

Secondly, 'formal adult education' could be dissected into 'formal' – a particular type of – 'adult education', which would provide the main framework. We would study 'formal' compared to other ways of 'nonformal' adult education or – in a broader framework – between any type of 'instruction' for adults, wherever instruction may be held. Consequently, the rise and development of 'adult education' would serve as the backdrop to studying formal adult education.

In this chapter, I will start to show that we cannot simply choose between the two understandings, because systematic links exist between the historical and contemporary development of both formal education and adult education. 'Formal adult education' *is* the most visible result of this linkage. In Chapter 3, I will further explore this link.

Consequently, we have to recall what we know about the modern history and current development of both the education system and 'adult education' as a field and how it emerged outside and in opposition to formal education. Let us take Fritz K. Ringers (1979) landmark study 'Education and Society in Europe' as our guideline.

Ringer refers to five types of education, namely (1) elementary education, (2) 'general' education (preparing for higher studies, higher services or serving as the basis for class identity of the wealthy classes), (3) vocational education, (4) engineering and (5) professional education at higher education institutions such as universities. Five main actors have directed education and fought to preserve or expand their influence: (I) the churches, (II) local communities ('the citizens of a town' and so on) (III) the trades and professions, (IV) the emerging large industrial corporations of the 'railway period' and beyond, and, finally, (V), the rising modern nation-state and its bureaucracies and standing armies. During the 19th century, the modern nation-state came to dominate all branches of education, forging a system out of a patchwork of historical elements. Control over education even became a main fibre of modern nation-states, integrating a scattered citizenship and controlling access to any position of symbolic power; the rise of the nation-state itself, thereby, propelled the system's expansion. This account barely includes 'adult education', because it remains outside of and serves as an alternative to the emerging stratified and firmly controlled education system.

The state-led rise of the 'education system' (Müller et al. 1987, Stichweh 1994), achieved in the second half of the 19th century in most European societies, created the *educational ladder* as a principle for stratification of both educational providers and societies. This coercive framework has clear criteria for entrance, progression and the value of credentials offered. An educational institution and a graduate became positioned in a strictly hierarchical, strongly segmented space. Entry requirements were defined for a particular level and type of education beyond compulsory education – lower secondary, higher secondary or university level, *general* or vocational. Some types of education provided eligibility to progress on the ladder and other types were *terminal*. The clear steps on the ladder ruled out other possibilities to use the education system in a legitimate, socially acknowledge way. By linking particular steps and pathways in education with particular social and occupational careers – in state bureaucracies, in the military, in the emerging private organisations – a competing principle challenged 'noblesse' (ancestry), 'inheritance' (wealth) and 'vocation' (spiritual) as guiding principles for access and progress in any type of socially privileged careers. Competing for control over the including and excluding principles that created the 'educational ladder' became equivalent to fighting for power and privilege in the emerging 'credential society'. (Collins 1979)

At the same time as the educational ladder rose as a modern principle of social stratification, the universe of available social positions turned upside-down. The new wealth resulting from high industrialisation and extended European colonialism resulted in many desirable social positions based on higher secondary or university education and created a new 'middle class'. Work in traditional crafts and agriculture deteriorated, which fed into desperate working classes that later became a political power fighting for their share of wealth if not the 'whole cake'. The available social positions along with the educational credentials preparing for them have constantly changed in the past 200 years. The phases in modernity's social development can be seen when connecting the evolution of the modern employment system with the education system. (Ringer 1979, see also Brint 1998 for a different approach) Ringer discerns between an early (1800–1860), a high (1860–1930) and a late industrial (1930–1980) phase in the employment system's interaction with the education system. Clearly any phase has winners and losers; education becomes more important for some, yet others have skills – no matter how achieved – that become less important.

Many believe that we are currently in a fourth phase of modernity, different from the 1930–1980 period. However, there is little agreement as to where the previous period actually ends, because of the challenge of identifying the current period with such descriptions as post-industrial, post-Fordist, knowledge-based and service or network societies. However, both the universe of social positions and the functioning of education have changed qualitatively within the past three decades. We are uncertain of how to grasp the characteristics of today's education systems and their institutional changes because today's most cited sociological theories on education emerged in the 1970s and described a rising tension in traditional education systems, new worlds of work and new societal values, as represented by various social movements. Moreover, when describing the relation between education and available social positions, we have become aware of their co-dependence; far from simply answering the demands of the employment system, education also provides employment categories. In challenging contemporary theories of credential inflation and over-education, John Meyer argued already in 1977 that education produces the 'demand' for graduates as much as it reacts to it.

Educational policymakers and administrators take for granted the existence of an educational ladder. In the first version of the International Standard Classification of Education (ISCED) of 1976, no one doubted the existence of educational hierarchies. Difficulties arose only with country-specific hierarchies between general and vocational education and in attaching newly available particularised educational programmes to the levels established in national education systems. Finally, the rise of qualifications frameworks marked the highpoint in forming the 'ladder' metaphor by claiming that all forms of learning can be mapped against ascending levels of requirements.

Although there are many predecessors, adult education arose in the space left empty after the formation of the state-dominated education system, roughly during late 'high industrialisation' in many European countries. This adult education offered non-degree courses (not formal ones) for adults (not for the youth) in liberal arts (not professional or vocational) and often forcefully excluded anything suspected as 'politics' instead of 'education'. Formal education for adults definitely arose after the education system had established comparatively strict age limits for entering in and progressing on various routes. As 'second chance' education, it reintroduced a level of flexibility, allowing for new alternative routes to particular credentials. At the same time, the use of credentials to limit and structure professional careers clearly added a field for 'professional adult education'. However, for 'late industrialisation' and our current stage, the picture becomes much more blurred: Adult education – for various reasons and at different points in time – starts to include formal adult education, starting with 'second chance education'. Moreover, instruction for adults traditionally confined to the workplace and not understood as adult education, gained considerably in extent and legitimacy; this blurred the borders between 'formal' education on the one side and 'liberal' adult education on the other.

Overview 1 shows a synopsis of co-evolutions in European education, which highlights the point that formal adult education could be understood only in its interrelation to education, the employment system and other organised educational opportunities for adults.

Section 2.1 will offer an overview of the history of the triad formal/nonformal/informal education and the discourses in which it was embedded. However, national and later international comparative educational register statistics had taken note of formal adult education before adding on the newly established role as one of the three components of lifelong learning. The UNESCO, the OECD and EUROSTAT jointly established the UOE statistics on education, which used national statistics for a global system of educational statistics that also included formal adult education. Almost all comparative statistical data, present in research and in everyday media coverage, derives from the UOE system, but even experts rarely used the figures on formal adult education. I refer to the UOE approach, therefore, in more detail in Section 2.2. In Section 2.3, I discuss some implications of the peculiarities of the English notion of 'formal' already mentioned in the introduction. Finally, I give an overview on the available statistical accounts on formal adult education and assess comparative results, discussing their appropriateness and pitfalls.

A note of caution: this chapter deals with (classification of) education, not with types of adults' learning. The formal/nonformal/informal distinction has also developed into a highly influential typology for ways of (adult) *learning*, playing with the exchangeability of 'education' (instruction) and learning. The prominent use of the triad for classifying learning in the European Commission's Communication on Lifelong Learning 2001 adds much to the confusion (European Commission 2001, 32–33). Various scholars have provided in-depth critiques and proposals for a way forward, which typically include dropping the formal/informal distinction for learning (for a review, Simkins 1977 or Colley et al. 2003). I return to this point in Sections 4.1 and 4.2.

Overview 1: Periods in the co-evolution of forms of education: Formal education, Formal adult education, Adult education, Workplace instruction

Periods	[1] Societal developments	[2] Changes in the employment system	[3] Formal education	[4] Formal adult education	[5] Adult education	[6] Workplace instruction
1800–1860	(Failing) democratic revolutions; Factory system becomes dominant; Rise of nationalism as basis of the nation-state (Germany, Italy …)	Sharp decline in crafts and trades; Increase of unskilled workers in the industry system; Evolution of early state bureaucracies (including standing armies); Rise of large corporations (railway era)	'Elementary' education – state controlled for the non-privileged; State experiments coexist with a variety of non-state institutions – domination of churches in higher secondary education or even universities prevail in many countries	Practically nonexistent, however, weaker age grading of educational pathways allow access of existing organisations	Predecessors (e.g. religious movements)	Crafts and the workplace are the most important learning areas for vocational skills
1860–1930	Economic crisis and nationalisation of railways; Victory of representative democracies; Civil liberties; Rising laicism; Rise of social democracy and communism; First World War; Great Depression	Formation of large-scale monopolistic trusts; Internalisation of vocational education challenges drive-system* for skilled work; Rise of large public and private bureaucracies (e.g. insurance companies, banks) with internal labour markets for white-collar work; increased level of coordination as a result of war economy; Rise of trade unions; Rise of social insurance (accident, health, retirement, unemployment)	State control and funding; Age grading; Standardisation of curricula; Hierarchisation; Rationalisation of selection mechanism; Creation of the 'educational ladder' ; Initial vocational education become partly or fully incorporated in the state supervised system	Early 'second chance education'; Cooptation of craft/professional (non-university) degrees as 'formal'	Rise of 'liberal adult education'; Adult education of social movements	'Continuing' vocational education and learning remain outside the 'education system'
1930–1980	European fascism, Stalinism, Second World War; Cold War; *Wirtschaftswunder*,1960 onwards – de-colonisation completed; New social movements (e.g. women's movement, peace movement), Oil-Shock	War economy; Rise of internal labour markets for blue-collar work; Increase in internal labour markets in large organisation; Delegitimisation and outlawing of marriage bans and unequal pay; outlawing of racial discrimination	Rise of co-education at higher secondary and tertiary level; Strong increase of female participation rates; overall strong expansion	Expansion of 'second chance' education and 'bridging courses' allowing for access to higher education; Expanding access for non-traditional students to higher education; Promotion of 'recurrent education'	Expansion of social movement-based adult education by state support; Faure Report (1972); Rise of LLL as a policy	As components of the 'skill formation system', strong increase of corporate training and educational programmes
1980-onwards	Economic crises (1980–82) Transformation form state socialism to democratic capitalism in Eastern Europe; end of Cold War	Weaking of trade unions; decreasing employment security for mid career men, increasing security for women; new types of careers; rise of precarious employment	'Curricula revolution' – enhancement of legitimate contents (Meyer 2006); Multiculturalism; Credit-based provision; Expansion of length of compulsory education; Rise of accreditation of prior learning; Educational standards; Extension of public funding	Expansion of 'continuing higher education' and 'continuing professional education'; basic education become accepted; modularisation of programmes, APL and credit-based qualifications start to change the field	Reduced lump-sum funding raises market-oriented activities; Expansion of fields of activity (e.g. within active labour market policy), More project-based work	Rise and fall of 'corporate universities'; Outsourcing of HRD and training; Increased training activities for a reduced work force

Source: Own description * The 'drive system' refers to an organisation of work frequently in place prior to the introduction of internal labour markets, where supervisors or craftmasters act as subcontractors for industrial enterprises while hiring, managing, supervising and paying their own small teams of unskilled or skilled workers (Jacoby 1984).

2.1 The Formal/Nonformal/Informal Triad

Throughout the world, the classifications of educational or learning activities distinguish between 'formal', 'nonformal' and 'informal' activities. This distinction is applied by surveys introduced by national or supranational statistical organisations as well as by research-based approaches. Any educational activity potentially fit in one of the three types characterised by the 'triad'. Yet, where does this triad actually come from?

Literature on the formal/nonformal/informal distinction (Simkins 1977, Colletta 1996, Tuijnman & Boström 2002, Rogers 2004) attribute educationalist Philip H. Coombs (1915–2006) with successfully introducing the triad to global, educational policy research. President John F. Kennedy appointed Coombs as the first Assistant Secretary of State for Education and Culture (between 1961–62). Later he became the founder of UNESCO's International Institute for Educational Planning. Coombs then promoted the further use of his and his collaborators' definitions in several publications on educational development policy for the adult rural poor and the youth in developing countries. These studies formulate the triad in a way that has become a basis for various later definitions by global educational and statistical institutions. Coombs & Ahmed (1974, 8) states:

> We found it analytically useful and generally in accord with current realities, to distinguish between three modes of education (recognizing that there is considerable overlap and interaction between them): (1) informal education, (2) formal education, and (3) nonformal education.
>
> Informal education as used here is the lifelong process by which every person acquires and accumulates knowledge, skills, attitudes and insights from daily experiences and exposure to the environment – at home, at work, at play; from the example and attitudes of family and friends; from travel, reading newspapers and books; or by listening to the radio or viewing films or television. Generally, informal education is unorganised and often unsystematic; yet it accounts for the great bulk of any person's total lifetime learning – including that of even a highly 'schooled' person.
>
> Formal education as used here is, of course, the highly institutionalised, chronologically graded and hierarchically structured 'education system,' spanning lower primary school and the upper reaches of the university.
>
> Nonformal education as used here is any organised, systematic, educational activity carried on outside the framework of the formal system to provide selected types of learning to particular subgroups in the population, adults as well as children. This defined, nonformal education includes, for example, agricultural extension and farmer training programmes, adult literacy programs, occupational skill training given outside the formal system, youth clubs with substantial educational purposes, and various community programs of instruction in health, nutrition, family planning, cooperatives, and the like.

Coombs in other publications states similar definitions. Before following the fate of the distinction through other literature and trying to understand the meaning of this early introduction of the formal/nonformal distinction, we need to briefly consider the dominating educational discourses of the late 1960s and early 1970s. In particular, we need to consider why the triad classification became widespread without exploring the meaning of formal adult education.

Coombs promoted nonformal education in his highly influential *The World of Educational Crises* (1968) as a way out of dead-end educational expansion (for details of the prehistory and history of the concept, see Roger 2004, in particular, 71ff.). The chapter *'Nonformal Education: To catch up, keep up and get ahead'* recommends to expand or rely on nonformal education for developing countries, and the industrialised nations. The former should develop nonformal education to provide adult literacy and improved skills used in agriculture and related activities, instead of spending their resource for advanced education for small elites. The industrialised countries should remedy shortcomings in any possible initial formal education system by expanding and systematising 'life-long education', as already established in multiple facets. As an echo of the 'Sputnik shock', Coombs even considered that the 'West' may learn from the socialist countries in 'breaking down the artificial barriers that have perpetuated for too long an unwholesome separation between formal and nonformal education.' (Coombs 1968, 141). Social mobility and inclusion, economic progress and individual well-being are already introduced for justifying the essential character of 'lifelong education':

> Life-long education is essential in a rapidly progressing and changing society for three primary reasons: (1) to ensure the employment mobility of individuals, and to make unemployable 'drop-outs' of the past employable; (2) to keep already well-trained people abreast of new knowledge and technologies essential to their continued high productivity in their respective fields; and (3) to improve the quality and satisfaction of individual lives through culturally enriching their expanding leisure time. (Coombs 1968, 139)

Where the initial education system was highly developed, nonformal education is consequently proposed as a means for overcoming limitations that cannot be resolved by further expansion of 'schooling'. For industrialised countries, the expansion and systematisation of post-compulsory *adult education* meant promoting 'nonformal' education, which later become the core of the lifelong-learning policy. Where poorly developed education systems lacked study places and services, nonformal adult education was proposed as the more viable way forward.

Early in the 1970s, two influential policy reports promoted the idea of 'nonformal' education as a remedy for problems with formal education and as a blueprint for lifelong learning; both reports extensively consider both nonformal and formal adult education, but provide considerably different interpretations. UNESCO's Faure Report, *Learning to Be: The World of Education Today and Tomorrow.* (1972) and OECD's *Recurrent Education – A Strategy for Lifelong Learning*' (1973) both provide answers to 'the world educational crisis'. The two reports are often characterised as strictly opposing each other, representing the 'two faces of lifelong learning', the 'empathetic' humanistic one (Faure Report) and the 'cold' human capital one ('recurrent education') (Rubenson 2009). However, both reports mirror the 'Zeitgeist' and are more responsive to 'leftist' criticism than one would expect to find in later documents of global organisations. Both reports obviously add to the 'breakthrough' of the 'formal/nonformal/informal' triad as a widely used classification.

UNESCO's 'Faure Report' – written under the guidance of France's influential and controversial politician Edgar Faure – continues Coombs' analysis of a crisis of the initial education system; the report stresses the educational system's inefficiency and detrimental effects on social equality. The scope is widened by new critiques of formal education, from the centre (Ivan Illich's claim for 'de-schooling society' (1970)) and the periphery (Paulo Freire, promoting a 'pedagogy of the oppressed' (1970)). The educational crisis results from an over reliance on regulated and school-based instruction for achieving learning throughout life. By bringing back everyday learning in the family, the local community, the workplace, the leisure activities and social movements, learning arises as a lifelong activity independent of schooling. Informal learning has to become respected as the basis for lifelong education, supported by planned intervention of all kinds, including taught courses, but governed by the needs and preferences of the participants. The formal education system has to be reformed to become less elitist and exclusive and more in line with the lifelong learning needs of its participants. However, even a reformed formal education system is not expected to play an important role for adults later in life: they should pursue their learning pathways freed from the restrictive nature that formal education necessarily implies. Formal adult education appears as something undesirable and resulting from a lack of more appropriate means for achieving the underlying goals.

OECD's *Recurrent Education – A Strategy for Lifelong Learning* (1973) shares the main assertions of both the Coombs' and the Faure's report and presents itself as a 'systematisation' of policy implications made by the other reports. Sweden's president Olaf Palme introduced 'Recurrent Education' as a genuine reform agenda for educational policy in 1968 (Tuijnman 1996). Authors involved in forming the strategy echo this social-democratic vision of a 'lifelong learning' approach. At its core, 'recurrent education' proposes not only to offer nonformal education throughout a person's life, but to 'postpone' investment in initial education in favour of 'returning' for spells of full-time education (alternation principle) later in life when convenient for individual and societal purposes. Formal education should remain central, yet be substantially reformed. Instead of standardised, selective, multi-year programmes that determine individual social positions early in life, a system of educational provision should flexibly allow for any educational pathway, at any time over the life course in accordance with actual needs of individuals and their employers. Teaching-centred provision of traditional formal education should be transformed to learner-centred provision, where mature learners bring their professional and personal experience into the classroom. Consequently, a reformed system of formal education, absorbing what nonformal education has to offer, should become the backbone of lifelong learning: formal adult education thereby should become the single most important component of a LLL strategy. While the concept of 'recurrent education' has never been successfully implemented, lifelong-learning policy frameworks later absorbed several of its recommendations (for example, free movement between tracks, accreditation of prior learning) and proposed instruments (for example, educational leave programmes). The focus on 'formal adult education', however, did not make it into later policy paradigms.

To summarise, by the mid-1970s, the 'formal/nonformal/informal' triad was firmly established and 'nonformal' education was introduced as a notion for any planned activity that overcomes the shortcomings of formal education by implementing or strengthening educational alternatives.

2.2 Defining by constructing oppositions: the 'cons' of formal as the 'pros' of nonformal education

Some early contributions on the 'triad' defined 'nonformal' education by its differences to formal education. This strategy achieves two goals. Firstly, 'nonformal' education covers a vast range of highly different educational activities varying from literacy and numeracy programmes to 'theatre of the oppressed', from courses on typewriting to skills training for subsistence agriculture, from puritanical Sunday schools to safer sex education, from needlework groups to multi-year programmes educating working class counter-elites. Therefore, a 'negative' definition, working along the established model of formal education, seems much more feasible than extracting common features out of various nonformal opportunities. Secondly, the legitimacy for nonformal education was co-constructed by demonstrating how it overcomes the 'register of sins' of formal education.[3]

King (1976) formulates the development of nonformal education as a set of shifts or movements within education: from teachers towards animators, from academic subjects to developing areas, from diffuse fields of knowledge to modular units, from centralised control towards devolved control and from paid personnel to community control of resources (cited in Fordham et al., 1983). Simkins (1977) provides an early, exhaustive table comparing the 'ideal type' of formal to an 'ideal type' of nonformal education; this comparison has frequently been reproduced in an abbreviated form.[4]

3 Paolo Freire's 'capital sins' of formal education provide a highly influential prototype for what nonformal education has to overcome and is consequently defined by. (1) Teacher teaches, students are taught; (2) teachers knows everything, students nothing; (3) teachers think, students are thought; (4) teachers speak, students listen; (5) teachers discipline, students are disciplined; (6) teachers choose, student comply to the choices made; (7) teachers act, students join the illusion of acting though their teachers' activities; (8) teachers choose programmes' content, the students adapt to it; (9) teachers proclaim their claims for professional authority and the authority of knowledge, violating the students' freedom; (10), teachers are the subject, the students are the object of the teaching (and learning) process. (Rogers 2004, 51)

4 Formal education has been described as long-term and general, credential-based, based on a long cycle, preparatory, full-time, input-centred and standardised, academic, having a clientele deter-

Nonformal education was ideologically constructed as a superior alternative to formal education. The reality of the claims that 'nonformal' education forms the 'better half' of education often remained uncontested. (Rogers 2004) Criteria of formal education were not evaluated in their advantages, only in their likely disadvantages. Education analysts have only occasionally emphasised that formal education might have something to offer not available by nonformal education. (Bock 1976, see Chapter 3)

However, while the triad of formal/nonformal/informal education and its presence in statistics became widespread, the debate hardly left its main context, the field of development policies. Even within the wider research on adult education, the 'debate' of nonformal provision versus formal provision had played no important role (Rogers 2004, Hoopers 2006).

To my knowledge, the single most important contribution on the contrast between 'formal' education and 'nonformal' training only poorly contributed to the 'great debate' on nonformal education. W. Richard Scott and John W. Meyer wrote 'The Rise of Training Programs in Firms and Agencies – an Institutional Perspective' (1994) and made no direct link to the formal/nonformal opposition; however, the authors might have been aware of the literature.[5] To consider the *institutionalisation* of company training, they also construct an opposition between 'education' and 'training'. However, both are taken for subtypes of a more general institutional pattern: instruction.

> Instruction connotes a set of activities, arrangements, categories, and cultural forms that supports activities across a wide array of contests. Whereas 'learning' is something one does, 'instruction' is something that is done to one. Thus, instruction calls up the clear notion of differentiated roles: teacher or instructor versus students or trainee. It suggests a set of activities distinguished from 'work' or 'play'. It implies an outcome – the learning of subject matter or the acquisition of skills – that is expected to occur, an output different from any tangible product that may result from performing the activities. This outcome is often socially constructed to appear to be more tangible: It may be accompanied by the assigning of scores or grades, the specification of credit units, the granting of certificates, or other tangible evidences of successful completion. (Scott & Meyer 1994, 235)

'Formal' and 'nonformal' education therefore share a common core and differ according to various dimensions. The differences are more fluid. Instruction appears in various societal fields, besides 'traditional education', such as in business, in the military or

mined by entry requirements, institution-based, isolated (from the socioeconomic environment and from social action), rigidly structured, teacher-centred, and resource-intensive, as well as controlled external and hierarchical. Nonformal education, to the contrary, is portrayed as short-term and specific, non-credential-based, based on short cycle, recurrent, part time, output-centred and individualised, having practical entry requirements determined by clientele, environment-based and community-related, flexibly structured, learner-centred, resource-saving, self-governing and democratic. (Fordham et al. 1983, based on Simkins 1977).

5 John W. Meyer, for example, was the supervisor of John Bock, who has written extensively on the subject.

in religion. In all contexts of adult instruction, Scott and Meyer assert the existence of more or less clearly discernible levels, running from clearly 'formal' education like 'degree programmes' to more mixed 'certificate' programmes to clearly non-degree, nonformal programmes. Each societal field has thereby organised instruction in a way that spans 'formal' to 'nonformal' and created different institutional effects for participants on each level of instruction. (Scott & Meyer 1994, 236f, in particular Figure 11.1) The properties of 'formal' or 'nonformal' education are no longer classified as the 'bad' or the 'good' side of education, instead they are seen as variations of instruction that coexist and take on different functions and follow different institutional logics.

Overview 2: Ideal type for 'Education' (formal adult education) versus 'Training' (nonformal adult education).

Education		Training
Learning as an end in itself *Future utility* *Understanding*	*Goals*	*Learning as a means to an end* *Present utility* *Results*
Theoretical *Subject-oriented* *Concepts emphasised*	*Cognitive frames*	*Practical* *Problem-oriented* *Skills emphasised*
Teacher active, students passive *Students dependent* *Student differences minimised*	*Teacher-student relation*	*Both teacher and students active* *Students independent* *Students differences emphasised*
Cooperation forbidden *Learning only from teacher*	*Student-student relation*	*Cooperation encouraged* *Learning from each other*
	Own additions	
Many hours long period (2–10 years)	Time required	Few hours (for a single training event) within short time frame
Access (on higher level) typically restricted Selection as an accepted social function ('drop out' as an individual failure) Exclusion as a social sanction of misbehaviour	Selectivity	Access typically open No selection foreseen within the process ('drop out' as an organisational failure) No regularly established sanction of misbehaviour
Examination of outcomes against standards Proof of competences (e.g. thesis)	Rules for rewarding credentials	Attendance (measurement of improvements use for self-assessment)
Government bodies Professional bodies	Locus of control	The providers *and* the participant eventually public agencies (providing funds)
Public and eventually private (households)	Source of finance	Enterprises and households, eventually public co-financing
Universal (institutionalised) recognition throughout social fields for standardised outcomes Social agreements between social partners may restrict employers choice in wage setting Various rights of being treated differently from non-graduates	Claims connected to credentials	Negotiable appraisal by various agents Employers may explore fully their power (paying 'market prices' or below) No rights granted for different treatment
Defined starting points for social trajectories; opening access to social upwards mobility Fulfilling access requirements of professional fields	Impact of credentials on social stratification	Further exploration of opportunities on a given social place (a given social trajectory)

Source: Scott & Meyer 1994, 238; own additions

Meyer and Scott put formal and nonformal education on one level, comparing them for their particularities instead of taking nonformal education as a remedy for the shortcoming of formal education. They point towards the need to understand both the way forms of instruction are institutionalised and the types of institutional effects they create. Meyer – together with some colleagues – made outstanding contributions to an institutional theory of education, which I discuss in Section 3.2.

While typologies imply that empirical cases more or less strongly derivate from the 'ideal type', however, the appropriateness of the formal/nonformal oppositions suffers from the effects of their own critical stance. No formal or nonformal adult education fit the typologies. However, the constant critique of the social organisation of schooling and educational approaches has introduced considerable change within the initial education system and even more changes in formal education provided for adults.

Particular important change processes since the late 1960s include:

- expanding choice within established programmes, allowing for programmes to adjust to individual preference at the price of reduced standardisation;
- introducing the modularisation of programmes, allowing for more flexible completion and more easily transferring modules between providers or types of programmes;
- accrediting prior learning, either of learning within the educational system only or of any learning, no matter where and when it took place;
- introducing credit-based qualifications replacing the link between a programme and a qualification by a link between a standard and a qualification, allowing individuals to freely follow their preferences in earning the credits required for a qualification;
- introducing qualification frameworks, which typically increase the number of available qualifications and the access routes for acquiring them.

Countries differ widely in how and to what extent they have established any of these innovations. Moreover, the system of qualifications does not remain untouched by the implementation of any of the reform strategies for initial education. Typically, reforms imply a 'de-standardisation' of the qualifications, as more access routes lead to the same 'certificates'. Concurrently, however, introducing outcome-related measures and procedures for a more tightly controlled qualification may enforce 'core' standardisation of qualifications: standardisation of 'learning outcomes' substitutes curricula based on standardisation of inputs. These policies could not be understood without references to a country's overall skill formation and employment system and the place of qualifications within the systems (see Chapter 6).

To sum up, the strategy of defining 'nonformal' (adult) education by stylising an opposition between 'formal' and 'nonformal' education has been flawed from the beginning, yet became even less convincing by changes within formal adult education itself.

2.3 Formal adult education 'within' the education system – the concept of the para-education system in the UOE statistics

Since the medieval era, European students have been carefully 'registered' by educational organisations run by the churches. The modern nation-state – working towards monopoly control over education – continued this tradition. Being a pupil or a student, typically, required registration and implies being counted. As late as 1975, UNESCO proposed 'requiring registration' as a sound basis for defining 'formal education'. (UNESCO 1975, 4f). Thus, adults in formal education were also 'counted'. Yet, who counts as an adult?

Before the 19th century, educational organisations served (mostly male) students of broad age ranges. However, *any* 'student' was regarded and treated as an adult, regardless of his age and reflecting his typically elevated social position, coming from a noble or a well-off bourgeois background. 'Higher' education in 'colleges' and 'gymnasiums' were understood as part of the 'university' system, providing 'undergraduate' entrance qualifications for the 'upper' faculties of law, medicine and theology. Students in preparatory institution ranged from about 10 to 30 years old. With expansion, standardisation and state-control of higher secondary education in the 19th century, the age range for lower secondary and higher secondary education became more standardised. In (prosperous) Europe, more mature students became more exceptional at first, and then later not acceptable.[6]

Thus, the official educational statistics included adults in formal adult education in two ways. Firstly, they are counted together with students of traditional age. Any available age information allows them to be identified as a particular group within the participation statistics. Secondly, any 'formal' educational programme reserved for adults has statistics of those who have registered. 'Adult' could stand for 'being older' than a certain threshold (such as 16, 17 or 18 years) or a certain 'out-of-school' experience (for example, being out of school for more than two years; having worked for at least two years). When a public authority either offers or controls these programs for adults, a governmental body should collect statistics on these programmes. Moreover, increasingly widespread laws require educational providers to report on participation for a defined set of programmes.

Therefore, accounts for adults registered in institutions of the 'normal' educational system provide a long established 'blueprint' for understanding 'formal adult education'. For statistics on adult education, the 'formal' part has long seemed easier to document. However, the emergence of more and more programmes reserved for adults, either as 'second chance education' or for further professional training (for example, in the health professions), requires the introduction of the concept of 'paraformal education' (Chu 1996). This concept 'draws into' the map of the education

6 In many developing countries, up to the 1970s, schools served both children and adults alike.

system, any formal programme, not available within 'initial' education, yet related to the logic of the education system. Programmes of this type could often be found 'at the border' of the age-graded graphical representation of a country's education system. However, over the decades, programmes belonging to the 'para-formal education' increasingly came into existence – in many countries, several hundreds – and make it difficult to provide an overview even for insiders.

Any country, therefore, has its own procedure of counting adults in formal adult education. Even before the rise of transnational surveys that follow a common methodology, we find figures based on registers on 'formal adult education' on a national level. Accounting for formal adult education means little more than discussing these available figures. However, statistical accounts were and remain a mess of idiosyncratic developments of what is in and what is out, what type of information is available and what type is missing. Changes in the availability of register data significantly alter a country's concept of what 'formal adult education' means.

In a world of standards, (Boli & Thomas 1999) global standardisation of educational statistics came comparatively late. However, global institutions active in educational policy have, for decades, focused on standardising 'incomparable' educational data coming from national register statistics. The 'inauguration' of the International Classification of Educational Statistics in 1978 (ISECD 1976, revised in 1997 and again in 2011) marks the definitive breakthrough in comparative educational statistics. Although national idiosyncrasies remain strong (Schneider 2008), global standards allow for measuring the deviation of national accounts from the set model (for example, for ISCED in Europe). Since the mid-1990s, the three dominating players in educational statistics – the UNESECO, the OECD and EUROSTAT – jointly operate the most influential statistical system on education; they require the educational administrations of their member countries to report educational data following a common, highly elaborated framework. All three organisations publish results from this common data collection – known as *UOE*[7] *data collection on education systems* – within their database (UEO 2010a).

The UOE carefully addresses formal adult education for one primary reason: many important indicators (for example, percentage of a cohort attending) for initial education must report on the proportion of 'non-traditional' students included in the data. Information on adult students within formal adult education is seen only as a by-product, because definitions are too narrow to represent the whole of 'adult education'.[8] This claim comes as a surprise, because no comparable source of informa-

---

7 [U]nesco[O]ecd[E]urosat

8 *'It is recognised that in some countries there are, in addition, adult education programmes which are NOT reported in the UOE. (…) Therefore, these tables are not an attempt to collect comparable data on all adult education in countries. The UOE includes only partly the adult education which exists in countries: The adult education with subject content similar to initial education, leading to similar qualifications as corresponding initial programmes. The new tables will mainly be used to exclude adult education from initial education in presentations.'* (UOE 2010b, 34–35).

tion is available for formal adult education and much more information is collected on formal adult education than reported. Therefore, the UOE provides the most elaborated 'specification' of what should be counted for available 'formal adult education'. Given its importance, I outline the specification's most important features of 'formal adult education' as stated (virtually unchanged since 2005) in the 2010 UOE manual edition (see Overview 3).

Overview 3: Definition of formal adult education according to the UOE manual

Element	Definition
'Adult'	'*the learning activity of those returning to education after having left initial (or 'regular') education.*' [2010a, p. 7] – yet, there is no age threshold and no further specification for 'leaving' initial education (such as a minimum of two years)
'Age'	Exact age should be reported as for any student *('age as of 1st January 2009 for academic year 2008/2009'* UOE 2010a, p. 37)
'Programmes' to be included	'*The activities involve studies with subject content similar to regular educational programmes, or – that the underlying programmes lead to similar potential qualifications as corresponding regular educational programme.' [2010a, p. 8]* – programmes should be included irrespective to their general or vocational orientation or their provision within *'the same educational institutions which provide initial education or by educational institutions (or components of institutions) specialising in adult or other continuing education' [2010a, p. 8]*
'Programmes'* not to be included	Any programme not similar to initial education, in particular '*courses or classes for adults that are primarily for general interest or personal enrichment and/or for leisure or recreation' [2010a, p. 8]*. Following the general rules, any work-based programme with less than 10 percent school attendance should be excluded.
Classification on ISCED levels	'*Students in programmes designated as "continuing education" or "adult education" should be assigned to the most appropriate ISCED levels. Adult education should not be treated as a separate level of education*' [2010a; 8]
Minimal length/'workload' of programme [since 2005**]	*At least* the equivalent of one semester full-time study (as for all educational activities reported ***
Full-time or part-time programmes	Participation in full and part-time programmes has to be reported; in case of part-time programmes, full-time participation equivalent has to be calculated (2010a, 42ff).

Source: Own description based on UOE 2010

* '*Educational programmes are defined on the basis of their educational content as an array or sequence of educational activities which are organised to accomplish a pre-determined objective or a specified set of educational tasks. Objectives can, for instance, be preparation for more advanced study, qualification for an occupation or range of occupations, or simply an increase of knowledge and understanding*'. (OECD 1999, 8)
** UOE 2010b, 16 'A new requirement on a minimum duration of one semester for programmes (1/2 of the Academic year as defined nationally) is introduced. Enrolments in programmes of shorter duration than one semester, full-time equivalent duration, should not be included in the enrolment statistics. This applies to adult education as well as to initial education.'
*** 'Programmes of shorter duration than one semester, full-time equivalent as defined nationally. This applies to programmes specifically designed as adult education as well as to any initial programmes of this short duration.' (UOE 2010a, 5)

By excluding any programme fully in the workplace and not under external control and by introducing (in 2005) a minimal workload, the standard strongly shapes what is regarded as 'formal adult education'. However, data reported by the countries might be as close as possible to the 'administrative' understanding of formal adult education in participating countries. Data on formal adult education collected by the UOE statistics urgently need in-depth analysis, which is beyond the scope of this chapter. However, a significant proportion of adult learners (25 years+) lies among all participants in formal education (ISECED 2–6): in the LLL2010 countries, the proportion of adults among registered participants varies between 8 percent (Ireland) and 18 percent (Flanders). As a percentage of the 25–64 years old age group, participation rates ranges between roughly 2 percent (Bulgaria) to roughly 5 percent in Belgium.

2.4 Distinctions in the English language between 'formal' education and 'formal' learning

In many languages, formal adult education appears as something like an oxymoron – at least in the light of available definitions in thesauri, lexica and handbooks. Other than entries on the 'formal/nonformal/informal' triad (Colletta 1996), recent handbooks on adult education have no entry – not even in the subject register – for 'formal adult education' or 'formal education' of adults.[9]

When European nation-states gained control over education, other actors within the field of educational services had to withdraw from 'formal education'. In many countries, the field of adult education gained its identity by (and was often forced to obey) a double negation: the adult education did not include 'formal education' or 'vocational education', yet provided various fields of 'self help', 'homemaking' or 'liberal education' in the tradition of the 'liberal arts' curriculum that focused on history, languages, arts and expanding to modern curriculum such as natural sciences or foreign languages. Changing political pressures determined whether or not adult education covered social sciences and political issues: in more liberal periods, adult education may include urgent social issues; in more authoritarian periods, anything interfering with 'politics' must be either carefully excluded from the courses provided or become a state-controlled activity with a tolerated field of 'self-organisation' of citizens. Thereby, formal education became equalised to 'initial education': adult education became liberal (non-vocational) further education.

UNESCO's first manual (1975) on the statistics of adult education reflects this 'division of spheres' very clearly. Statistics on adult education should supplement the statistics on 'formal' education in schools and universities (p. 1). However, the first edition of terms in adult education of 1979 already considered a 'traditional' narrow and a 'UNESCO promoted' wider definition of adult education, including both 'formal' and 'vocational education'.[10]

---

9 There is, for example, no entry on formal adult education in Aspin (2001), Merriam et al. (2007), Jarvis (2009), Kasworm et al. (2010) or Rubenson (2011).

10 Adult education refers to
1. Any organised and sustained communication designed to bring about learning for the benefit, and adapted to the needs, of persons who have completed the continuous cycle of initial education

English (and many other languages) use 'formal' within further and adult education to express another distinction. Most frequently, 'formal' education of adults indicates 'taught courses' that follow some kind of curriculum and leads to some kind of certification, compared to more 'informal' or 'nonformal' learning opportunities. A typical example for 'formal courses' within adult education is language courses, because such courses typically end with some kind of 'test' or 'certification'. Many countries, however, maintain clear differences between a certificate gained for a language course within adult education and a certificate issued by an institution of formal education. Examples for nonformal courses include any taught classes without certification (beyond stating mere attendance), without clear and staged curriculum. Informal (yet organised) adult education includes regular meetings, where group members work on particular subjects or engage in a particular activity such as groups exploring the local nature every Saturday afternoon.

In the literature on vocational and further training, 'formal' is used for 'taught courses', outside the workplace, while 'informal' is used for the plethora of planned or non-planned activities allowing for learning in the workplace. Surveys on training in companies try to measure some of these 'informal' ways of supporting learning; for example, the CVTS framework classifies activities such as 'job rotation' or 'quality circles' under the heading 'other forms of training' (CEDEFOP 2010).

Finally, 'formal' could become not only an attribute of an 'educational programme', but an attribute of a type of 'learning'. Here, 'formal' marks understanding a pre-defined body of knowledge (for example, European history) taught in an explicit curriculum or acquiring abilities (for example, correct use of grammar in a foreign language). 'Formal' learning refers to 'curriculum' and 'school-knowledge', where 'informal' learning refer to non-codified learning or even strictly 'tacit' knowledge such as learning to respond to group dynamics or to clearly make one's own point. Typically, 'informal' learning refers to the 'hidden curriculum' and the structural effects of educational organisations on the learning and socialisation of individuals. When used within a typology of learning, we find typically 'formal', 'nonformal', 'informal' and 'accidental' learning. However, as often emphasised, types of 'learning' do not equate with types of 'education': any formal educational programmes include 'for-

---

commenced in childhood. Higher and post-school education undertaken before entering the labour market is not normally considered to be adult education.

2. In the UNESCO Recommendation on the Development of Adult Education, the term denotes the entire body of organised educational processes, whatever the content, level and method, whether formal or otherwise, whether they prolong or replace initial education in schools, colleges and universities as well as in apprenticeship, whereby persons regarded as adult by the society to which they belong develop their abilities, enrich their knowledge, improve their technical or professional qualifications or turn them in a new direction and bring about changes in their attitudes or behaviour in the twofold perspective of full personal development and participation in balanced and independent social, economic and cultural development.(UNESCO 1979, 33)

mal', 'informal' and 'accidental' learning. Most 'nonformal' courses also use 'formal' learning (see Simkins 1977).

The literature offers various and partly competing meanings of 'formal' in the field of adult education. Definitions of 'formal' education and learning in global and European glossaries co-exist with different definitions given in statistical manuals of the very same global and European organisations. Other languages partially have the complex use of 'formal' as in English. However, given the role of English as the common language of researchers and practitioners with the European Union and beyond, all members of the fields participate in the confusion.

To sum up, while 'formal adult education' clearly refers to a statistical entity, policy documents and the research literature on adult education hardly use the expression in the same manner.

2.5 Three statistical concepts and data sources: UOE, AES, and LFS

Three concepts and three data sources cover the definition and implementation of formal adult education; these also represent three historical layers of accounting for education of adults within 'the system of schools'. We have learnt that measures for 'formal' education of adults were already in place when the triad of formal/nonformal/informal education took centre stage in the world of global (adult) education. 'Formal' education requires registration, this allows for statistical reports on participants and – if that information on the participants is made available – the representation of adults 'participating in the system of schools and universities'. Collecting data on formal adult education occurs within the ongoing translation of national register data into statistics that follows standards set by global organisations engaged in educational policies. This leads to the introduction of the UNESCO-OECD-EUROSTAT approach, which has become the world standard for statistical reporting on education. Quantitative surveys within adult education, however, focus in their methodologies on the 'nonformal' part of adult education because information could not be taken from any registers for the many courses scattered over the social space.

Consequently, European Union surveys on adult education leave formal adult education in the shadow. The Labour Force Survey (LFS), and, consequently, the 2003 Ad-hoc Module on Lifelong Learning, tried to identify participation in formal adult education by providing a list of institutions; however, no further information was gathered beyond participation or non-participation in one of the selected types of education. Lists of education organisations represent a narrow definition of 'formal education', also present in the UOE-tables. Therefore, the LFS approach remains bound to nationally established visions of 'formal education' and their subsequent developments.

While remaining under the influence of 'register-statistics' for formal adult education, the Adult Education Survey (AES) breaks with the tradition of taking for granted the 'formal' parts; it collects various data on formal adult education, but not as much as for nonformal adult education. The range of activities which could become visible and could be classified as 'formal' expanded, because the AES increased the number of learning activities to be reported (up to 15 instead of up to 3 in LFS-Ad hoc Module) and allowed for a close revision of the 'formal' or 'nonformal' status of any course taken by adults. Its definition sticks to the 'triad' approach, yet reflects ongoing developments by including 'representation' within a kind of 'framework of qualifications' that served as a new 'proxy' for 'within the education system'. Changes in methodology and definition led to a fundamental change of learning activities represented as formal in some countries, but it changed little for others.

Overview 4: Comparison of the three main statistical concepts within comparative statistics on formal adult education

	UOE-system Traditional school statistics ('inscriptions')	**LFS (LFS Ad-hoc module 2003)**	**AES**
Introduced	1970s	1960s	2005–2007
Dynamic of 'breaks' in time series	Continuously (multiple breaks) on country level	Considerably stable	Changing understanding of the framework's contents
Definition of 'adult'	Having finished initial education	Older than 25 years	Older than 25 years
Proxy for 'adult'	Various age breakdowns	-	-
Range of programmes	Within the officially recognised system of schools and universities or leading to a qualification represented within the system or provided by an organisation of the initial system	Provided with the system of schools and universities	Within the officially recognised system of schools and universities or leading to a qualification represented within the system, respectively a *National Qualifications Framework* or provided by an organisation of the initial system
Time frame of observation/units	'inscriptions' for a programme at a given point of time (no matter, how many courses making up the programme)	Participation within a 12 month period	Participation within a 12 month period
Workload of the programme (total length)	Minimum of a 'term' full-time education	No criteria	No criteria

Source: Own description

The statistical concepts have small, yet important, differences with each other. All three concepts have the same core – provision within the system of schools and universities. The UOE and AES both expand the concept to anything provided within the formal system or leading to a recognised qualification. The AES more closely defines 'recognised' as 'represented by a framework of qualifications', while more traditional views (as 'provided or controlled' by a public authority) remain in places for the UOE and LFS. The UOE defines 'adult learners' as anyone having left schools: because no data are collected on this point, age breakdowns identify adults. The LFS and AES use, but do not define, the category of adults. The UOE requires a minimum workload of 'one semester of full-time education'. The LFS does not ask about any minimum level, yet not much difference should arise from this point, because it asks about attendance in schools or university programmes, usually implying a considerably high work load. The AES also does not seek information on any 'minimal workload', but first asks about courses then classifies them later with plenty of opportunity to potentially label 'short' courses as 'formal'.

When comparing the results of the three statistical sources, we note that the UOE and LFS report formal adult education as at approximately the same level in Belgium, Norway, Estonia, Lithuania, Hungary, Austria and Bulgaria. Only in the United Kingdom (England and Scotland) and in Slovenia, does the LFS indicate considerably higher participation rates among adults than by UOE. The AES reports higher participation rates in formal adult education rates in most countries (with the exception of Hungary). The methodologies and concepts actually lead to an extraordinary expansion of formal adult education in Belgium, Norway, the United Kingdom and Lithuania. However, when using a proxy of 200 hours of reported coursework for meeting the UOE minimum requirement, the picture changes again. Figures for formal adult education become much more in line with the two previous representations: outstanding differences between countries, however, disappear.

Diagram 2: Results for three measures of formal adult education

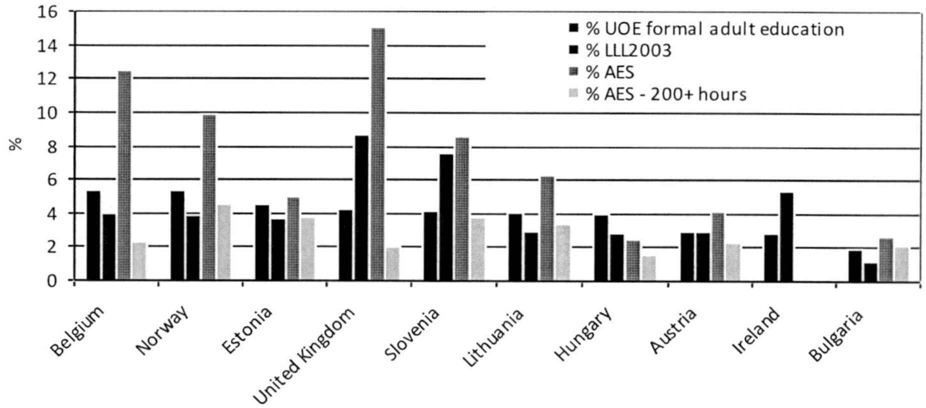

Source: LFS 2003; UOE 2007; AES 2005–7; own calculations

As we have seen, the statistical methodologies are ambiguous and cause considerable bias. For methodological reasons alone, figures must differ when we consider the likely effects of 'register counts' (cross-sectional, one moment in time) and surveys (collecting participation rates within a 12 month period).[11]

11 The three concepts cover, first, different participant groups of adult learners, reflecting their different conceptual basis, yet, secondly, fail considerably to meet their own intentions by more or less important 'measurement errors', which are far from negligible. The UOE statistics perceive con-

2.6 Outlook: Understanding country figures on formal adult education

Ongoing changes in statistical representations and differences between countries must not be taken as mere 'artefacts': Beyond causing difficulties in measuring, these changes represent ongoing developments in the understanding and organisation of education, and, consequently, formal adult education, within particular countries. While particular countries clearly participate in transnational trends, they also vary greatly because of the history of their national education systems and their institutionalised embeddedness into the wider society.

As we have seen, the following institutional developments of initial and formal adult education directly change what potentially does or does not count for formal adult education:

1. allowing more organisations to provide education regarded as 'formal' (for example, organisations providing programmes to prepare for external examinations);
2. classifying more programmes as 'formal' by including education provided within active labour market policy (Sweden, Norway) or financed by the Ministry of Education (Flanders);
3. offering much more different qualifications and preparation programmes on different educational level, in particular, within vocational education on ISCED 3 level and, post-secondary or post-tertiary level (ISECD 4, 5a, 5b);
4. offering more modularised programmes;
5. allowing more qualifications to be achieved by collecting credits within or outside the formal education system so that any course providing credits can be reported as 'formal' adult education.

Countries differ considerable on how the five shifts become vital for their systems. Diagram 3 provides a tool for clarification by distinguishing between two sorts of diversification.

On the one hand, particular new organisations may arise without a presence in initial education but providing formal adult education. Examples include 'evening schools' for adults, controlled by the educational authorities present in all countries or some organisations run by public employment services that award formal degrees. The number of organisations providing education, regarded as formal, could considerably increase by various mechanisms, such as offering 'external examinations' or

siderably broad ranges of programmes as 'formal', yet reporting ministries lack data and therefore cannot report them. The LFS results intend to represent available formal opportunities, yet there are too many for implementing them in any questionnaire. The AES reports various credit-providing courses as 'formal', yet participants do not intend to gain 'qualifications' at all. Even where data provided by different sources seems more similar, considerable parts of formal adult education may not be reported. However, some activities reported as formal definitely do not interest us when analysing formal adult education as a particular social institution.

forming a system of credit-based qualifications. Countries differ clearly in the range of organisations involved in formal adult education.

On the other hand, the number of programmes or courses that provide credits for acquiring qualifications may increase. The programmes' content may become more narrowly defined. In addition, workload could become more variable and include short courses. When credit-based qualifications become available, even short courses potentially contribute to them and could (although not necessarily) be counted as formal. Countries differ clearly in the range (content, length) of available programmes regarded as 'formal'.

Different levels of diversification among programmes (and, certainly, groups of participants) within formal adult education result from the range of organisations entitled to engage in formal adult education and the many programmes, different in content and workload. While we find countries with considerable low differentiation (Bulgaria, Estonia, Hungary, Russia), we find countries with medium (Slovenia, Lithuania, Austria and Norway) and considerable high variation (Scotland, England, Ireland, Belgium). High diversification results primarily from varied credit-based qualifications or rules from different important institutions. Medium diversification, for example, comes from distinguishing between available qualifications provided by an ever-increasing number of highly specialised organisations. In countries with low diversification, we typically find restrictive control by educational authorities for the 'scarce' good of acknowledged qualifications that labels various existing educational opportunities only as 'nonformal'.

Diagram 3: Grouping of countries according to the degree of diversification of the formal adult education system

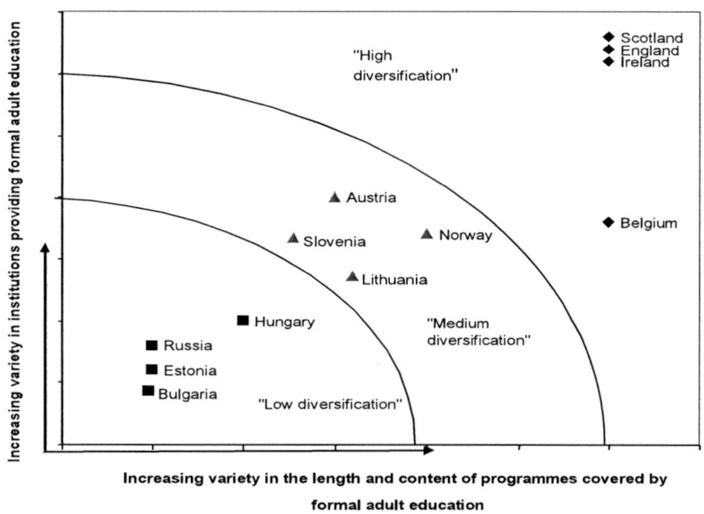

Source: Own description

Without reflecting on the diverse perceptions of formal adult education, statistics on formal adult education could not be interpreted, for example, with regard to the social composition of the student body. Figures reflect both the overall level in participation in lifelong learning and the narrower or broader understanding of formal adult education resulting from different pathways in control and reform of educational systems. Overview 5 provides an order to the countries represented by the LLL2010 project. The AES reports of extraordinarily high participation rates in formal adult education do little else but represent obvious differences in the meaning of 'formal adult education'.

Overview 5: Provisional grouping of participating countries

		Understanding of formal adult education		
		Clearly Narrow (more than 70 % + 200 hours)	'Medium' range (40 %–70 % more than +200)	Clearly Broad Less than 40 % more than 200
General activity in lifelong learning	Low	Bulgaria Hungary		
	Moderate	Estonia	Lithuania	
	High		Austria Norway Slovenia	Belgium Ireland England Scotland

Source: Own description

However, while the scheme helps us to avoid mistakes in using statistical data, it tells us little about the actual meaning of low or high participation rates or the actual reasons represented in the data. We need, firstly, to understand the particularities of formal adult education as a social institution and apply a definition independent of idiosyncrasies of national educational statistics. Secondly, we need to know what types of formal adult education are actually present and show their particular logics and tendencies for expansion or contraction. Actually, we need a typology of formal adult education. Providing a new conception of formal adult education and a typology of organisational fields, given the rise of formal adult education, are consequently the goal of my next chapter.

Chapter 3: Formal adult education as a social institution

3.0 Introduction

When non-formal education – for young people as well as for adults – was promoted in the late 1960s as an alternative to a strongly criticised formal education system, critics highlighted what might be lost for non-formal learners. Although they might acquire knowledge, skills and competencies, they may not gain the wider social benefits that the institutionalised education system delivers for its graduates. Opting for 'formal' or 'non-formal' education has an impact on the *institutional effects* of the education system beyond any learning opportunities. John Bock already emphasised in 1976 that as long as the institutional logics of the formal education system remain in place any non-formal education suffers from its lack of institutionalisation:

> [I]f schools are seen as serving an important mobility management function, strictly controlling access to elite status through the application of certification rules, then nonformal education is viewed as potentially even more inhibiting of the mobility prospects of lower status groups. For, by not providing either the accepted and socially valued certification or the non-cognitive attributes necessary for 'promotibility,' nonformal education locks workers into the lower segment of the occupational structure. (Bock 1976, 349f.)

References to the institutional dimension for differing formal from non-formal education have virtually disappeared in the more recent literature. More recent contributions (Roger 2004, Hoopers 2006) on the formal/non-formal distinction, while noting the literature of the 1970s, do not explore the institutional effects of education. Yet, in my opinion, the most satisfying, problem-oriented way of justifying the distinction between formal and non-formal education refers to its institutional aspects. While non-formal adult education typically has few institutional effects, we could explore the institutional effects for formal adult education and identify their intended and unintended consequences for the participants and the non-participants. Institutional theories on schooling and higher education provide a promising starting point for the analysis of formal adult education.

In this chapter, I start with an introduction on institutional accounts of formal education, which I will use throughout the book. I intend to fill the gap left in the discussion on 'formal' adult education that does not characterise 'formal education' (Roger 2004, 76) beyond a list of its allegedly inappropriate features. In the next section, I start with a short clarification on the different meanings of education as a social institution. In Section 3.2, I provide an overview of important themes of an institutional theory of education. In Section 3.3, I continue to discuss selected institutional motives on the school-employment link. Next, I introduce two lines of analysis of organisational institutionalism, which I will use to build up my theoretical argument (Section 3.4). In Section 3.5, I discuss the possibility to define formal adult education by its 'social charter'. In Section 3.6, I propose a typology of seven organisational fields, responsible for the institutional characteristics of seven types of formal adult education. In the outlook (Section 3.7), I use my approach to outline further steps in comparative research on formal adult education.

3.1 Three meanings of formal (adult) education as a social institution

Addressing 'education' as a social institution provokes little opposition. Everyday language naturally refers to an 'educational institution' or an 'educational institute', meaning a particular school, academy or university.

Defining formal adult education as a social institution requires declaring what 'social institution' actually means and what should be analysed. The analysis of institutions, certainly, is at the heart of social-science disciplines since their founding in the late 19th century. The notion 'social institution' has numerous competing meanings that oscillate between social institution as – in the Durkheimian tradition – a '*fait social*' (for example, 'unemployment', 'marriage', 'private property', 'universities') and as perpetually ongoing *institutional processes* creating what becomes 'objectified' as the social institution in question.

In the early 1980s, various 'new' approaches within institutional analysis mark 'an institutional turn' (Nielsen 2007) within social theory, notably in political science, economy and sociology. Using the attribute 'new' (Powell & DiMaggio, 1991a) has caused much confusion, because it works quite well in some contexts as 'older' traditions of institutionalism fell out of fashion (for example, economics of markets or organisational research), while in other disciplines institutional approaches have never lost their central positions (for example, sociology of education, industrial relations). With the expansion of approaches quite different in scope and arguments, positioning 'old' versus 'new' hardly works for gaining an overview; therefore, recent approaches in institutional analysis become typified in alternative ways (Hall & Taylor 1996, Campbell & Pedersen 2001). All three main strains of neo-institutional research – 'rational choice institutionalism', 'historical institutionalism' and 'organisational institutionalism' – are relevant for my purpose of studying formal adult education.

However, 'sociological' approaches have faced what has been called the 'economic imperialism' (Baron & Hannan 1994), following the rise of economics to become the dominant social discipline, shaping policy and public discourse on nearly any social issue, notably education (Fourcade 2006, Lebaron 2000). The outstanding success of 'human-capital theory' to justify public spending on education as 'the best economic policy we have' (Tony Blair, 1997, cited according to Gorard & Rees 2002, 4) threatens to marginalise any other approach to education. Policy driven studies repeatedly ask for the individual reasons for participating in and the societal outcomes of education: a dominating framework based on 'methodological individualisms' becomes institutionalised in the wider society together with the belief in the benevolent qualities of education. While the sociology of education has overcome mainly individualistic accounts for explaining the world of education, highly simplified rational choice and human capital models, often provided by professional economists, prevail because of one social discipline dominating others.

While sociological research on education accepts institutional approaches, widely different concepts exist on the meaning of education as institutions. In Overview 6, I distinguish three understandings or levels of analysis.

Overview 6: Three meanings of education as an institution

	Initial Education System	**Formal Adult Education**
Particular Type of organisation or type of programme	Gymnasium Dual apprenticeship	Evening Gymnasium Executive Master of Business Programme
System Approach Functional and hierarchical relations between types of organisations/ programmes	Levels of education Entrance permissions Opportunities to change between tracks Differentiated qualification levels of teaching personnel	Preparation for higher education Permissions to enter a profession
Formative Categories and Symbolic Systems	'Membership' in a category of graduates 'League tables' of 'good' and 'average only' Legitimated/non-legitimated speaker positions Feelings of superiority/inferiority towards members of other membership groups	Changing membership categories in adulthood (becoming eligible for positions otherwise out of reach) Holding of 'state of the art' expertise legitimised supervision

Source: Own description

(1) Types of organisations and programmes

Institutions could be defined as particular types of educational organisations, such as ('elementary school', 'gymnasium', 'university') or a programme of education ('apprenticeship', 'study of medicine'), that stay 'institutionalised' in the sense of 'founded' and 'arranged in a permanent manner'. Typically, these are studied by examining their historical foundations and any change in their legal and regulative basis. Types of organisations or programmes can be studied within a society over time and as 'institutional forms' which diffuse internationally and potentially become a 'world standard'.

Studying formal adult education clearly requires accounts for the 'institutionalisation' or emergence, regulation and evolution of types of organisations and programmes on local, national and transnational levels. Some types are highly diffused across groups of countries (for example, 'evening gymnasiums'); others are more specifically bound to a few countries ('preparation for craft-master examination'). Different kinds of programmes could meet various system functions (for example, access to higher education). Some types and organisations and programmes in formal adult education mirror existing counterparts in initial education; however, others only occur for adult education (for example, Executive Master of Business Administration programmes, vocational retraining programmes).

Any institutional approach on formal adult education must explain the existing varieties of types of organisations and programmes. Explanations of participation in formal adult education require an exhaustive description of the 'menu available' that includes a theoretically justified clear distinction between 'formal' and 'non-formal' educational activities.

(2) Relations between organisations and programmes: the system level

Studying education as an institution refers to the system of relations between educational organisations and their programmes. The system consists of elements such as types of organisations and programmes, types of rules connecting elements ('admission rules'), organisations of supervision and funding, types of governance and standardisation instruments ('curricular', 'grades', 'examinations') and types of qualifications and graduates. Moreover, the system relates to other societal institutions such as particular modes of governance (centralised versus decentralised system) or teacher-employment systems (public versus private employment).

An organisation has a place within the 'educational ladder', understood both as a functional system and a system of symbolic hierarchies. Organisations and programmes accept students prepared by lower level of organisations and allow or do not allow students to progress to higher levels. Particular 'institutions' may serve particular social groups and link their faith with their students' faith. Various groups of stakeholders – the students, the parents, the future employers, the teachers, the educational administrations – exert their influence for continuing or changing the status quo. Organisations and programmes with similar 'functions' or 'products' compete with each other for resources, students and placing graduates in the labour market. Existing organisations and programmes, which fear marginalisation, could oppose new ones. Any introduction of new elements potentially alters the 'rules of the game' and established hierarchies. In short, to study education as an institution implies carefully considering how introducing a new programme, changing admission rules or expanding student bodies affects the education system.

Studying formal adult education also requires clearly focussing on the 'system level'. Formal adult education undoubtedly depends on the characteristics of the initial system. There are three principle ways how programmes of formal adult education connect to the initial system. Programmes of formal adult education try, firstly, to *imitate* initial programmes and follow any change of their initial system counterparts. Secondly, many programmes of formal adult educational look for their place within the wider system by simply *subordinating* to existing programmes in the initial system, becoming a second-best, second-chance alternative for anyone who may have missed the more prestigious opportunity within initial education. Thirdly, within niches – for example, closely connected to occupations or professions – formal adult education *expands* the spectrum of available educational opportunities beyond the scope of the initial education system. The modes of how programmes of formal adult education relate to the initial systems make up an important dimension for understanding different types of programmes (see Section 3.6).

(3) Formative categories and symbolic systems for the wider society

In its most comprehensive sense, formal education as a social institution refers to the effects of education on the wider society. It includes the issue of how to coordinate the 'education system' with other 'functions' of social life, in particular, employment. However, education does not only influence other parts of the society through its graduates, but also by changing the fundamental categories and symbolic systems of any part of the society. Effects studied include the creation of formative *social categories* (1) and comprehensive *symbolic systems* (2) and social *belief systems* (3) or social myths, orientating the behaviour of society as a whole.

(1) The education system creates and is built on *social categories* – for example, the creation of 'school classes', of logical continuation between 'grades', of membership categories such as '*Maturant/in*', 'university graduate' and 'dropouts', of disciplines, of knowledge in or outside the curriculum, worthy or unworthy of being taught or being accepted as a proof of performance – and make them universal for modern societies. They become social categories in a neo-Kantian (Cassirer) or Durkheimian/Maussian sense and change the way members of a society see each other and themselves. They change a society's possible ways of 'thinking' and behaving. While modern sociology of education has at its heart the study of 'structural effects' of education (for example, Dreeben 1968), the institutional approaches argue that 'structures' become institutionally reinforced and thereby symbolically over-determined.

(2) 'School knowledge' produces symbolic systems, particular worldviews, where everything fits into various categories that become related to various groups of students on various levels of education. For a certain group, anything could be either 'to be known' or 'not relevant'. Knowledge becomes inscribed in a

hierarchy of 'low' or 'elementary' and 'high' and 'advanced', with vast areas classified as 'irrelevant' or even 'inappropriate'. Challenging knowledge becomes a 'practical function' but also a prerogative for particular groups of educators and types of students.

(3) Education shapes *belief systems* that orientate behaviour of members of the society. The education system asserts, for example, that higher ranking graduates of the education system possess more abilities required for working effectively than members holding lower degrees. These claims are taken for granted and orientate behaviour in, for example, hiring, rewarding (according to payment schemes) or promotion. Individuals know about appropriate behaviour – for example, in their cultural consumption – that reflects their 'educational background' and, independent of their preferences, governs their every-day behaviour. Deviation from appropriate behaviour sanctified by education requires explicit strategies.

Studying formal adult education requires a comprehensive view on education as a social institution. Formal adult education could only use the social categories introduced by the education system. Their own curriculum symbolically interacts with the systems established by initial education. To be socially relevant, formal adult education has to enact beliefs in the value of education, instilled by the education system in general. However, adults participating in education, not children or adolescents, create tensions between various elements institutionalised by the initial education system and what actually took place within formal adult education.

Formal adult education, consequently, *imitates* initial education's categories, symbolic and belief systems and demonstrates cognitive isomorphism. Formal adult education has to partially accept *subordination* for applying institutional mechanisms inherent in initial education, yet, not in line with the adult status of its participants. 'Latecomers' in achieving qualifications may be labelled as 'second best' among graduates, yet remain better off than those of lower educational status groups. Finally, formal adult education clearly *expands* the scope of education as an institution by providing social categories, symbolic orders and beliefs not available within initial education. Formal adult programmes, requiring professional experience, establish patterns of 'legitimised' supervision or management functions within occupational or professional groups – the 'craft mastership' or the 'master of business administration' (MBA) are both examples.

3.2 Elements of a theory of schooling

Consequently, understanding formal adult education requires reviewing the most important elements of an institutional account of schooling. Therefore, I discuss some 'fibres' of the 'fabrics of schooling' in the following and relate findings to formal adult education. Steven Brint's (1998) excellent introduction to institutional theories on schooling ('old and new') will serve as a guide through one of the most expanded fields of sociological research.

Fabrics of schooling

'Schooling has three major purposes in contemporary societies: the *transmission of school knowledge* [...], *socialization*, the training of values, attitudes, and habits of conduct; and *social selection,* the sorting of people for higher- and lower-level jobs in society' (Brint 1998, 100, author's emphasis). Unlike short courses where socialisation or selection effects might hardly be an issue, for formal adult education, all three purposes of schooling deserve reflection.

Transmission of knowledge: For formal adult education, transmission of knowledge, skills and competences seems to be the most vital issue. Yet, the tasks involved are far from trivial. For young people, acquiring 'school knowledge' competes with knowledge and attitudes towards knowledge from other life spheres, particularly, the family and community life. However, for adults, any claims made by 'school knowledge' to be right and relevant, must also meet the accumulated knowledge of previous working life and more general life experience. Justification for acquiring the 'knowledge' to meet examinations requirements become more demanding, as adults know from personal experience what is or is not relevant in the real world life. The cocoon of schools as an upside-down world does not unconditionally function any more. Moreover, adult learners know very well about the poor survival prospects of any knowledge acquired just for examination purpose. 'School knowledge has a short half-life [...], when it has a life at all.' (Brint 1998, 102). They might be less prepared to acquire knowledge that will be immediately forgotten afterwards. The curricula should require better justification and favour learning outcomes more commensurable to the current interests of adult learners. However, adults may also reactivate their survival strategies of earlier schooldays, focusing on little else than passing examinations, seeing credentials earned the only promises formal adult education has to offer to them (Asselmeyer 1996).

Socialisation: Socialisation in pre-, elementary and secondary schools is a key issue, because schooling interferes with core developmental processes of childhood and adolescence. Schooling made an impact on the unfaltering self of the young, for the good and for the bad, yet, deals with 'students' whose cognitive abilities are evolving and whose ego development go through a series of fundamental changes within short periods in a fairly predictable manner. We expect adolescent development to be completed before adult education, so that any socialisation has to deal with already developed adult identities. Nevertheless, we clearly want adult education to have socialisation effects on their participant and support developmental steps in adulthood (see Chapter 4). Second-chance education should develop the same attitudes towards knowledge and learning expected from higher secondary education. 'Continuing professional education' should deeply instil values of the related occupations or professions. Moreover, because development processes are conceptualised as continuing beyond adolescence, formal adult education will use 'windows of opportunities' ('teachable moments', Havighurst 1972) for promoting personal growth.

Social selection: Formal adult education – contrary to non-formal – could be defined as fully immersed in the issue of social selection: perhaps in this dimension, formal adult education most resembles initial education of young people. As with initial education, various social groups measured for their social origin ('the long arm of the family') and for the type of present work place ('the long arm of the job') have unequal access to more prestigious tracks in formal adult education. (Rubenson & Desjardins 2009) The increasingly important diploma in formal adult education redefines groups eligible for promotion, employment as an expert or progress to higher levels of education. Formal adult education thereby contributes to the education system's selection function by expanding possibilities for participants and restricting the opportunities for non-participants.

Far from monopolising 'education' or 'learning', the system of schools provides particular structures with which the modern society builds its institutions (for example, the rule of law, representative democracy, the bureaucratic work organisation and the labour market).

The 'logic of school organisation' could be summarised (Brint 1998, 8ff.) by the headings (1) 'selectivity', (2) 'sequencing' and (3) 'boundaries'. Schools do not teach everything to everyone, but choose what might be learnt (stated in a 'curriculum', converted in a 'grid' of subjects and hours) to selected individuals eligible for schooling. Schools address various issues and individuals may fail to meet requirements for becoming pupils of a particular type of school. School orders everything into a logic of progression, first teaching 'elementary' courses and then 'advanced' subjects. Consequently, schools could penalise individuals for not having the expected knowledge and could exclude questions on matters 'too complex' for a given level. Finally, schools erect clear boundaries between an inner space and an outside world; these borders potentially allow for a fresh start of socialisation process, for and against any forces of the pupils. Schools necessarily create 'worlds upside down', ruled by moral orders substantially different from its environments.

Formal adult education clearly participates in the 'logic of school organisation' and often applies the same instruments (for example, curricula). A dominating feature remains exclusion of themes and issues. Sequencing of knowledge learned is common; however, the more heterogeneous entrance levels of adult participants call for more flexibility. Because of greater prior knowledge and experience, adult learners could less easily than adolescents be denied the right to advance to any desired level of complexity. When developing programmes in formal adult education, we clearly face more complex issues than with ordinary schools. Teaching habits perfectly adjusted to 'initial education' may show their 'dark sides' when applied to adult learners. Boundaries between the school world and the wider society are more difficult to erect for formal adult education than initial education, because students typically have more involvements outside their education. While andragogy involves responding to and working with the quotidian experiences of adult students, adult education also requires crafting and defending space for learning, untouched by any other demand of adult life. Adult learners may demand – consciously or unconsciously – to return temporarily to the incubator such as that typically provided by schools of children and adolescents.

The idea of schools as 'upside-down' worlds governed by a 'moral order' (Brint 1998, 11ff.) refers to 'a set of share norms of conduct, orientation, and identity' (ibid, 12) responsible for many of schooling's socialising and institutional effects (Kamens 1977, Meyer & Rowan 1978).

Firstly, schools strictly organise 'time and space' for maximum efficiency as an organisation. 'School bells' dissect time devoted to various subjects and allow for movement between rooms of pupils and teachers. Neither the learning process nor the individual, but an organisational blueprint regulates time and movements in space, socialising participants into a perfectly rationalised, impersonal order. However, children as adults may exactly demand an alternative organisation for their learning process, providing plenty of opportunity for educational reform.

Secondly, schooling includes *differentiating* and *integrating rituals* that allow for a sequencing and classifying of pupils according to their adjustment to various values superimposed by schooling. This forges an emotional bond among members of the school community and particularly pupils and the organisation. For adults, most traditional school rituals do not apply but have to be replaced in one way or other.

Thirdly, schooling imposes *status hierarchies*. Pupils have to both accept and 'naturally obey' status hierarchies and also compete for rank in the various status hierarchies. Everyone ranks high or low in any balanced hierarchy, the school – by definition – gives something to every child in exchange for the pupil's support for the established order. Competing informal hierarchies, developed by pupils in hallways and the playground complete the indoctrination and provide alternative rankings, rewards and punishments. Adults have not only been socialised into status hierarchies during their initial education, they have experienced more and competing social hierarchies during their adult lives and careers. Formal adult education thus faces much more complex conditions for inducing their status hierarchies within the socialisation process of participants.

Fourthly, schools create *standardised membership categories*, which 'allow unequal people to be treated more or less equally' (Brint 1998, 13). Any holder of a certain educational certificate is regarded as being more similar to the category of 'graduates' and fundamentally different to all 'non-graduates', no matter, how much anyone in these categories actually knows or can do. Yet, types of courses ('Macroeconomics'), number of credits ('four credits') or categories of teaching personnel make incommensurable educational 'input' measurable and institutionalise their very meaning. Good formal education provides access to *standardised membership categories* – irrespective of the relative position within these categories – in exchange for minimum levels of devotion and hard work from students. Formal adult education aims at a change – a progress – from one membership category to another. However, the institutional force mobilised by formal adult education compete with the initial education systems to exert power over any individuals' life course. For further exploration of this idea, I turn to two further works of John W. Meyer.

The 'Charter': Institutional effects of education (Meyer 1970, 1977)

'What is learnt at school' (Dreeben 1968) depends not only on the formal and hidden curriculum, but also on anticipating a student's future role and place in the society. Knowing what one is institutionally designed to become shapes individual perceptions of and practices within school socialisation, for the good and the bad. Individuals that know their schools prepare for prestigious positions requiring knowledge, skills and 'morals', typically work towards this imagined future and accept the school's claims as necessary for achieving a preset goal. On the other side of the spectrum, schools preparing students for uncertain futures have little to offer in exchange for their students' acceptance of their demands, so the students will consequently socialise themselves according to alternative patterns available in their life world, developing an identity independent or opposed to school values and their few available opportunities.

Meyer (1970) introduces the term 'social charter'. By social charter, Meyer understands 'the agreed on social definition of [an education organisation's or programme's] products' (p. 565). An educational programme owes its effects not only to its contents or its way of provision, yet, 'include effects the [providing] organisation has by virtue of its charter in the larger society.' (p. 568). This 'social charter', however, is highly independent of any other feature of a programme or organisation (such as the curricula or the teacher-student ratio), because schools with highly comparable educational techniques connect institutionally to both promising and disappointing social careers. However, the 'charter' itself becomes a major socialising instance.

In this way, the 'social charter' self-reinforces the institutionalised effects of education attached to a particular combination of programme and providing organisation. All programmes with charters for favourable outcomes most likely lead to favourable outcomes. Students learn more when expecting a more prosperous future and they become eligible for more advantaged careers even without any proof of their superior potential or performance. For programmes with charters for less favourable social positions, the 'charter' may not only result in negative socialisation, but the low prestige of the graduates' educational achievement may result in powerful social discrimination that impedes career progress.

Consequently, the 'charter' attached to an educational programme in initial or in formal adult education represents the social effects of education, both on individual socialisation and on the perception of a graduate in wider society. This makes an individual *eligible* for entering or progressing in available social careers that lead to more advantaged or more disadvantaged social positions. While *eligibility* may not be enough for progressing to more favourable, but more competitive positions, the exclusion effect of not belonging to prestigious categories can hardly be overcome by any individual effort (perhaps by 'second-chance education', when institutionally available and valued). Moreover, charter effects could be highly general, such as becoming an 'academic' or 'college graduate'; this offers eligibility for a broad selection of advantageous careers, or highly specific eligibility for a particular career in public administration or profession.

In his seminal contribution, *'The Effects of Education as an Institution'* (1977), Meyer generalises and systematises his assumptions. The institutionalised beliefs on education shape socialisation in schools and 'lagged' socialisation throughout adulthood; this socialisation produces categories of personnel with varied scopes for individual development, as perceived by themselves and their social counterparts like employers, superiors, co-workers or family members. However, the nature of categories of personnel, the quantitative relations between 'elite' and 'mass' position and the range of 'possible futures' for them is not predetermined through 'technical' requirements for a defined number of available places. While 'allocation theory' observes only how defined social positions awarded to credential holders, Meyer stresses the effects of the educational system *creating* social positions. Education could produce either a small successful elite and masses virtually robbed of any opportunity for social progress or masses with competences developed for progress and only a few individuals excluded from education and social advancement. However, by specifically relating categories of society members with charters for career opportunities, reforms and changes of the educational system imply considerable alterations for groups, not only for participants. Any expansion of education – including formal adult education – produces both winners and losers.

Formal adult education, not explicitly present in Meyer (1977), deepens education as a social institution: It can correct for negative charter effects by creating alternative pathways to eligibility for more 'empowered' social positions. Moreover, it expands the available pathways, allowing entrance into a specific type of formal adult education. Thereby, more people become eligible for the more advantageous positions. At the same time, it incites 'social closure' and de-legitimisation mechanisms: holders of particular educational credentials can monopolise competences achieved in various ways.

3.3 The education-to-work link as a social institution

John Meyer's concept of 'social charter' was originally introduced to explain an independent component of socialisation within educational organisations. Independent of any 'knowledge', skill or competence transmitted and therefore any functional and human-capital-based explanation, Meyer also suggested a theoretical link between education and the world of work: within societies, social groups fight for the ways to institutionalise the link between education and the world of work. Meyer explicitly aims at providing a more comprehensive theory that includes contemporary Marxist (Bowles & Gintis 1976) and credentialists positions (Bourdieu & Passeron 1996, Collins 1979). Ideas of 'educational capital' (Bourdieu) or the 'span of qualification' (Maurice et al. 1986, see Chapter 6) represent comparable ideas of how to theorise the connection of 'education' and ' work', when the functional argument fall short. A particular test case for developing an institutional theory of the school-employment link is the faith in vocational education, which is immediately useful yet devalued in many societies.

The great divide between general and vocational education

The cultural divide between intellectual work, proper for high-status members of the society, and 'manual' work, only appropriate for low status groups, has powerfully shaped education systems. Traditionally, any 'higher' education has excluded more practical, vocational subjects. Early compulsory, 'terminal' education offer practical instruction for pupils working in agriculture or domestic work, yet, vocational education remains mainly outside education. By the middle of the 18th century, only state-funded, highly specialised military engineering and professional schools, where science and mathematics allowed for enough social distance of 'lower' manual activities, represented 'vocationalism' within education.

Until the late 19th century, a craft or a trade was learned outside the educational system and not regarded as 'education'.

> After completing a number of years of primary schooling, – when it was available, working-class children sought apprenticeship training in artisanal and industrial trades under the tutelage of a master craftsman or worker. The character of apprenticeship frameworks, in contrast to schools, was both distinct and informal: few were differentiated by age or ability level and there was little emphasis on formal certification and credential conferral (Benavot 1983, 64).

However, medieval traditions of guilds, providing apprenticeships, were substantially weakened by early industrialism, where division of labour and mechanisation reduced dramatically the required numbers of *Gesellen* (journeymen). In the 19th century, members of skilled occupations in the crafts and trades represented a small minority that formed the lower middle class. To enter a trade, considerable fees have to be paid to the craft-masters for vocational education provided 'on the job'. Moreover, training in crafts and trades – for example, teaching bookkeeping and practical arithmetic – was provided on a for-profit basis by various organisations, which may be called 'schools', yet remained strictly outside the legitimate 'general' education, defined and controlled mainly be the churches. Up to the 20th century, 'skilled workers' defined themselves more frequently as 'small entrepreneurs', than as part of organised industrial labour (Streeck 2011, Thelen 2004). With a few workers and apprentices, they provide services for the industry and for private customers alike. Achieving high levels of expertise in various fields of vocational competences remain their particular capital; yet beyond the more general 'titles' (Master, PhD), these Dreyfus-type '*ladders of expertise*' (Dreyfus et al. 1986) remain strictly informal and undocumented: economic success of the individual enterprise defines the social status of the 'skilled worker', which may become rich or stay poor.

During the 19th century, the rise of the state education system and – during the first half of the 20th century – internal labour markets within the corporate economy fundamentally changed the acquisition of vocational skills. Moreover, the transformations had highly different outcomes for various societies.

The systematisation of education and the rise of different tracks of 'secondary education' incorporated vocational training – both apprenticeships and schools – into the system. Schools accepted state-control in exchange for state funding and a new mixture of curricula elements of 'general' and 'vocational' orientation. In some countries (for example, England, France or the United States), 'vocational tracks' became or remained 'terminal', and represent only lower ranges of the 'educational ladder'. However, in other countries (for example, Germany and the successor countries of the Austrian-Hungarian monarchy), 'vocational tracks' formed an educational ladder of their own, leading up to 'professional' higher secondary and tertiary education. Where vocational tracks do not allow access to the higher ranks of the education system, the society demeans vocational learning. However, even in countries with prestigious vocational education tracks, only some segments of vocational education have high symbolic value, while other segments charter only for low-status, low-income jobs.

To sum up, the social charter of vocational education depends on their institutional link to occupational careers – to entrance points and job ladders that lead to the more favourable positions – and not at all in their usefulness. Therefore, any institutional theory of (formal) education has to observe the organisation of work and how it allows for particular types of careers.

Institutionalising careers: organisational, vocational and professional career patterns

Career patterns become institutionalised, that is, subject to stable and shared expectations by all parties involved in the labour contract: the individual seeking employment and the hiring organisation, yet, also trade unions, business-interest organisations, regulatory authorities, courts and many other parties (Jones & Dunn 2007,

Lawrence & Tolbert 2007). The social charter could also be expressed as the promise that a particular education functions as a 'building block' within career patterns. Following Arthur's broad definition of career as '*the evolving sequence of a person's work experience over time*' (Arthur et al. 1989, 8), career involves any social trajectory in the world of work. This includes highly restricted careers (Guest & Sturges 2007) promising stable positions after a short introductory phase for a unspecified time as well as highly structured pathways that lead from entrance positions in more peripheral areas of contributions to top management position in the functional centre of organisations. Education and further formal adult education become an expectation – a symbolic function – within the *visions* of careers, as institutionalised in regulations ('minimum standards', 'equal opportunity' procedures), norms ('identifying a rank order of qualifications when choosing the formally best qualified candidate') and cognitive, 'taken for granted' assumptions ('mathematics is harder to master than literature').

Research in institutionalised career patterns had its heydays in the late 1970s and 1980s. It particularly described the emergence of 'internal labour markets' between approximately 1940 and 1970 for the United States and the advent of firstly, white-collar career patterns, and, secondly, blue-collar job ladders (Jacoby 1984). Internal labour markets emerged as a dominating structure in large U.S. corporations as a result of wartime economic policies and a new government-supported compromise between employers and empowered labour unions (Baron et al. 1986). In democratic European states, labour unions in post-war economies gained in state-supported strength and institutional legitimacy. Lifetime employment, constant pay raises and regular career ladders become projected as the 'normative' employment model for the 'golden age' between 1950 and 1975. However, 'internal labour markets' have been established mainly in public services and in large (1000+ employees) and major enterprise (10,000+), which have never employed a majority of all employees (Osterman & Burton 2006). Even large companies had never matched fully to this model for white, male, non-migrant employees and had openly excluded women, migrants, and members of discriminated race or minorities from this model. 'Internal labour markets' could be used as a tool for suppressing workers, who may remain excluded from stable employment after losing their contract with the employer where they had started their career. By allowing or denying access to organisational career trajectories for particular groups of workers, enterprises became key players for social stratification (Baron & Bielby 1980, Baron 1984, Bielby & Baron 1986): they still play this role. (Lounsbury & Ventresca 2002, DiTomaso et al. 2007, Stainback et al. 2010).

Interest in the theory of internal labour market and other forms of institutionalised careers had sharply declined by the middle of the 1980s, presumably as a consequence of the 'dramatic decline' of job stability, which become the hallmark of public opinion and research since the 1990s. What became 'the new employment narrative' (Hollister 2011) explained how a sequence of fundamental shifts in employment practices undermined the stable employment relationship serving as the foundation for traditional career models. Practices such as 'automation' (1970s) and 'computerisation (1980s) reduce the demand for skilled blue-collar work. 'Business-reengineering' and new approaches in quality management allowed for dramatic 'downsizing programmes' and eliminating layers of middle management, fundamental for the career ladders of white-collar workers. 'Outsourcing' allows for radicalised versions of segmented internal labour markets and off-shoring for an economy that requires no domestic blue-collar workers. Global trade and production networks have radically transformed industries (for a populist account, see Deal & Kennedy 1999; for a more balanced overview Osterman & Burton 2006). The dominating post-modern sociologists such as Ulrich Beck or Richard Sennet strongly supported this view. They argue that institutionalised career patterns and their institutional basis such as the trade unions will probably give way to highly individualised career patterns, where the individuals make the best out of a 'brave new world' (Beck 2000) of unavoidable risks and unprecedented opportunities. Career research provides new metaphors for this type of 'individuated' career patterns that takes the 'model' and the 'reality' as identical: concepts include the 'protean careers', 'boundary-less careers', or 'hybrid careers' (for a review, see Sullivan & Baruch 2009).

Comparative cross-sectional and longitudinal studies on the relative stability of career patterns, however, reveal a more limited change in life-course employment and career patterns. In the U.S., for example, average employment tenure has decreased for mid-career men (from 40–44 and 50–54 years), yet, increased for mid-career women at nearly the same rate (Osterman & Burton 2006). The downsizing and dismantling of U.S. economy for the 20 largest 'old economy' giants has reduced their workforce from 4.5 to 1.9 million employees between 1977 and 2002. However, the same period saw the rise of major enterprises of the 'New Economy': in 2002, the 20 largest corporations already employ 600,000 employees (Lazonick 2006). Although different for groups within the labour market, the employment stability in the United States declined in the 1990s, but was also comparatively low in earlier decades (Mills & Blossfeld 2008). For Europe, comparative longitudinal studies show slight or no decline in job stability for mid-career men and increasing stability for women – employment regimes with traditionally high levels of job security tend to prolong the pattern throughout the 1990s, while employment regimes with low security tend also to continue their overall pattern – there is clearly no common trend toward decreasing job security through Europe (Bernardi et al. 2006, Blossfeld & Hofmeister 2006). The observed changes in employment patterns do not support the rhetoric of dramatic decline in job stability.

Relative changes and public discourse on job stability, however, have certainly changed the institutionalised expectations for occupational careers: the promises of 'life-time' employment no longer embody the ideal of 'good' employment relationship. Feelings of insecurity have risen everywhere, in particular for groups of employees (for example, male, middle-management university graduates) who have traditionally not suffered job instability. Nonetheless, surprisingly 'small' changes in job security over birth cohorts reveals that even in the 'golden ages', stable careers were the prerogative of some groups of employees and not a reality for everyone. Yet, despite a loss of institutionalised legitimacy, employment stability still provides space for more institutionalised career patterns (Mayer 2009, Mayer et al. 2010). Models developed in the 1970s and 1980s, therefore, could still provide a starting point for investigating the institutionalised patterns of career pathways in today's societies.

The institutionalisation of career patterns is at the core of studying the institutionalisation of governance of work and industrial relations, a field with a strong tradition in institutional analysis (for a broad overview, see Blyton et al. 2008). Business associations, chambers of commerce, trade unions and interest organisations of the professions typically represent employers and workers who fight and collaborate with each other in establishing institutional orders. All parties seek state support for their cause. This institutionalisation interacts with other sets of institutions such as the welfare state, the typical family patterns, the division of family work and homemaking between the sexes or the discrimination against genders, ethnic minorities or migrants.

Typically (for example, in Fligstein & Byrkjeflot 1996), three types of careers are delineated:

Organisational careers: Within organisations, belonging to one area of institutional life, typical career pathways for groups of employees or types of workplaces become established, legally enforced, normatively expected and cognitively taken for granted. Work requiring no particular skills could be organised, for example, in 'dead-end' jobs that allow for no *institutionally foreseen* progress after the probation phase. Jobs could, however, also be organised within ladders, leading from more simple, more inconvenient, lower-paid jobs to more complex, more convenient, better-paid jobs: organising any jobs into career ladders become thereby an institutionally expected organisational practice, including various institutional complementarities (as for example, closed internal-labour markets and long-term employment). For skilled and highly skilled labour, particular career models establish professional ladders that lead either to more managerial authority or to wider areas of technical contributions. Educational credentials legitimate career patterning. Effects on individual life chances of institutionalised organisational career patterns come not only from a single employer, but also from the interaction of employers, shaped by the institutionalised rules for organisational careers.

Occupational (or vocational) careers: Occupations organise skills and capabilities to exercise *institutionalised* bundles of pre-defined tasks: as an institutionalised rule, only trained members of an occupational group can legitimately do the tasks. The levels and nature of institutionalisation of occupations and their relevant vocational training vary widely between societies; however, at least some occupations have occupational career patterns present everywhere. Career patterns consist typically of an extended initial training, school-based, workplace-based or in a combined (dual) mode. Phases of practical experience, overseen and supported by more advanced members of the occupation, provide for 'deliberate practice' to gain higher levels of expertise in the various field of competences, bundled together by the occupational profile. The 'craft-master' examination serves as the most traditional example of the formal assessments of professional expertise, governed or co-governed by various occupational bodies. Occupational careers interact with organisational careers because employer organisations must sufficiently respect the task bundles institutionalised by a singular occupation; furthermore, members of a certain career level (typically, level of qualification) must not be employed for work requiring a lower level of expertise. Institutions could value educational credentials within occupational career patterns in various ways: returning to formal education – for example, on the higher secondary or tertiary level – could mark an expected step for anybody striving for more advanced positions within occupational career ladders.

Professional careers: Professions control and codify a body of knowledge and state of the art practice, securing the exclusive rights for providing related service for their members. Access to professions typically requires higher education in a defined discipline as well as satisfying other qualifications requirements, defined by the professional bodies: professions, therefore, control the 'production of producers' (Larson 1977, 49). Professions typically seek state support to secure exclusivity: binding and enforceable regulations require states. Areas of state regulation include the boarders between related professions, access routes to the profession and criteria for moving to senior positions with a field. Institutions have rules, often legally enforced, on relations between organisational career patterns and professional career patterns: Employers must respect areas of work reserved for members of professions; this requires hiring properly trained professionals for any posts. Beyond more traditional professions (lawyers, medical doctors, architects), employment systems may have a higher or lower number of professional groups. Typically, countries with a strongly institutionalised occupational system have a less strongly institutionalised system of professions and vice versa.

In all three institutional career patterns, formal adult education – as initial formal education – could become an institutionalised 'step' that provides eligibility for entering a career track or making progress on one track. By becoming institutionalised, particular programmes in formal adult education receive their particular charter, relevant for the particular career pathway – a mechanism, I will explore in a cross-country comparative perspective in Chapter 6.

3.4 Selected core concepts of 'organisational institutionalism' preparing a theory of formal adult education

While I cannot provide an introduction to organisational institutionalism (for introductions see Scott 2008b, Walgenbach & Meyer 2008, Senge 2011; for an in-depth overview, see Greenwood et al. 2008) I quickly introduce two lines of argument, which I will use for developing both a theory on and a typology of different forms or fields of formal adult education. As I argue in Sections 3.5 and 3.6, educational organisations belonging to one *organisational field* deliver various programmes of formal adult education. The institutional charter of programmes is achieved by various institutional mechanisms, among them various types of isomorphisms, a concept that I will explore.

Organisational populations, organisational sets, organisational fields

No matter how far reaching their influences, institutions typically arise, are shaped, reproduced and changed in more local orders, not in the society at large. Shifting the focus for institutional analysis from societal level to more discrete, more strongly connected, more specifically knitted local orders marks the most important breakthrough within organisational institutionalism (Scott 2008b, Chapter 8; Wooten & Hoffman 2008).

Institutional life takes place within *organisational fields* – according to the seminal paper of Paul DiMaggio and Walther Powell (DiMaggio & Powell 1983):

> *By organizational field we mean those organizations that, in the aggregate, constitute a recognized aera of institutional life: key suppliers, resource and product consumers, regulator agencies, and other organizations that produce similar services or products. [...] The virtue of this unit of analysis is that it directs our attention not simply to competing firms [...] as to the totality of relevant actors.* (DiMaggio & Powell 1983, 148)

Scott inserts the terminology (taken from organisational ecology[12]) of *organisational population* for any organisations providing a service in question and competing with each other, and *organisational set* for all the other types of organisations crucial for institutional life as regulatory authorities, organisations administrating public (co-) funding, collective interest organisations or customers.

To identify an organisational field as an area of institutional life, DiMaggio and Powell require a minimum and steady increase of interaction between all parties, re-

12 The organisational ecology approach was developed by Michael T. Hannan, John H. Freeman and others in close interaction and collaboration with the protagonists of emerging 'organisational institutionalism' and provide much of the empirical approaches for studying organisations over time in carefully design longitudinal studies, also fundamental for institutional research. The interaction between the two contemporary schools and their partly converging, partly competing claims, must not be overlooked. For an excellent overview on the approach and an exhaustive review on empirical studies, see Baum & Shipilov 2006.

sulting in a reciprocal awareness of behaviours demonstrated, requiring the development of minimal infrastructures for managing information observed within the interaction processes. The strongly increasing interaction between the members of a field results in the development of structures of dominance, subordination and exclusion; this compounds institutional processes with power relations. Most importantly, organisational fields replace the more vague, more general notion of organisational environment: particular organisations share and interact with their particular organisational fields as environments, *as they become relevant for them*. Therefore, any potential institutional influence, coming from 'outside' the organisation (for example, a management fad, a new regulation), become 'filtered' and 'translated' by the organisational field and its particular established institutional order.

The idea of *organisational fields* builds on the rich tradition of field approaches in social sciences (for a review, Martin 2003), in particular on Pierre Bourdieu's concept of *social field*. Alternative formulations of related ideas appearing about the same time, include Scott and Meyers proposal for 'societal sectors' (Scott & Meyer 1991) or Whitely's idea of 'business systems' (Whitley 2007). However, there is a risk of confounding the organisational field concept with functional systems and miss its focus on institutional processes[13].

Within their organisational fields, organisations are not doomed to passivity, but could strategically respond to institutional pressures (Oliver 1991) and work purposefully towards a change of the status quo, turning into *institutional entrepreneurs* (DiMaggio 1988; for a review Battilana et al. 2009). While most organisational actors

13 Two caveats are crucial for not losing the outstanding capacities of the organisational field concept. Firstly, organisational fields should not be confused with more traditional ideas of 'functional systems', which have become differentiated as more independent areas in the advancing division of labour. This danger looms large, when addressing the 'organisational fields' of general hospitals, higher education or adult education that as part-systems also become present in a functionalist account. However, organisational fields arise around much closer defined 'products' (for example, museums of contemporary fine art (DiMaggio 1991), academic publishing (Thornton & Ocasio 1999) or haute cuisine (Rao et al. 2003) or even social issues (for example, environmental protection Hoffman 2001). Typical 'functional sub-systems' could actually be found in highly disparate organisational fields, with contradicting institutional processes, logics, rules and consequently outcomes. How many organisational fields actually 'populate' one wider area of societal life, could not be forecast theoretically; they remain to be detected by empirical research. From a comparative perspective, countries probably have different amounts of clearly distinct organisational fields for one type of 'product' ('second-chance education') or issue ('promotion of equal opportunity in education'). Secondly, organisational fields function as economic markets only as far as any economic market is itself an institutionalised area of organisational life, such as an organisational field. Important aspects of organisational fields include economic competition and 'technical' feedback processes rewarding or penalising organisational behaviour. However, they interact closely within the institutional order established within an organisational field. Moreover, any economic sector (for example, according to the classification of economic activities) is a candidate for becoming an organisational field, yet, typically, one economic sector contains more than one field, and the subfields may hardly be connected at all. To sum up, the statement that organisational or social fields work like 'markets' is true only insofar as an institutional view on economic markets replace simplified economic models (Fligstein 2001, Fligstein & Dauter 2007).

can not influence institutional processes on the societal level, they generally can influence processes at the organisational level. While radical institutional change is comparatively rare on societal level, competitions for change and persistence are daily issues within organisational fields. After becoming locally established, institutional innovation could diffuse among fields and build momentum to eventually change society. By adopting the organisational field level, organisational institutionalism shifts away from accounts of 'persistence' and isomorphic (ritual) 'compliance' to the study of conflicting interests and power (Lawrence 2008), 'change', strategic behaviour and institutional innovation.

Finally, the organisational field approach allows for overcoming typical divides such as the 'local' and the 'global' or the opposition between 'inside' (for example, competition processes within the field) and 'outside' (for example, influences of another organisational field) drivers for current developments. Any 'institutional power' such as the normative claims of professional organisations or attempts for trend setting by transnational policy organisations such as the UNESCO or the OECD, could be modelled as 'within' the organisational field under study to the extent that members of the population or the set create representations for them within the field. Any global-scale-policy recommendation could influence organisational fields when local players adopt successfully their claims for their own strategic purposes, becoming institutional entrepreneurs by reusing what external organisations brought into the game. By their 'co-optation', potentially any organisation outside an organisational field could create a 'virtual branch' inside the field and becoming influential as a kind of intruder. However, when no players make 'external' institutional claims a matter of the field, or when the strategy for adopting positions fails because of too strong resistance, then more 'macro', more 'global', institutional processes might have no impact. 'Importing' institutional claims requires no ladder, running from more local to more societal or more global levels or vice versa: any local actor can potentially borrow from global organisations, without any transmission by societal level actors. Following the same argument, any more macro, more global, institutional prescription will produce highly different institutional outcomes in local organisational fields.

Cohesive (regulative), normative (professional) and mimetic (cognitive) isomorphism (DiMaggio & Powell 1983)

Any organisation must secure its legitimacy by at least partly obeying to institutional claims. Beyond introducing the concept of organisational field, the DiMaggio & Powell's article (1983) proposes three types of interrelated and overlapping processes that shape how organisations could participate in the institutional legitimacy established in their proper 'arena of institutional life', could add legitimacy to their own products and could secure acceptance as a member organisation of the field. By sharing collectively established sources of legitimacy, organisations make themselves consciously or become unconsciously more similar to each other; therefore, the authors speak of *isomorphic processes* that lead to greater similarity of organisations and their behaviour within an organisational field.

Organisations providing formal adult education have three available options for securing their legitimacy and the legitimacy of their 'products', the social charter of their programmes. They could, firstly, participate in the institutional legitimacy of initial education, claiming to be a (special) member of the relevant organisational field of initial education. Secondly, they could participate in the social legitimacy of occupational and professional fields, and, to a lesser extent, the organisational fields – the 'economic sectors' – for which they prepare their participants. Thirdly, they could model themselves according to the most legitimate organisations established in a particular field of formal adult education, yet, the strategy requires a considerable development of the field, strong enough, to produce and safeguard its own legitimacy. The three strategies might be occasionally conflicting, yet not generally exclusive, and might be pursued simultaneously by a single organisation or a group of organisations that provide a type of formal adult education (see Section 3.6).

DiMaggio & Powell (1983) describe three types of isomorphic processes:

A first *coercive* isomorphic process implies that organisations model their structure and processes according to existing formal laws or less enforceable rules and regulations relevant within a proper organisational field. Educational providers could, for example, orient themselves on ways to define their curricula, to choose and assess their personnel or to report on their output and quality-control procedures. Various authorities or the organisational populations could establish regulations in formal adult education. Their business-interest associations may define various kinds of accountability guidelines. For example, expectations for quality-control systems resulted in introducing quality-management systems within (formal) adult education. Various approaches are imported to the organisational fields or further developed; moreover, funding organisations or regulating bodies negotiate the establishment of their own quality-control approaches within the fields (Hartz 2009). Organisations in formal adult education, therefore, could be required to demonstrate a quality-control approach even without any formal requirement.

These more formally governed coercive processes are complemented by a second, more informal, *mimetic* (or cognitive) isomorphic process, where organisations model themselves according to visible examples of organisations that enjoy high level of legitimacy within an organisational field. By mimesis, organisations avoid being perceived as illegitimate when entering into new fields of activity not highly structured by regulations or explicit prescriptions for good practices. Practices of prestigious organisations in initial education – for example, leading universities in their field – could be copied for preserving or achieving legitimacy. Expert committees, safeguarding professional excellence, could be modelled according to panels established by professional associations, which reflect their views of which discipline must be represented and which sub-fields might be ignored.

The third isomorphic process is called *normative* and refers mainly to the homogenising impact of professions on organisational fields. Organisations gain legitimacy by creating positions and organisational units (for example, for quality management, equal opportunity and diversity, for counselling, etc.) and by employing properly trained experts for the established fields. By sharing a common training, experts import their worldviews and cognitive structures into the organisations. By exchanging professionals over their employment careers and by established exchange platforms such as professional societies, journals, symposiums or continuing education, more idiosyncratic innovations in one organisation spread over organisational populations. Professionals also change between organisations of the population and members of the organisational set such as regulatory authorities or funding organisations (cf. DiMaggio & Powell 1983, 152f).

All three isomorphic processes – which became the basis for Scott's three pillar framework of institutional analysis (Scott 2008b) – contribute to particular types of formal adult education. However, as I will show in Section 3.6, different types of formal adult education differ considerably on the relative importance of initial education, the professions or future employer organisations and the models available within the own field.

3.5 The existence of a programme 'social charter' as defining criteria for formal adult education

By putting into effect the institutionalised qualities of initial education or other sources of institutional legitimacy, formal adult education *charter* its participants for achieving social positions in a way not possible by non-formal adult education. The existence or inexistence of a particular charter is therefore proposed as the most vital defining criteria for dividing formal from non-formal adult education.

Diagram 4 summarises the elements of my framework for understanding formal adult education. As a social institution, formal adult education represents *institutional processes* creating a particular range of *institutional effects (B)*, not in place for non-formal adult education. I focus on institutional effects on the eligibility for particular further steps in educational and in particular occupational careers (I, II, III). Beyond their more general symbolic value, particular types of programmes in formal adult education could thereby become institutionalised within organisational, occupational or professional career patterns.

The 'social charter' of formal adult education is created within *organisational fields*; namely a field of the programme (a) and a field of the adult participant's occupational career (b), thereby requiring an overlap between two fields.

Institutional effects of formal adult education could be studied as attached to particular educational opportunities (A), consisting of programmes (*type of programmes(x)*) provided by a particular *educational organisation (y)* for a *group of typical participants (z)*. While institutional effects are mainly attached to the institutional qualities of the educational programme, the 'symbolic' (institutional) value of the providing organisation and the particular group of participants cause considerable variation.

Diagram 4: Framework for defining formal adult education as a social institution

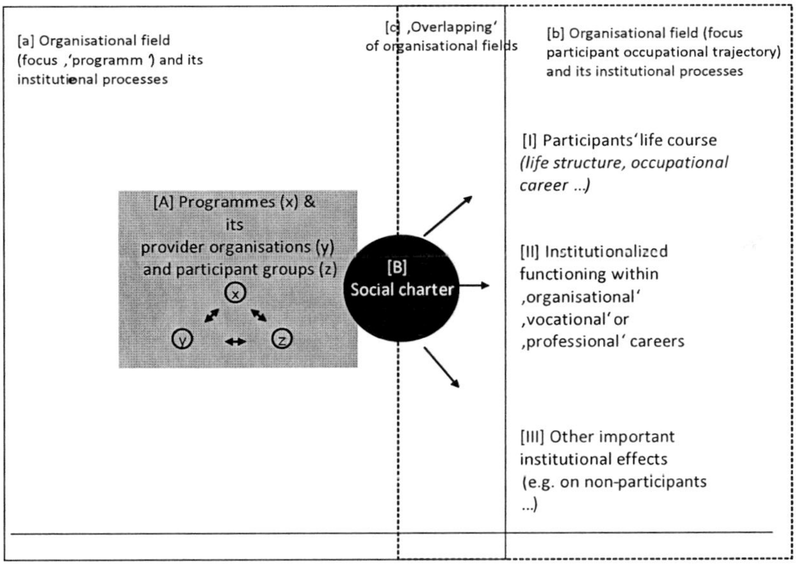

Source: Own description

A preferable starting point for analysing and understanding formal adult education would be an exhaustive account of all *formal* educational programmes[14] open to adults [A]. The UOE criteria provide a feasible definition (see Chapter 2.3) that covers formal programmes of initial education open for adult students and programmes separated from the initial system offering comparable content.

The social charter relies partly on the type and status of a particular provider organisation. (Think about the difference between an 'Ivy-League' university or a 'no-name', for-profit provider both offering programmes in, for example, marketing.)

14 For educational programmes, I use the definitions available in statistical manuals of the global statistic system, namely 'educational programme is defined as a collection of educational activities which are organised to accomplish a predetermined objective or completing a specified set of educational tasks' (OECD 2004, 80).

Thus, the provider organisation offers a kind of 'index' to a formal programme. Typically, programmes attract particular types of participants, speaking of their social and professional background. Moreover, the provider organisations anchor formal programmes in particular organisational fields (for example, the field of higher education organisations; the field of for-profit training providers, etc.).

While also comparatively short programmes could have important institutional consequences (for example, providing permission for particular occupational activities), only programmes of – compared to years of schooling in initial education – a significant length should be considered as formal. We expect more extended institutional effects only for longer programmes. The UOE criteria of 'at least the equivalent of *one* semester of *full-time* education' seems an acceptable proxy.

Finally, we must consider accessibility for 'adults'. UOE provides a feasible criteria for adulthood ('having left the initial system'). Programmes described as formal adult education could engage both adults and initial students.[15]

While UOE criteria provide a clear guide for discerning between formal and non-formal programmes and for organising an exhaustive list of formal programmes, the criteria offer little help for analysing the meaning of 'formal'. If a programme fails to produce the institutional effects connected to its 'social charter' for formal (adult) education, then it is not formal education. If a programme regarded as non-formal has a clearly visible social charter (for example, preparing for promotion), then it should be considered as formal.

The social charter of a programme and related institutional effects of participation [B] and/or completion of formal adult education affects the following.

(1) *an individual participant's life course:* It expands not only the institutionally available or expectable moves within the life course, but also the programme's institutional 'charter' imprints the socialisation during participation. While a programme includes socialisation and requires adaptations, the 'mutual expectations' connected to the 'charter' exerts an influence, independent of the specific educational setting.

15 Contrary to other possible connotations I particularly stress the requirement of an explicit 'decision' (no matter how motivated) to return to education later in life. Formal adult education must imply this decision to 'return'. Because typical 'interruptions' of initial education might take place (for example, traditions of 'gap years', 'voluntary services' or 'military services' after higher secondary education), the definition of 'returning' implies a longer interruption (for example, an interruption of at least two years as proposed in the LLL2010 project definitions.). Moreover, age thresholds may be required for overcoming missing data (for example, on interruptions). This definition excludes, for example, non-standard educational careers, where multiple, yet, unrelated educational programmes overlap in the world of education. 'Multiple training episodes' with initial education occur when programmes on the same hierarchical level are completed. In addition, scarce employment opportunities lead to a prolongation of initial education as a more legitimate 'waiting status' than unemployment. (Hillmert & Jacob 2003)

(2) *eligibility for steps within career patterns:* Formal adult education creates 'building blocks' within organisational, occupational and professional careers. Institutional effects include wageraises, access to types of careers, eligibility for promotion, and legitimacy for management authority or applying expertise. The institutional effects typically connect to graduation/completion of a programme, yet are independent of the learning or competence development achieved or learning effects' persistence over time.

(3) *'non-participants':* Any institutionalisation of formal (adult) education affects the life chances for individuals, comparable in their starting positions, who do not participate in a programme of a particular 'social charter'. Eligibility for particular career moves is either reduced or simply over-ruled by the institutionalisation of particular programmes within career patterns.

The varying institutional effects of programmes' social charters are substantial enough to justify their systematic exploration. Studying the emergence of the 'social charter' of formal programmes requires examining the organisational fields – the areas of institutional life – that serve as the source of the charter.

Creating the social charter of a particular programme involves both the organisational field (or fields) of an educational organisation and the organisational fields of potential employers for which a programme prepares.

The provider organisation (a) anchors a programme within one (or more) organisational field(s), where providers of comparable services interact with enterprises, employing graduates and various other types of organisations. Local characteristics of organisational fields are key for understanding the institutional effects of formal adult education programmes. Changes in the organisational field may alter fundamentally the institutional qualities of formal programmes, even when their content and provision stay the same.

Potential employer organisations, for which a programme prepares, also belong to particular organisational fields with their legitimate employment practices and career trajectories. However, different from initial education, adult participants work or have worked for one or a series of enterprises, belonging to various organisational fields. With the exception of attempting a 'new start' – after wiping the slate clean – the participant's individual life course anchors the participation event in a particular organisational field, respectively institutional environment. The effects of a formal programme depend on the overlap between organisational fields responsible for creating a programme and the organisational fields providing employment. Without a link between the two fields, an individual may not benefit from the institutionalised career opportunities promised by a 'formal programme' – a case seen as a 'skill mismatch' for initial education.

Exploring typical features of programmes in formal adult education

When reflecting on typical programmes in formal adult education – a four-year, evening gymnasium, a two-year, part-time preparation course for craft-master examination, a part-time, university master programme, a part-time master course in health care, a two-year part-time Master of Business Administration – we could outline some typical characteristics of formal adult education programmes, which we would not expect for most non-formal courses. Overview 7 presents an ideal type of programmes in formal adult education, which I will discuss in more detail.

Overview 7: Typical characteristics of formal adult education programmes

a) are of substantial length (several months to several years) involving a significant number of learning units and related tasks
b) provide potentially one step upward on the educational ladder, in regards to an existing hierarchy of qualifications
c) require an authority acknowledging them (often the state)
d) require regulation of its relations with the initial educational system
e) support – as part of a socialisation experience provided – a substantial gain of competences in a range of fields, marking a clear difference between before/after the program
f) provide – compared to the starting position – a significant improvement in the competitive position on internal/external labour markets (no matter if realised or not)
g) overcome potentially the symbolic consequences of being excluded from progressing to higher levels of education

Source: Own description

Programmes of formal adult education *are of substantial length involving a significant number of learning units and related tasks:* One programme normally lasts for a longer period, starting from several months (for example, six months) to several years (for example, four years). Many programmes open for adults preparing for vocational qualifications on the ISCED 3 level often take 9 to 18 months. Vocational schools on a higher secondary level take three to four years in many countries. Part-time programmes in higher education take four to six years. Within the timeframe, teaching involves many hours and related assignments require even more time. While the shortest programme may involve not more than 200 hours, many programmes have up to several thousand hours of instruction.

They *potentially provide one step up on the educational ladder with respect to an existing hierarchy of qualifications:* This implies, firstly, a close connection to the structures, provided by the initial educational system. On a first level, the 'size of learning packages' relate to the 'size of packages' in the initial educational system (for example, an equivalent of three to four years of learning from ISCED 2 to ISCED 3, respectively, a shorter period when prior learning is acknowledged). Higher level of qualifications results in more formal rights (for example, access to higher education, access to certain professions) and more prestige. Secondly, this implies a hierarchy of qualifications or 'membership categories' (Meyer & Rowan 1978): formal adult education receives a particular profile only with differently valued educational levels requiring different personal investments.

Programmes *require an authority (exerted by one organisation or by a collective of organisations) acknowledging them:* The need for acknowledgement implies a standardisation of the curricula (input) and/or the expected learning outcomes (the skills and competencies acquired by the graduates). Authorities can acknowledge only when programmes exist that meet standards. As in initial education, often the state or its agencies recognise a programme as formal adult education. Any authority legitimating initial education could possibly legitimate formal adult education. However, within formal adult education, additional bodies may serve this purpose; such as business associations or professional bodies that build up alliances (for example, with educational administrations) and have enough legitimacy to make claims for the value of programmes. Finally, as in the case of educational programmes becoming an 'industry standard' prior to any legal enforcement, dominant organisations within organisational fields could collectively provide acknowledgement and allow for 'formal' status even without any state intervention.

Formal adult educational programmes *support a substantial gain of competences in a range of fields, marking a clear difference in skill and competence level between before/after the program:* Programmes both 'teach a lot' (for example, demanding the reading of several thousand pages), and, by completing a programme, individuals are expected to develop further in several dimensions of competencies and personal abilities. In short, programmes should have a lasting socialisation effect and an impact on a participant's knowledge and competencies. Regardless of whether programmes are more general or more vocationally oriented, traditional academic skills should be expanded; for example, the capacity to read, to extract information, to write and to communicate about their findings and their ability to reflect critically. Normally, the 'hidden curriculum' of working through the actual subjects should improve personal skills such as coping with stress, frustration and uncertainty. Completing a certain level of formal education connects to a set of expectations of type of tasks a graduate normally could handle or could learn to handle in a reasonable time. The initial system provides 'membership categories' of educational attainment signalling (more) 'elite' positions and (more) superior potentials; these provide the blueprint for expecting 'progress' to be made for justifying an adult's 're-labelling' from a non-graduate to a graduate (Meyer & Rowan 1978). Organisations providing formal adult education, however, must not awarding formal credentials too easily, otherwise they risk the overall legitimacy of their credentials.

They provide – *compared to the starting position – a significant improvement in the competitive position on internal/external labour markets:* Graduation in formal adult education should clearly enhance opportunities such as access to the labour market. Both improved competences *and* the symbolic value of credentials create the better opportunities. However, given the importance of experience and on-the-job learning, many participants in formal adult education may already have a position that corresponds to the expected level of formal education. Therefore, new credentials could legitimate an already completed career step.

They *potentially overcome the symbolic consequences of being excluded from progressing to higher levels of education:* Completing formal programmes in adult education could signal that participants belong to a group with certain abilities and shared values, who deserve symbolic recognition. By awarding a degree, formal adult education can certify a level of knowledge, skill and competence already achieved before entering the programme: it helps to overcome the symbolic consequences of being without formal qualification. Although varying considerably between societies, the educational system divides populations into three categories: a group of low qualified ('unqualified'), who could claim nothing based on their education and could become an openly discriminated-against minority (Solga 2008); a group of medium qualified, who symbolically own a right to qualified employment, recognition for their contributions and positive discrimination against all 'unqualified' in any form of job competition; and a group of 'highly qualified', who can compete for the most prestigious and enjoyable positions and are considered to have superior ways of working and living. Even accepting that qualifications are only one ingredient in the symbolic infrastructure of class societies, formal adult education could overcome the symbolic discrimination connected to a lack of formal qualification and provide access to the competitive areas reserved for highly qualified within a society (on membership categories, see Meyer & Rowan 1978).

3.6 Seven types of formal adult education and their organisational hybrid fields

The challenging task of gaining oversight of educational provision and particularly adult education implies difficulties and shortcomings (frequently discussed in such works as Carron & Carr-Hill 1991, see also Merriam & Brockett 2007). Many typologies and classifications have been developed to classify adult education, both at the individual country level and at a comparative or even global level. Classification can be done by the *content* of educational programmes (for example, classification of learning fields), the *level* of education (ISCED), the *types* of educational organisation (running from more simple typologies, for example, 'state' and 'non-state' provision, to more complex classifications that map the whole diversity of providers), the *type of provision* (for example, full-time/part-time), the *target groups* or groups eligible for programmes, the *funding organisations* (for example, various types of public actors on national or local levels; various types of agencies) or the *purposes of education* stated by individual learner or by third parties. Existing typologies represent the 'historic achievement' of the theoretical and conceptual considerations of the field of adult education. Therefore, it would seem natural to start the analysis with some of the established typologies.

Despite outstanding efforts, isolated classifications often lead to poor results. Simply too many different entities belong within any group of programmes, providers, etc. These classifications do not properly represent anyone or anything; this becomes an even more pressing problem when using classifications and typologies in cross-country comparative research. The typologies and classifications produce mainly 'descriptive' data 'unable' to disclose the underlying social processes that explain the displayed differences, in short, the very meaning of the data collected. Therefore, despite the abundant typologies, dissatisfaction leads to ever more typologies and to inconsistent use of existing ones, which often do not survive the narrow project framework for which they were originally made.

Today's 'formal adult education' could hardly be perceived as a 'system' compared to the system of initial education; various types of formal adult education derive from different organisation fields and societal sectors and therefore have diverse cognitive frames (including forms of instruction), professional standards and normative regulations. As mentioned above, particular types of formal adult education arise as a co-production of various fields and form a 'hybrid' field with one or more centres of gravity. Variations in organisational fields may explain differences between types of formal adult education.

All classifications and typologies generally developed for education and adult education could also clearly apply to formal adult education. Every available data source on formal adult education in Europe (LFS, AES, UOE) uses core classifications such as the 'field of education manual' or the ISCED levels; therefore, further use of this information seem indispensable. The typology inherent in UOE definition for formal adult education provides a useful starting point, because it relates initial and formal adult education to each other and stress 'areas' that requires particular attention on the new programmes of formal adult education likely to emerge, independently of the initial education system and its educational organisations. However, even when combining various dimensions and classification, results are expected to be disappointing, because none of the current classifications can grasp the institutional life, the institutional processes, logics and players.

Therefore, I propose a new typology of formal adult education, which focuses on areas of institutional life that give birth to particular types of formal adult education and I specify their particular institutional characteristics within one country. Because these areas of institutional life often do not fit to established societal sectors or organisation fields, I refer to 'organisational hybrid fields', where various types of formal adult education emerge. Hybrid fields of one type may be coherent, yet may also consist of poorly coordinated, highly independent sub-fields that may be addressed as distinct organisational fields by empirical research. However, even if there are comparable sub-fields – for example, organised around independent funding sources, all sub-fields deliver services that could potentially replace each other. Each hybrid field may have hidden or temporarily suppressed conflicts about legitimate provision or (public) funding and about the 'charter' attached to its credentials.

The typology addresses ongoing institutional processes, not their immediate outcomes (for example, particular programmes of formal adult education). Consequently, characteristics of types of formal adult education could be highly different between countries and at different times within one country. The typology therefore functions more as a research framework explaining the emergence and social significance of programmes than as a classification of educational programmes. Existing typologies of educational provision are used for describing the outcomes of the institutional processes shaped by the fields.

Formal adult education in Europe could be analysed as emerging in seven main types, representing seven organisational fields (or more loosely integrated groups of sub-fields), namely.

I. Basic Skills and Remedy Programmes
II. Second-Chance Education
III. Higher Education Programmes – accessible for non-traditional (adult) students
IV. (Occupational) (Re-)training Programmes
V. Customised Vocational Programmes
VI. Post-Tertiary Continuing Higher Education
VII. Continuing Professional Education – governed by professional bodies

The headings stand for organisational fields, not 'types of programmes'. I will briefly characterise each of these fields by focussing on how the institutional qualities of 'formal' status are achieved, how the organisational populations and sets are composed and how institutional processes feed the expansion of the fields. Moreover, I refer to the following aspects selectively summarised in Overview 8.

Examples for typical 'forms' of programmes: Particular programmes illustrate a type of formal adult education (such as 'evening gymnasium' for second-chance education). Often available in many countries, they demonstrate diffusion of 'forms' across borders (for example, Master of Business Administration programmes for continuing professional education).

Relation between formal and non-formal: Often, formal and non-formal provision closely co-exist within one organisational field, an existing 'non-formal' programme will add formal qualities. Moreover, the perception of programmes as 'formal' or 'non-formal' of similar characteristics may differ between countries and periods of time: Programmes that clearly demonstrate all characteristics of formal education are not labelled as formal, while those that hardly differ institutionally from non-formal counterparts are described as 'formal', at least by statistics. However, labels are important: the opportunity for 'formalisation' of groups of programmes by representing them, for example, in newly established National Frameworks of Qualifications could itself become a motivation for institutionalisation.

Institutional processes for securing formal status and isomorphic processes: At the core of the typology is the characterisation of how isomorphic processes shape formal status – including its social charter – through participating in the legitimacy of the educational system, the professions or other established fields.

Role of employing organisation institutionalisation within career pattern: For understanding how the social charter is achieved, the role of the employing organisations and the embeddedness of formal adult education in institutionalised organisational, occupational and professional career patterns are reflected.

Organisational population and organisational set: This provides a short characterisation of the composition of the organisational populations and sets. Note, both change with time and clearly differ between countries.

Organisational fields of (adult) education present in the organisational fields: Formal adult education is provided as one of various adult education activities that build separate 'areas of institutional life'. By bringing in their particular history, professional ideologies and cognitive models, at least ten organisational fields of adult education contribute to one or more types of formal adult education (Hefler 2010a, Chapter 9.4). Consequently, more fields of adult education increase diversity in organisational fields of formal adult education. Institutional requirements may conflict with requirements established for a type of formal adult education (for example, when liberal adult education or trade unions must accept various regulations on examinations). Moreover, the rise of organisational fields of formal adult education by for-profit providers (profit-orientation) potentially alters competition by introducing more 'technical', 'business-like' elements. Finally, established players in adult education import particular traditions and normative models of instruction for adults. Principles of andragogy may, however, conflict with the ways the formal status of programmes is symbolically secured.

Groups of participants typically attracted and levels of education (ISCED) available: Fields generally cater for selected groups of adult learners and virtually marginalise or explicitly exclude others. The kinds of participants, however, may influence the legitimacy of types of formal adult education and their credentials awarded. Moreover, vulnerable groups (for example, those holding low levels of initial formal qualifications, working in low-paid, dead-end jobs) are clearly restricted to fewer fields of more precarious status than well-qualified employees in stable career trajectories. For them, fields provide qualifications on a more narrow range of ISCED levels.

Relations/overlapping with other types: Organisational fields and therefore types of formal adult education interrelate and overlap; partly they compete with each other, as programmes potentially replace others.

Social dynamics inducing growth/contraction: Various institutional processes, coming from within and from outside the organisational fields, shape the growth and dynamics within organisational fields. Analysing the institutional drivers increases understanding of particular types of formal adult education (for exemplary analysis of growth/contraction see Markowitsch et al. 2012 forthcoming)

Overview 8: Seven types of formal adult education and their related (hybrid) organisation fields

	(1) Core Issue(s) supported by formal adult education	(2) Isomorphic process mainly oriented towards:	(3) Organisational population – fields of adult education	Aspects of organisational set (selection): (4) Funding sources	Aspects of organisational set (selection): (5) Main participation groups:	(6) Typical ISCED level	Examples
I. Basic Skills Programmes	a) overcoming exclusion and stigmatisation by low literacy; b) providing access to credit-based qualifications c) integrating migrants	Initial-education system	Typically heterogeneous, highly different between countries; liberal adult education; trade unions; general education, providers linked to ALMP	- local municipalities - welfare-to-work agencies - public employment policy	- people in routine jobs (having low literacy) - unemployed -formally low qualified - migrants	1–2 (however, often embedded in 3)	- basic literacy, numeracy and IT-skills - languages courses
II. Second-Chance Education	a) providing access to higher education b) access to higher secondary vocational qualifications (terminal)	Initial-education system	Typically more homogenous; general education, vocational education, higher education (bridging courses); more rarely, adult education, active labour market policies	- educational authorities - public employment services - public co-funding agencies for LLL - households	- young adults (18-24) - adults in early mid-career (well-established) - migrants (well educated abroad)	3 a,b 4 a,b 5 a, b	- Evening gymnasium - access course for higher education
III. Higher Education Programmes	a) providing membership among graduates b) vocational specialisation on tertiary level	Initial-education system	Exclusively higher education institutions (state-run/private)	- educational authorities different between countries: households	- young adults (18-24) - adults in early mid-career (well-established)	5a, 5b	- part-time programmes in HE
IV. (Re-) Training	a) re-entering the labour market b) changing to the non-disadvantaged core segment of the labour market	Occupational fields and their initial vocational education Organisational fields (fields employing disadvantaged groups e.g. temporary work agencies)	Typically heterogeneous, active labour market policy, vocational education, adult education, on the job/off the job training,	- public employment services - municipalities - joint employer-employee organisations	- (long) term unemployed (including mature (50+); low qualified, individuals with outdated skills, etc.)	3 b	- retraining for another occupation
V. Customised Vocational Programmes	a) broadening validity for securing shared commitments/contributions of employer/employees b) internal career patterns	Organisational fields (employment) for acceptance Initial-education system and professional fields (for minimal requirements)	Mainly management training, vocational education, higher education, professional education, various combinations	- employers - public agencies for business promotion - public co-funding agencies for LLL	- mid-career employees and skilled blue-collar workers (core segment)	3 b 4 b 5 b	- customised programmes in mechatronics (ISCED 3b, 4)
VI. Continuing Higher Education	occupational/ professional specialisation	Autonomous field of continuing higher education; Initial-education system Alternatively, organisational fields (sectors)/ professional fields	Mainly management training, higher education, professional education	- households - employers	- mid-career employees with higher education/ higher secondary education	5 a, b (6)	- Master in Marketing - MBA
VII. Continuing Professional Education	a) access to professional-status groups b) professional specialisation	Professional fields and autonomous field of CPE; initial education (minimal requirements)	Besides the particular field Higher education Management Training	- households - employers	- mid-career employees with higher education; specific groups of skilled workers and semi-professionals (e.g. work master examinations)	5 a, b 6	- bar exams - certification psychotherapy - work-master examination

Source: Own concept

(I) Basic skills and remedy programmes

Formal programmes are increasingly used to overcome the risk of social exclusion due to low literacy skills, including low official-language skills for native speakers of another language. Most countries have programmes that teach basic skills and run over several months or years, with highly variable number of teaching units per week. The programmes generally target adults with comparatively low levels of formal schooling, who have never attained or have lost skills usually delivered by compulsory schooling. However, while some countries follow the UOE recommendation to classify these programmes as formal, many others see the related courses as non-formal.

This uncertainty also reflects comparatively weak isomorphic links of this type of programmes to the institutional qualities of formal education. The claim that basic skills and remedial programmes are formal may be supported by one or more of the following possibilities: public funding for mandatory courses; individual rights or requirements to participate may be established for particular groups (for example, migrants or individuals receiving social aid); the courses' content may be mapped against the backdrop of primary and lower secondary education curricular and credits may be awarded that could help attain higher levels of education in subsequent programmes. 'Formal status' is thereby both a requirement for public funding and the result of public funding; this makes 'basic adult education' a new area of state-supervised educational activity. However, providers are mostly private non-profit entities and mostly do not belong to the initial education system, instruction is not given by persons holding degrees comparable to those of teachers in traditional schools, programmes do not exactly follow any curriculum and tests and examinations play a more subordinated role.

In any case, basic education generally has a weak formal charter. Any adult having left compulsory schooling is institutionally expected to hold some essential competences. Therefore, before a person participates, basic skill programmes could not simply award credentials to expand the given level of skills. Programmes often effectively expand participants' abilities and provide empowerment and social inclusion. However, institutions hardly support the transformation of achieved competences into social mobility. Consequently, this does not particularly justify the label 'formal', because any kind of non-formal provision could achieve comparable outcomes. The formal status of 'basic education' seems fully justified only when developing basic skills results in credits that can be used to acquire higher levels of qualifications. This is exactly the case in many countries that regard basic education as formal (for example, Norway and Scotland).

Because of their positive effects, 'literacy' programmes have traditionally been a key part of various social movements of non-formal adult education. Programmes are generally labelled on ISCED Levels 1 and 2. Various traditional organisations in liberal adult education or 'workers education' (trade unions) form – together with more specialised non-profit organisations – the core of the organisational populations. For-profit provision is rare. To avoid repeating negative experience with previous schooling, they typically use 'non-formal' styles of instruction. They encourage personal interaction among small groups of learners. Providing basic skills requires considerable expertise and therefore professional development of specialised instructors: however, levels of professionalisation of the field differ widely between countries. Organisational fields arise around one or a few public funding sources; their variations likely explain the differences between countries. Private financial contributions are negligible. Enterprises frequently co-operate in basic education programmes, because newly acquired communication skills add to productivity while participation typically does not result in demands for higher wages.

Greater public engagement in migration policies and welfare-to-work programmes, as well as the acceptance of a prevailing problem of 'adult illiteracy', resulted in an increase in programmes. However, the programmes can have ambiguous institutional qualities. To add institutional value, basic-skills programmes can be combined with vocational elements essential for formal credentials. They can deliver credit-points that lead to institutionally valuable qualifications. Programmes may even decide to hide their main purpose by using alternate headings and thus becoming more attractive to learners and avoiding the potentially negative effects for their participants of being labelled 'illiterate'.

(II) Second-chance education

The organisational (hybrid) field of 'second-chance education' arises around the tasks of allowing access to higher education or providing terminal, higher secondary vocational education. All countries have programmes that allow adults to acquire lower secondary and particularly higher secondary educations. Traditionally, the term 'second-chance education' was reserved for programmes that provide access to higher education (Schleicher 1990). Today, the notion also covers other programmes and degrees, corresponding to initial education up to the ISCED 4b Level and usually finished before the age of 19 years. Typical examples include 'evening gymnasiums', programmes that prepare for entrance permission for higher education or part-time vocational schools on a higher secondary level. In most countries, numerous types of programmes and providers populate the field and compete for student populations. Modularised provision or availability of credit-based qualifications may add substantially to the institutional complexities.

This organisational field caters to comparatively large, student populations, dominated by young adults (16–25 years old) enjoying a socially institutionalised, extended adolescence. Adolescents may experience 'second-chance education' more as a variation in 'initial-educational careers' than as an overall distinct pattern. Second-chance education generally demonstrates a high level of regulative, normative and cognitive isomorphism with corresponding programmes and organisations in initial education. Consequently, differences between national education systems strongly shape the specific composition of the organisational field. For example, initial-education organisations may also provide adult education. The curricular closely match the curricular of 'traditional students'. Teachers often share the same professional background as their initial system counterparts: they may even work with both children and adults. The initial-education model typically has a uniform procedure to organise teaching and testing. Organisations focused only on adults may follow a curriculum comparable to the initial-education programme. However, important variants demonstrate significantly lower levels of isomorphism. Isomorphism may be reduced to curricular content and types of monitoring, while the providing organisations, styles of instruction and professional status of teachers may or may not follow prescribed patterns. Organisation-bound programmes often show high levels of isomorphism, but only limited isomorphism may be demonstrated by various alternatives (preparation for external examinations, modularised programmes offered by various providers, etc.).

The 'charters' of programmes reflect their main purpose and the degree of isomorphism with initial education. Alternative access routes to higher education may have little institutional value beyond granting permission to enter higher education. However, competitive entrance procedures for higher education may limit the value of this institutionalised right of entry. Any further charter effect connects to later completion of the higher education programme. General programmes (for example, evening gymnasiums) and vocational schools, which are highly isomorphic with initial education, offer a charter comparable to qualifications earned in initial education. However, earning the status as an adult may reduce the credentials' value. Alternative routes to vocational qualifications may be highly devalued compared to their traditional counterparts. This aspect would differ greatly between countries because of different educational organisations and the varying prestige of vocational education.

As a hybrid field, 'second-chance education' covers independent sub-fields that arise around particular governing and funding bodies. The state funds educational opportunities more isomorphic to initial education and organised within the educational system, thus forming sub-fields such as 'evening gymnasiums' or 'part-time higher vocational schools'. Authorities define members of the organisational populations. In sharp contrast, providers of alternative, less isomorphic pathways include various organisations such as liberal adult education or for-profit educational providers. Although alternative routes may have state (co-)funding, private sources provide substantial financial contributions that allow for the emergence of a demand-led market for educational services with weaker isomorphism to initial education; these services do not go beyond mastering codified requirements (for example, passing a set of examinations). However, competition for student populations will integrate various sub-fields into one organisational hybrid field structure. Student populations turn out to be highly volatile. Groups seeking access to higher education might find more attractive programmes that require less efforts ('loss of time') than more 'in-depth' programmes. Participants may willingly pay high fees for 'time-efficient' private tutoring. More traditional 'schools for adults' may lose clientele and thereby risk legitimacy necessary for their lump-sum, state funding. The availability of new programmes may revolutionise the organisational field within a few years (for an example, see Markowitsch et al. 2012).

The ongoing expansion of educational participation translates into paradoxical tendencies within 'second-chance education'. The constantly increasing pressure to attain at least a higher-secondary-level certificate leads to expanding student populations. However, higher education has become increasingly dominant and become the 'natural' goal for any 'second-chance education'. The comparable weak 'charter' of many available qualifications reflects four decades of 'credential inflation' that significantly reduces the legitimacy of terminal qualifications provided by the hybrid field. Second-chance education provides a knowledge that could be seen only as something required for the exam to start substantial learning later in higher education. The field could experience a crisis because of fading legitimacy and loss of institutional power of available vocational credentials. In this case, second-chance education would then become an ideal field for studying both 'institutional entrepreneurship' and processes of 'de-institutionalisation' (Harney & Koch 2010).

(III) Higher education programmes accessible for non-traditional (adult) students

For adults, higher education provides either membership among 'graduates' – no matter if this still signals an elite position – and allows for a professional specialisation. Higher education of 'adult' students traditionally does not belong to 'adult education' but is seen as a sub-field covered by higher education policy and research. However, the space of higher education also forms the single most important organisational field for formal adult education, when one considers the number of participants and the goal sought by participants in 'second-chance education'.

Traditional universities owe their legitimacy and their power to determine valuable credentials to their own 'institutional model': their position was institutionalised in society even before the rise of modern education systems. However, universities are entrenched in a dense network of coercive, normative and cognitive institutions. Moreover, by the late 19th century, all European states had fully integrated universities into educational bureaucracies. Strong regulations generally control private universities and add to isomorphic pressure within the organisational field. Consequently, to remain a 'degree programme' on a predefined level, a set of criteria has to be met, no matter how 'ritualised' the compliance may be. Virtually the same rules apply to adult-oriented programmes that lead to certificates with comparable institutional value.

The organisational field has become more complex with the rise of 'non-traditional' universities that cater to new groups of students or employers and that divert student from more prestigious 'old' universities. 'Newcomers' have to struggle for high levels of isomorphism to earn sufficient legitimacy. Yet, new organisations partially fail to become full universities and must distance themselves from the leading model in order to find their niche in a strongly expanding, highly expanding market for prospective students and their graduates' prospective employers.

The tensions between 'old' and 'new' universities – such as the presence or absence of 'doctoral level' education on ISECED 6 – are highly significant for formal adult education within higher education. 'New' universities are more inclined (partly as their *raison d'etre*) to cater to 'non-traditional' students, while 'old', 'elite' organisations enjoy more discretion. Any abbreviation of the 'gold standard' of university education that intends to help adult students to proceed may be interpreted as devaluing credentials. When adult students become diverted to less prestigious types of organisations or programmes, their credentials may be devalued in comparison to the more prestigious educational tracks. As a result, explicitly serving adult students is risky and, to avoid marginalisation, non-traditional students may even opt for the traditional fulltime programmes.

Among higher educational institutions, we find organisations with and without programmes designed or even reserved for adult students. University systems differ widely in their competition for students, for public funding, for private tuition fees and for mere legitimacy. The most typical examples are part-time programmes that deliver the same curriculum as full-time studies, yet extended over longer periods, and provided mainly in the evening. Moreover, some programmes are available only for adult students. In many higher education systems (following the 'German-university' model), employed adults could attend full-time programmes and, on an individual basis, lengthen the duration of their study. In other systems, adult students must complete a full-time educational programme within a predefined period.

Ongoing expansion of mass higher education towards universal higher education (Trow 1973, 2005; Meyer et al. 2007) will certainly bring more students that are adult into higher education. Already, a viable field of research focuses on the consequences of shifting the overall composition of higher education students – making non-traditional students the majority – on the institutional foundations and the everyday operation of universities. An under-researched area involves the institutional processes that enhance or limit adult participation in formal adult education. Changes in the institutional and 'exchange' value of higher education credentials have been discussed since the late 18th century; however, our own vocabulary for describing 'credential inflation' and 'status competition' stems mainly from the 1970s. Newer concepts, reflecting an additional three decades of expansion, are still in short supply.

(IV) (Occupational) (re-)training programmes

These formal programmes help (long-term) unemployed to re-enter the labour market or to overcome their marginalised position by entering the labour markets' core segment. All European countries have public employment services and related welfare institutions that initiate varied forms of occupational retraining programmes for workers who could not stay in their previous occupations. The programmes' governance and orientation vary over time and between countries. When programmes lead to acknowledged qualifications, they should be seen as formal adult education.

Various countries follow this view, while others do not understand retraining programmes as formal.

Occupational programmes take place in highly complex institutional environments that require securing sufficient isomorphism with the education system and particularly with the vocational tracks. The funding organisations such as employment services, public health agencies or local communities have a clear-cut purpose: bring beneficiaries of welfare payments back to work, yet within their field's legal and normative requirements. Typically, they are allowed to provide support only for clearly defined eligible groups. Therefore, participants can be highly pre-selected and consist of multiple disadvantaged social strata. The legitimacy of the publicly funded intervention depends on the re-employment of most participants. Programmes thereby directly involve organised interests in the world of work. Business-interest organisations must accept programmes for their 'technical' and/or 'institutional' outcomes. Trade unions have to accept that more 'skilled workers', whose training costs are strongly co-funded by public means, may have an impact on the employment prospects of members of their trades, both those currently employed as well as the unemployed not eligible for the programme. Challenges are further exacerbated by the multiple vulnerabilities and needs of the typical participant groups that often require professional support beyond mere instruction. Finally, participation is often de facto mandatory, undermining the voluntary-participation principle fundamental for adult education. Even when training organisations fail to meet their participant needs, they could not protest by simply walking away.

As a solution for complex, competing institutional claims, programmes may be defined as a temporary compromise established for a set period. Over the decades, a steady flow of temporary programmes may be introduced; this establishes a highly informal, institutional ordering of the possible and the impossible. Alternatively, new vocational-training organisations, typically controlled by employer-interest organisations or/and trade unions, could cater to various groups and provide both formal programmes and short non-formal training. Within a particular country, one solution typically dominates; however, both approaches can be combined.

Although some isomorphic links to initial vocational education may be present, the previously described institutional compromise shapes the capacity of retraining programmes to provide qualifications. Frequently, we find 'second-tier' qualifications: substandard credentials awarded for meeting clearly reduced requirements. The qualifications often lack the institutional qualities expected and hardly help find employment, beyond what has been 'technically' learned by participation. While programmes deliver formal rights of specific qualifications (for example, entitlements for 'skilled workers' set by binding collective agreements), they often fail to satisfy expectations for their educational credentials. They only transmit skills. To fight against the consequences of negative stereotypes of their clientele, they usually offer various placement services based on stable collaborations between educational providers and selected employers.

The organisational fields for (re-)training programmes vary across countries. Public spending is high in many countries and – by comparison – among the highest for formal adult education. Private contributions are negligible. When public retraining organisations are institutionalised, they may absorb most available funds, restricting the entrance of competitors. However, without permanent structures, huge 'training markets' may arise that attract organisations with various backgrounds to compete in the market. Preferred suppliers are often training organisations related to the trade unions or to employer interest organisations, because the social partners interests are crucial for forging compromises. Vocational schools are partly involved for matters of legitimacy and expertise. Various non-profit organisations with strong background in social work are also often present. However, substantial public funds could also attract 'for-profit' providers with experience at organising large-scale programmes. Modes of instruction vary with the institutional background of providers and the professional standards required for the instructors.

Occupational retraining programmes expand with rising levels of long-term unemployment, when the pension system tries to reduce early retirement by expanding occupational rehabilitation and when work-to-welfare programmes seek to reduce costs for communal welfare. Shifts away from specialised programmes periodically happen when large-scale retraining poorly integrates participants into the labour market. Moreover, mandatory programmes threaten to discredit lifelong learning among the most vulnerable social groups, overrepresented in retraining programmes. However, creating programmes can hardly be replaced by educational vouchers, which typically do not fit opportunities available for the particular target groups.

(V) Customised vocational/professional programmes for organisations

Formal adult education is used to improve the balance of the competing interests attached to company training of employees and their employers and to justify internal career patterns. Education providers may customise their programmes for employees of a single or a group of organisations. Alternatively, education providers can cooperate with companies in adding formal status for existing non-formal training programmes. In both cases, customisation and restricting access to predefined participants do not necessarily conflict with symbolic requirements for formal education. Countries vary in their institutional frameworks that allow for tailored formal programmes. Moreover, countries have different ways to grant formal status.

Securing formal status of customised programmes requires a minimal level of isomorphism with initial programmes. Typically, the providing organisations belong to the legitimate organisations of initial education, such as a higher secondary technical school or a university of applied science. Moreover, counterparts available in 'open' (non-customised) programmes of formal education model the firm-level programmes' subjects, workload and duration. While the subjects' names may remain unchanged, the contents may be completely adapted to the current needs of the participants and their employer. Where required, other bureaucratic rules may be applied to secure the formal status. When non-formal programmes are transformed into formal ones, providers look for appropriate matches among existing formal programmes. An educational provider can certify a particular non-formal programme by increasing its isomorphism with comparable existing programmes. In case of transforming existing non-formal firm specific programmes into formal ones, an appropriate formal model has to be identified: next, amendments and slight changes of company programme make the programme sufficient similar, so that the educational organisation could certify graduation.

Customised formal programmes have increased because educational entrepreneurs and companies began to establish internal training programmes that closely follow formal education models. Traditionally, company-based educational programmes are 'non-formal'; however, as Meyer & Scott observe (1994), in the 1980s in the United States, these company-based programmes began to adopt typical forms and techniques of formal education for increasing their legitimacy. Companies arrange in various ways the certification of their programmes and generate organisation-specific credentials, which claim to be recognised informally within certain industries. The hype of corporate universities early in the 1990s represents only the most obvious development in the field (see Markowitsch & Jonach 2006; Dobbin et al. 1994).

Mainly on their own initiative, higher secondary vocational schools and universities provide customised programmes. These programmes deepen relationships with potential employers for their graduates and collect cutting-edge experience that may help develop curricula for open programmes. Moreover, for-profit providers in the 'market for corporate training provision' seek opportunities to formalise their customised educational programmes; to 'authorise' their entry in the market, they create networks with recognised formal-education organisations. Enterprises cover most of the fees for programmes that are partly supported by available public co-funding schemes. The field may also expand because of public funds available exclusively for supporting formal adult education in enterprises – with or without requirements to target particular groups. In extreme cases, some educational providers have the core business model of restlessly searching for companies prepared to receive free formal educational programmes for their employees.

The number of training programmes in enterprises may be somewhat stable, yet demand seems to be expanding for 'certifications' of education. Organisations within formal education are increasingly entrepreneurial; they seek to replace increasingly scarce public funds and to improve network relations with potential employers of graduates.

(VI) (Post-tertiary) continuing higher education

Continuing higher education supports vocational or professional specialisation. Organisations entitled to provide higher education generally could also provide continuing education programmes; their full control includes setting tuition fees, which usually cover full costs (or even allow for profits) and lead to high fees compared to regular studies. Entrance requirements often include an academic degree or a number of years of occupational experience. Flexible regulations for continuing higher education empower the organisations to develop market-oriented, niche products. Thus, programmes also change quite often. Even relatively small countries have available several hundred different programmes within continuing higher education; however, they have few students per programme (for example, 15 students per programme). Typically, programmes cater to adult students with some years of professional experiences. A particular organisational field is formed from formal programmes attached directly to occupational or professional groups that provide 'continuing professional education' (see Type VII below).

To secure legitimacy, the programmes' formal content and organisation are combined with models from 'non-formal' management training. However, differences in local traditions greatly blur the borders. Successfully distributed international models for 'continuing higher education', such as the 'master of business administration' (Mazza et al. 2005), often inspire the search for other opportunities in higher continuing education. These models typically include small groups of learners, frequent personal interaction between teaching experts and students and problem-based learning. Reflecting high tuition fees, they typically have higher quality service than initial education.

The status of the organisation (for example, a well-known, respectable 'full' university) adds much to any degree's potential value; this increases the horizontal stratification within higher education: participants or their employers may become attracted only for the symbolic value of the name of the organisation, not by the programmes' content. Because of their comparatively weak legitimacy, a new programme makes the key step of establishing links with the working world. Programmes can thrive in a highly competitive market only by satisfying the participants' expectations and by meeting employers' requirements.

In many countries, nearly all higher education organisations enter the market. Universities typically establish legally independent, 'for-profit' entities as specialised organisations. As a market, the field is particularly segmented by the programmes' contents, which allows for sub-markets including 'business education', 'technical education' or 'cultural' or 'health' sector programmes. While higher-education organisations can use their state-funded infrastructure and personnel, private households or the participants' employers typically contribute most to the fees. Through various schemes, some participants may be eligible for public co-funding of their fees. Attracting enough participants to make the 'break-even' level becomes the single most important criteria. Many advertised programmes never come into existence because of a lack of paying customers. Beyond state agencies with supervisory authority, monitoring includes local or international agencies that set and assess quality standards and also various professional organisations and business-interest organisations engaged in particular sub-fields.

The strong expansion of continuing higher education seems to be mainly driven by status-competition and the formalisation of eligibility criterion for increasingly specified careers. This formalisation has horizontally segmented labour markets for higher-education graduates. The symbolic status of the providing organisation and the programme content both add to the segmentation. However, the institutionalisation of degrees earned in continuing higher education does not match the level of formal degrees typically forming the 'educational ladder'. While programmes may work well and provide considerably benefits for established insiders, the same programmes may add little to career progress for outsiders. Continuing higher education therefore risks becoming a 'sequel' of the 'great training robbery', described for the expansion of higher education in the 1970s (Berg & Govelick 1973; Brown & Hesketh 2004).

(VII) Continuing professional education governed by professional bodies

Particular programmes control access to professional-status groups or fields of particular professional expertise. Professions develop their own systems of continuing professional education; particular programmes prepare for officially recognised degrees that entitle the practice of a set of professional activities. Professional or occupational associations provide or, at least, authorise programmes and claim the right to set, control and develop the standards for providing credentials. Members of the professional groups generally belong to the examination boards. Thus, continuing professional education forms an important mechanism within the 'control of the production of producers' (Larsson 1977, 49); this lies at the heart of the social closure required for controlling professional work. When leading to particular degrees and marking steps within professional careers, continuing professional education is typically understood as formal adult education within national frameworks. However, formal status for various professional programmes substantially differs within a country and in cross-country comparison. Because continuing professional education includes occupational or para-professional (non-academic) and professional (academic) programmes, the programmes have highly diverse requirements and participants.

Examples for the non-academic level include preparing for 'craft-master examination' or 'real-estate management' and preparing for 'bar exams' or for becoming a psychotherapist of a particular school of therapy. The social status of particular professions or occupations evolves over time and may differ between countries: an established profession in one country may be a subordinated, unregulated field in another country. (For example, psychotherapy has become an independent profession with its particular formal education in most countries; while in France, psychotherapy is still a prerogative of physicians (Strauß & Kohl 2009)).

Continuing professional education gains its legitimacy mainly by its relations to the professions. Faith in the value of its credentials depends on the professions' ability to defend their expertise against usurpation by competing professions and to regulate access to their own 'guild'. Programmes show a particular isomorphism with the regulative, normative and cognitive patterns of the various occupational or professional fields. Programmes within continuing professional education may be co-opted by the 'initial' education system: for example, the historic incorporation of the 'work master' in Germany or Austria within the 'education system'. However, institutional models for 'good' education within higher education certainly have an impact in continuing professional education. Moreover, occupational schools and 'professional schools' became major providers for continuing professional education; they merged the institutional logics of education and the profession. By balancing formal education requirements with institutional requirements from the professional field, the credentials can secure some value even outside their professional fields. However, as a rule, only a particular profession fully acknowledges specific credentials earned within professional continuing education. Although highly institutionalised within a particular profession, these credentials may lack any value outside the field.

Reflecting the strong linkage to various professional fields, the organisational field of continuing professional education is segmented into nearly unconnected sub-fields. Each sub-field typically has professional associations and their educational organisations, higher-education organisations, non-profit organisations established in various occupational fields (for example, mutual-welfare organisations) and for-profit organisations. Each sub-field has interaction and internal competition: a programme must legitimately provide access to a particular professional (sub-) field. The most important funds come from tuition fees of individual participants and their employers. The same organisation provides formal programmes (leading to a predefined step) and non-formal programmes that help satisfy requirements for compulsory continuing education as defined in various regulations. The organisational set will include regulators of the profession and organisations responsible for funding clients of the professions, such as the social insurance agencies for all medical and paramedical occupations.

The strong expansion of continuing professional education reflects the expansion of professionalism as an important way of controlling work. However, traditional non-academic provision of skills such as the 'work-master' programmes could also lose ground. Specialisation within professional fields is a major strategy to compete for particular sources of income. Balancing the costs and benefits for increasing educational requirements becomes a core tension within the professions. However, given the belief in the power of education, any perceived social problem – from misconduct in health care to poor counselling in financial services – results in calls for more and better continuing professional education.

3.7 Outlook: Towards a new definition of formal adult education

In this chapter, I have developed the argument that focusing on the institutional charter allows one to meaningfully discern between formal and non-formal adult education. Moreover, it allows for the argument that formal adult education is – although depending on initial education in a multitude of ways – a set of social institutions in its own right, providing particular social opportunities. Exploring the social charter of programmes and their institutional foundations also allows for a less arbitrary basis for classifying formal programmes as 'formal' or 'not-formal'. Overview 9 provides examples of considering programmes in the light of 'statistical' definitions applied in the Adult Education Survey (AES), the 'representations' of formal education provided within the UOE framework and an alternative approach, focussing on the charter. While deciphering the programmes' institutional charter certainly has its difficulties, at least some clarifications can be achieved; for example, the 'formal' label does not depend on the status of the educational organisations providing a programme. Therefore, formal adult education calls for careful analysis within an institutional framework and is far from being an artefact that we should try to get rid of – as occasionally argued (Hoppers 2006).

A reshaping of the applied definitions of formal adult education and their application within cross-country surveys, however, would only form a first, yet, indispensable step towards a framework for studying cross-country differences and similarities. Diagram 5 summarise the argument and displays a decision tree for (re-)classifying programmes counted by European statistics on adult education as formal or non-formal. For becoming classified as formal, programmes should cover a minimal workload *and* own a social charter. Consequently, they could be classified as belonging to one of the seven organisational fields of formal adult education outlined in the previous section.

Diagram 5: Reclassification of formal/nonformal taught programmes/courses according to the workload + social charter criteria

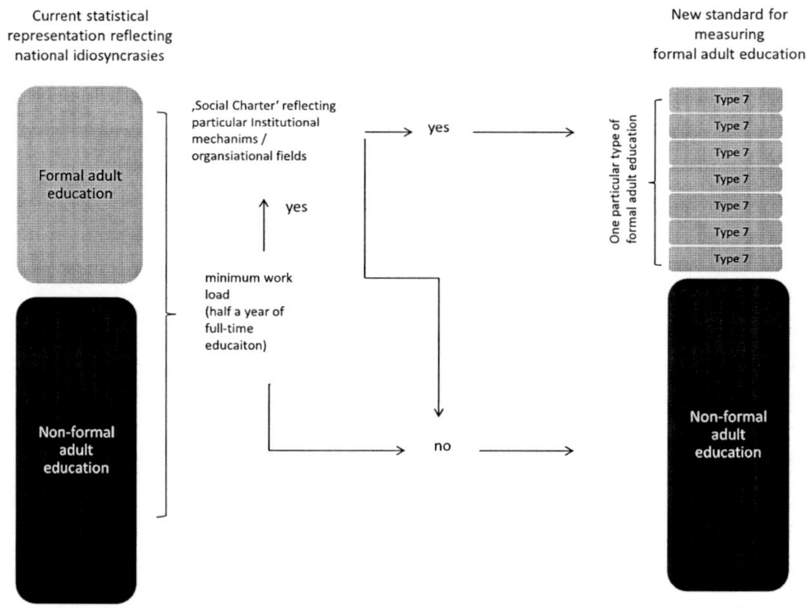

Source: Own description

Overview 9: Formal status for educational programmes with the seven types according to their 'statistical', 'country-system' or 'institutional' status

	Examples of programmes	Formal within AES	Formal within UOE	'Formal' for providing a particular social charter
I. Basic Skills and Remedy Programmes	One year part-time education programme, covering literacy, numeracy and IT for women	In some countries (England, Scotland, Norway, Belgium), not in others (Austria, Bulgaria, Estonia)	In some countries (England, Scotland, Norway, Belgium), not in others (Austria, Bulgaria, Estonia)	A weak formal status, only connected to educational progress, depending on the awarding of credits, accepted within second-chance education
	Short IT introductory course	In some countries, not in others	Not formal (too short)	Not formal
II. Second-Chance Education	Evening gymnasiums	Formal in all countries	Formal in all countries	Formal, linking to higher education and institutionalised careers
	Modularised courses leading to higher education entrance permission	Formal in all countries; however, even when understood as formal, potentially not measured as such (e.g. in Austria)	Understood as formal, yet, typically not reported in numbers; only counts qualifications awarded (not modules)	A weak formal status, only connected to educational progress
III. Higher Education	Adults in regular programmes	Formal in all countries	Formal in all countries	Formal status, differentiated charters
	Part-time study programmes	Formal in all countries	Formal in all countries	Formal status, differentiated charters
IV. Instruction Active Labour Market Policy	18-month, basic course vocational programme for 'care assistance'	Formal in some (Norway, England), not in other countries (Austria, Bulgaria)	Formal in some (Norway), not in others (Austria, Bulgaria)	Formal status, charting for selected position within organisational/occupational careers
	Short course in forklift driving	Formal in some countries (England, Belgium) not in others	Not formal (too short)	Not formal
V. Customised Vocational Programmes	Customised programme in mechatronics on higher secondary level	Formal in all countries; however, even when understood as formal, potentially not measured as such (e.g. in Austria)	Understood as formal, yet, typically not reported in numbers; only counts awarded qualifications (not modules)	Formal status, charting for selected position within organisational/occupational careers
	Producer-certified, modularised IT administrator course (120 credits)	Formal in some, not in other countries	Not formal in any country (does not include industry providers)	Borderline case; potentially formal, when institutionally supporting careers
VI. Continuing Higher Education	Master of Business Administration programmes (MBA)	Formal in some, not in other countries; mixtures are possible	Formal in most countries (yet, difficulties to provide accounts for)	Formal status; highly different charters
	Twelve-month, part-time course (post-secondary) in quality management	Formal in some, not formal in other countries	Formal in some, not formal in other countries	Borderline case; not formal without institutional link to positions
VII. Continuing Professional Education	Preparation for 'craft-master' examination	If available, formal in most countries	Formal in all countries	Formal status, with stronger/weaker charter within careers
	Professional qualification for psychotherapy of a particular therapeutic school	Formal (partly further depending of the type of provider) in some countries, not in others ; mixtures are possible	Formal or partly formal (depending of the provider) in some countries, not in others	Formal status; charter varies with the strength/weakness of the professional field of psychotherapy

Source: Own description

Formal adult education could be analysed only as closely linked to initial education, adding to the categories, symbolic systems and orientations for behaviour which provide the foundations of modern societies. It forms no system of its own, yet belongs to a greater part to the initial education system, and participates in its institutional logics by cohesive, normative and cognitive isomorphism. By following the institutional rules set by the initial system, formal adult education inherits the institutional power for adding a charter to its educational operations. However, the transmission of institutional mechanisms from initial to adult education knows its limitation: catering for adults is at odds with claims, successfully made for 'traditional age' students. Yet, formal adult education clearly expands the scope of educational effects. Beyond its legitimating effect (Inbar & Sever 1989, Inbar 1990), it adds to and alters the system characteristics of education and it expands available membership categories and codifications of knowledge, in particular by its extended interaction with occupational and professional fields.

However, by reviewing various institutional approaches, I have made clear that further analysis has to focus on the level of particular organisational fields for one type of formal adult education. Progress can be expected only by learning how a local field exactly manages to provide a charter for their programmes that interacts with the part of the education system, relevant for the organisational fields' purpose and the groups of potential employers, relevant for the career prospects of the graduates. Therefore, while I could indicate where a particular organisational field of formal adult education seems to be highly developed and where not, comparative research is actually at its beginning. I will address the task of developing a proto-framework for future comparative research in Chapter 6.

Chapter 4: Formal adult education as a life event

4.0 Introduction

> *'Everyone who has finished his senior years at school with the final matriculation examination complains how persistently he is pursued by the dream that he has failed, has to repeat a year, and the like. For someone who possess an academic degree, this typical dream is replaced by another, which offers the prospect of not holding his own at the viva for his doctorate, though he may object in vain in his sleep that he has been practising medicine for years, is a university lecturer, or head of a government department.'* (Freud [1899] 2008, 209210)

Past schooling experiences have deeply imprinted our conscience and unconscious lives alike. Formal education deeply contributes to individual socialisation in childhood, adolescence and young adulthood: beyond any social charter (although influenced by it), formal education changes the way we live, experience ourselves and others and perceive our opportunities. Our various experiences with formal education – no matter, if we are somewhat successful – become a deeply grounded structure of our personality. This structure influences – often unconsciously – what we believe, expect and fear about schools, universities or any other formal educational setting, no matter how this may become relevant in our later lives: as parents looking for schools for our children, as citizens supporting various programmes of educational change, as adult learners considering a formal programme.

The title of Willy Russell's play *Educating Rita* (1981), reaching a broad audience in its movie version, has turned into a catch-phrase (Wakeford 1993) for the pain and glory of formal education in adult life. The comedy considers class-based boundaries in higher education, anxiety and alienation prepared for minority students of all kinds or and the questionable worth of 'higher culture' for everyone not born for it. Becoming educated turns into a symbol for and against emancipation:

> *RITA [...] I'm educated. I've got what you have an' y' don't like it because you'd rather see me as the peasant I once was; you're like the rest of them – you like to keep your natives thick, because that way they still look charming and delightful. I don't*

need you [...] I've got a room full of books. I know what clothes to wear, what wine to buy, what plays to see, what papers and books to read. I can do without you.

FRANK Is that all you wanted. Have you come all this way for so very, very little?

RITA Oh it's little to you, isn't it? It's little to you who squanders every opportunity and mocks and takes it for granted.

FRANK Found a culture have you, Rita? Found a better song to sing have you? No – you've found a different song, that's all – and on your lips it's shrill and hollow and tuneless. Oh, Rita, Rita ...[Willi Russell, Educating Rita, Act II, Scene 7]

Accounts like *Educating Rita* remind us of the potential stakes of formal adult education in contrast to short 'non-formal' courses. Adults have achieved or been allocated a place in society, with all its possibilities, attachments and obligations. Educational attainment represents a powerful hierarchical, symbolic order potentially challenged by formal adult education that could revise initial education's verdict. Adults 'taking steps' on the educational ladder may become a different kind of person – *in the eyes of the world* and potentially from their own perspective.

In the previous chapter, I argued for taking as defining criteria a formal programme's *social charter*. In this chapter, I will explore the significance of 'returning to education' in adult's lives. I argue that participation in formal adult education marks a significant life event that brings an important change (or series of changes) required to cope with the demands of formal education. It makes sense to ask how the participant's life has actually changed by experiencing the formal programmes instead of short periods of non-formal education. This question remains important regardless of successful graduation or acquiring credentials to change one's occupation.

In this chapter, I start with a review of theories on participation in adult education, which, however, hardly discuss formal adult education as a special case (Section 4.1). I discuss Daniel Levinson's life-structure paradigm as an important yet discontinued framework for a more detailed understanding of formal adult education (Section 4.2). In Section 4.3, I summarise my points on the special position of participants in formal adult education as compared to any other participants in organised learning. In Section 4.4, I develop one typology of participation patterns in formal adult education. Finally, I outline directions for future research, by discussing how my proposed typologies in Chapters 3 and 4 could be combined (Section 4.5).

4.1 Awaiting systematic review – theories on adults' participation in education

In the 'adult learning and education' perspective, two complexes of theories have evolved. The first one deals with explaining the reasons for adults to participate in 'coursework' of any kind. The second one deals with any intentional learning activities beyond coursework that lead to learning outcomes, which stand alone or are embedded in other activities such as gainful work or civic engagement (see Fenwick

2000). Typically, these learning activities – often labelled as 'informal' – could potentially become the subject of educational planning or evaluation, although they might take place without any intervention by professional educationalists.

Coursework and other intentional learning activities could lead to comparable learning outcomes and could therefore partly replace each other. For example, to learn how to use new software, an adult could rely on learning by doing, support by co-workers or take a course. All these cases have similar expected outcomes of the learning activity. I propose to address 'informal' learning as a 'learning project' in order to highlight its goal and outcome-oriented aspect and the often overlooked explicit devotion of learning time and efforts. A 'learning project' includes the decision to devote time and efforts to mobilising required support for a roughly circumscribed learning outcome.

Given the exchangeability of 'adult learning' and 'adult education' in English and the programmatic stance of 'lifelong learning' policies, the borders unquestionably are blurred between theories explaining participation and concepts explaining 'adult learning' (in the sense of informal learning projects). Landmark contributions on participation in adult *education* have titles such as *The Adult Learner* (Knowles et al. 2005) or *Adults as Learners* (Cross [2]1992) or *Why Adults Learn* (Courtney 1992).

Why do adults participate in coursework? Research on adults' reasons for *participation in education* began in the 1920s (Merriam et al. 2007; for German-speaking countries, Bremer 2007), yet few theoretical contributions have been made within the past twenty years (Rubenson & Desjardins 2009, 189). In handbooks on adult education, reviews on (sociological) theories on participation are often subsumed in chapters on 'participation' and not independently presented as theoretical frameworks. These theories revolve around a common core, established in the 1980s (for example, Cross [2]1992, Courtney 1992) with a few recent amendments.

When explanations for participation are poorly linked to general sociological frameworks, the explanations risk isolation. In the following section, I discern three families of sociological theories on (adult) education by considering Meyer 1977, Collins 1971, 1979 and Rubinson & Browne 1994.

Functional theories: Participation in adult education is explained by a need met, a function fulfilled or an opportunity provided for the individual that participates. By assuming that effects of participation live up to the expectations, the 'demand' for adult education usually results from individual requirements (for example, learning the language of a host country), desires (for example, meeting other people) and rational-choice 'investment' decisions (for example, pursuing further education now for increasing later income). Within the framework of methodological individualism, 'environmental drivers' such as 'technological progress' or 'changing employment structures' could be easily translated into individual rational decisions. Because all course attendance seems justified, participation is typically assumed as a good thing (for a critique, Merriam et al. 2007, 70f.) not requiring any further scrutiny. However, constant non-participation becomes suspected as potentially deviant or a sign of an 'investment function' recommending non-participation for groups of individuals. This approach does not reflect social conflicts on further education or consider functional equivalents to achieving goals without adult education.

Conflict theories: Participation in adult education is understood as a means within a struggle for power, legitimacy and resources between social groups. It receives its significance by the particular use made of further education by the conflict parties. Social movements involve their followers in adult education to break the symbolic hegemony of their political opponents. Professions mandate continuing education in order to achieve social closure and entry fees benefit established members. Socially disadvantaged people must train within welfare-to-work schemes. Non-participants must accept their lack of credentials as the basis for legitimate discrimination. Conflict theories require both historical and structural analysis on meso (organisational) and societal levels beyond individual behaviour. Further education appears as one *enjeux* (in the sense of Bourdieu 1990) in ongoing conflicts among others; the position within the social space determines the relative meaning of both participation and non-participation. Participation becomes ambivalent and non-participation potentially loses its stigma, because both could be good or bad for people. However, conflict theories have difficulty in dealing with the ambiguity of adult education as experienced by the individuals, when something 'objectively' suppressive and subverting the proper group interest becomes experienced as 'subjectively' emancipatory and vice versa.

Institutional theories: Participation is explained by the emergence of a society-wide belief that (adult) education is a proper and preferable means for achieving a legitimate goal; this belief become institutionalised on coercive (legal), normative (professional) and cognitive (discourse) levels and buffered against any contradicting evidence. Apparent insufficiencies of (adult) education result in calls for improvements of applicable frameworks yet leave untouched the belief in adult education's benefits. Thereby, in the shadow of worldwide educational expansion, adult education participates in the 'educational gospel' (Grubb & Lazerson 2004), in education as a 'rational myth' (Meyer & Rowan 1977) of modern societies and evolves disconnected from its local precedents. The analysis focuses on how the belief in adult education spreads across countries and the globe and how multiple models of adult education become diffused. All involved parties, politicians, administrators, employers and individuals alike, participate in the shared belief systems and manage their role within it yet, beyond individual deviation, could not undermine what has become a constitute structure of modern society. Institutions predetermine whether adults participate or not. Changes in participation patterns result from changes in the institutionalised expectations, so that the latter must be studied in order to understand individual behaviour. While conflict theories could be taken as a special case (Meyer 1977) of institutional theories, understanding conflicting interest, strategic behaviour and the role of organised actors – although a dominating topic of more recent institutional research (Battilana et al. 2009) – remain weak points of (organisational) institutional approaches. Moreover, the rhetoric of 'education as a myth' is often simply ignoring instead of explaining the benign and malign effects of adult educaiton as reported by participants.

These families of theories are not completely distinct; for example, various types of institutional reasoning have aligned with the functional (rational-choice institutionalism) or conflict (historical institutionalism) perspective. However, as Rubinson & Brown (1994) point out convincingly, progress could be made only by integrating the frameworks, focussing on processes, and deciphering how functional, conflict, and institutional processes condition one other (ibid. 594; see for a similar argument Dobbin et al. 2007).

I use the three types of theories for quickly reviewing the most frequently used theories for explaining participation, which typically demonstrate no sensitivity for the particularities of formal adult education. Most of the theories reviewed in the following use only one framework (see Overview 10). While I could not make up for the lack of rigorous literature reviews, I start to outline a framework for positioning my arguments in this and the following chapters.

Overview 10: (Types of) Theories explaining participation in education of adults

Type of Theories	Disciplinary origin/important contributions (examples)	(Landmark) Contributions	Rational Choice/ instrumental	Conflict	Institutional
I Typologies of motives	Educational research	Houle 1961, Boshier 1971, 1985, 1991	☑		
II Expectancy-valence models	Psychology	Rubenson 1976	☑		
III Drivers/barrier models	Educational research	Cross ²1992	☑		☑
IV Socio-technical requirements and mandatory obligations	Sociology		☑		☑
V Investment decisions – human capital approaches	Economics	Becker 1975 Brunello et al. 2007	☑		
VI Rational-choice models; bounded rationality models	Sociology, Political economy	Rubenson & Desjardins 2009	☑		☑
VII Historical and organisational institutionalism approaches	Sociology Thelen 2004; Meyer 1977	Scott & Meyer 1994, Luo 2007		☑	☑
VIII Class-bound symbolic strategies	Sociology Bourdieu	Bremer 2007		☑	
IX Cultural consumption of consumer groups	Marketing	Tippelt et al. 2004, 2008	☑		
X Participation and social networks		Courtney 1992 Field 2005	☑	☑	☑
XI Biographical or life events, life-structure – life stage frameworks	(Social) Psychology, Sociology Levinson et al. 1978, 1996 Elder 1998	Antikainen 1996 West 1996 Biesta et al. 2011	☑		☑

Source: Own description

I Typologies of Motives: Since the early research on adult education, motives have explained participation: Adults intend to achieve something, so they begin an adult education programme. Classifications of participants vary from more simple – such as vocational versus non-vocational motives – to more extensive inventories of motives using qualitative (for example, Houle's 1961 threefold typology) or quantitative approaches (for example, Boshier 1971, 1976, 1985, 1991, 2006). Motives are taken as the elementary units without further discussion of their non/appearance. This approach does not reflect the nature and institutional embedding of the educational opportunity. Typologies of motives function as the backdrop of a functional and rational-choice framework. Conflict or institutional views are widely absent.

II Expectancy-Valence Models: Adapted from social psychology (Vroom 1964), the expectancy-valence models on participation allow for both ranking the importance of the likely outcomes of participation compared to alternative outcomes (valence) and ranking the expectation of the un/likeliness of achieving outcomes (expectancy). Introduced by Rubenson (1976), the model allows for combining an individual's motives for and resistance against participation, his/her assessment of the environmental – including institutional – conditions for participation as well as the certainty of achieving the desired outcomes. Any explanatory variable (such as prior experience with schooling) could be introduced in the model as 'dis/incentive' that increases or reduces the valence of participation but also as a factor 'de/increasing' the likeliness of achieving the desirable outcomes. The model could explain both participation and non-participation. Surprisingly, the type and the particular (institutional) qualities of a programme are often taken as a 'black box' and are hardly included in a systematic manner, although a programme's manifold features strongly affect both valance and expectancy. The overall model was strongly oriented on rational-choice assumptions, downplaying conflict and institutional perspectives.

III Drivers/Barriers Models: In continuation of motivation models, participation and non-participation have been explained as the result – similar to expectancy/valence models – of 'pros' and 'cons'. The starting point for today's research is still formed by Patricia Cross' (^{2}1992) typology on situational (such as costs, child care obligations), institutional (such as course schedules) and dispositional (such as lack of motivation) barriers (MacKeracher et al. 2006). These models generally do not discuss the type of education, which remains in a black box. Models are firmly constructed on the backdrop of rational-choice assumptions: by removing the barriers, non-participants would turn into participants, given the incentives available within adult education. The models do not consider conflict or institutional approaches.

IV Socio-technical requirements and mandatory obligations: While forming only a distant background for understanding individual participation, *differences* in the presence of socio-technical requirements and obligations for training form a frequent background in the cross-sectional and cross-country analysis of participation in adult education. Thereby, this analysis rarely explores the very nature and institutional qualities of the educational programmes. Explanations build mainly on rational-choice frameworks, because the benefits of arranging for participation outweigh the disadvantages of not doing so (for example, the exclusion from using a certain technology). This model typically considers (formal) institutions (such as health and safety regulations, legal regulations on the employment contract or the unemployment insurance), but it often lacks comprehensive institutional and conflict approaches.

V Investment decisions – Human Capital Approaches: The dominant view on the non/participation model has become the economics of education, which assumes that investment-like decisions determine non/participation. A rational actor participates in a training that provides better yields than any other investment opportunity available. This model generally takes nature and qualities of training as a black box and measured by crude proxies (such as the number of years of schooling). Becker's (1975) basic assumptions have been extended and applied in modified ways within myriads of empirical studies. The theory represents a pure form of (functional) rational-choice theory and considers institutions mainly as reasons for possible aberrations from ideal market equilibrium. It lacks conflict perspectives and more elaborated institutional perspectives.

VI Bounded rationality models: Human capital and expectancy/valence models are expanded by – usually formal – institutional frameworks that explain behavioural differences between social strata, sectors and countries. Models describe why adults may participate without any incentive and may not participate despite substantial incentives. These approaches hardly address the very type of education and combine rational-choice and institutional frameworks, while generally not including conflict perspectives.

VII Historical and organisational institutionalism approaches: Theoretical approaches within historical or organisational institutionalism explain participation without any rational motive. Historical institutionalism uses a conflict perspective; historic and ongoing competition for legitimate practice, distribution of material and symbolic goods, and the formation of social identities explain the rise of particular programmes and decisions to participate. Studies generally examine programmes of adult education related to particular social movements (such as worker education; trade-union education; feminist movement and so one). They assume that a social movement shapes a programme's content and motivations to participate. Organisational institutionalism focuses on the rise of beliefs in education and its legitimating effects within particular organisational fields and general society. Both approaches are rarely used to explain the general participation of adults but instead examine cross-sectional or country differences.

VIII Class-bound symbolic strategies: This approach builds on Bourdieu's framework for class analysis based on cultural consumption and educational investments. Therefore, competing social-class fractions use adult education to defend their privileged status (upper class), to strive for upwards mobility (middle class) or to defend the dignity within a disadvantaged position (lower class). Types of coursework may be analysed according to their symbolic (such as expensive MBA programmes) and practical value (such as a do-it-yourself courses with high practical and no symbolic value), yet they usually only explain participation rates, not particular choices. To avoid further defeat in an unequal competition, lower classes do not participate in adult education; they claim dignified work is more important than educational credits. The model downplays rational motives and institutional processes with similar effects throughout society.

IX Cultural consumption of consumer groups: This model assumes any adult may 'buy' appealing educational products. It frequently uses the long tradition of milieu studies in marketing – also explored by Bourdieu – to explain participation in education as a particular type of consumption: different social milieus prefer different educational 'products'. By assuming fixed consumption preferences, it allows for targeted educational marketing to various consumer groups. Coursework becomes described in its 'aesthetic' qualities; beyond any content and institutional charter, a chosen course may appeal to various groups, consciously designed by marketing experts. The refined rational-choice framework serves as a background and the key determinant becomes individual preferences.

X *Participation and social networks:* The main explanatory variable is the very act of participation, not the coursework and its likely learning outcome. Decisions on group or network levels trigger participation, turning whole communities into non/participants. The model generally does not examine types of education. However, only particular programmes may be available for a network; thus, specific social 'bridges' must link a social network to a particular opportunity for participation. Rational-choice, conflict and institutional frameworks explain participation of groups and networks.

XI Biographical or life structure/life course frameworks: Participation is explained as the result of ongoing developments and changes over the life course. Particular (marker) life events (such as expecting a child, the death of a parent, moving into another city) or life transitions lead individuals to look for opportunities of support; adult education could be helpful. As the life course further evolves, the reasons for participation may change or disappear; a multiyear programme may serve one issue in an early phase and other developmental needs in a later one. The explanations focus on why people start a programme at a particular moment in life (not earlier and maybe also not later). Various programmes may respond to a particular need (such as meeting other people to overcome a depressive mood and a strong feeling of isolation), but the model does not examine in detail the nature of the programmes. This approach expects programmes to be chosen mainly for their availability and social closeness. Biographical approaches use various theoretical underpinnings (including life-span development psychology).

This overview of theories on participation allows me three observations:

First, these theories do not differentiate between the decision to participate in the course and the desired learning – that may not have strong links to the course. They do not take seriously the possibility that a person may start a programme for reasons unrelated to its stated educational goals.

Second, the decontextualised theories mostly provide static explanations of the formation of interest in adult education. Only participation and life-course-based theories consider timing of participation as particularly important.

Third, theories on participation hardly explore specifics of the 'taught course': their length, workload, selectivity, prestige and so forth are taken as having no impact on a theory's explicative value.

Distinguishing between 'participation' and 'learning' involves considering various sites of learning beyond the classroom, such as the family, the workplace, the wider community and leisure activities. Participation in organised learning could result from a particular activity in a workplace, a civic organisation (such as mountain rescue service) or leisure activity (such as member of a brass band). Explaining participation in the more basic activities could also explain participation in organised learning (Courtney 1992). Consequently, to understand individual non/participation in organised learning, we need to study an individual's changing involvement in various social settings that may allow for learning and may trigger participation in organised learning.

We need a concept of the connections between the available, needed or desirable learning within various life areas and how all this may change during (developmental) a person's life, (institutional) social time and historical time (Elder & Shanahan 2006). Daniel Levinson concept of the 'life structure' catches the interplay of life areas allowing for learning over a lifetime. While discussing this framework in detail in Section 4.3, I only emphasise the crucial differences resulting from embedding educational experiences into one area of the life structure or if they temporarily constitute a component of the life structure.

Turning to the third observation, I argue that all theories of participation in organised education should classify educational programmes. I propose a typology using three bifurcations.

- *the place within an individual's life*: Is participation embedded in an existing area of the life structure or does it temporarily form an independent area?
- *the degree of institutionalisation of participation*: Is participation based on an individual decision not supported by any institutionalised expectations or should everyone participate that pursues a particular career, belongs to a certain community or active in a certain cause?
- *process versus outcome orientation of programmes*: Are programmes more orientated towards participant's needs or more orientated towards prescribed learning outcomes, even at the risk of excluding adults not matching the requirements from further participation?

Overview 11: Participation in organised learning as embedded in the life structure

		Institutionally foreseen for a taken/targeted occupational career		Individually arranged (not foreseen)	
		Orientation of the programme with examples			
		Participation oriented	Outcome oriented	Participation oriented	Outcome oriented
Place within the life structure	Strongly embedded in another area of the life structure	a first aid training for the members of a rambling club	a safety training for all employees of an enterprise	elementary lessons in playing an instrument	acquiring a boat driver permit (for leisure)
	Temporary formation of an own area of the life structure (requiring adaptation of the whole).	trade-union programmes to prepare for becoming/acting as job steward	preparation of craftmaster examination (e.g. Germany, Austria)	certified programmes in coaching or mentoring	adults in higher education unrelated to the current occupation

Source: Own description

Overview 11 provides examples for the types arising by applying the three dimensions. Theories explaining participation generally orient towards one or a combination of the eight resulting types. Theories of motivation explain 'individually arranged' participation, yet have difficulty explaining mandatory participation. Life-course and biographical theories could account for any programme that forms a temporary area of the life structure, but could not be used to investigate routine, refresher training institutionalised in many low-skilled service jobs. While any theorising of participation decisions must have a clear vision of a programme's qualities and their status within the life structure, these theories are also important for our overall understanding of participation in lifelong learning. Most organised adult education takes place within gainful work and is outcome oriented and institutionalised (often mandatory). Many of the most disadvantaged adults participate in organised learning only in a mandatory context. Formal adult education more likely will be outcome oriented; yet participation could be both strongly institutionalised in a type of career or only based on an individual decision; however, given the workload typically involved, in most cases, it temporarily forms its own life area, which hardly happens in any nonformal programme.

4.2 The discontinued paradigm – changing life structure over the lifecycle

In the 1970s and the 1980s, reflecting the likely impact of individuals' life stages and their connected challenges ('rush hour of life'), developmental tasks ('accepting the finite nature of life') and effects on identify stability and change, has been a legitimate and common feature in various disciplines such as career research (Cytrynbaum & Crities 1989, Dalton 1989), human resource management (Schein 1978) or consulting (Schlossberg 1984). Early overviews (Clausen 1986) on what becomes the life-course research certainly referred to the emerging field of research in adult development. For participation in adult education, only Aslanian et al. (1980) apply a life-cycle-developmental perspective and find considerable, although mainly critical reception (for example, Courtney 1992, 73f; Field 2006). In the study by Daniel Levinson and colleagues on stages in adult life, they ubiquitously refer to and build a connection between various applications of developmental thought in various fields.

The hallmark study by Levinson et al. (1978) explores the life course of groups of men and women (Levinson & Levinson 1996) over several decades. It identifies a continual building up and breaking down of an individual's *life structure* for pursuing (ever-changing) personal dreams.

The newly introduced concept of *life structure* denotes '*the underlying pattern or design of a person's life at a given time*' (Levinson & Levinson 1996, 22).

> The life structure is the pattern or design of a person's life, a meshing of self-in-world. Its primary components are one's relationships: with self, other persons, groups, and institutions, with all aspects of the external world that have significance in one's life. A person has relationships to work and to various elements of the occupational world; friendships and social networks, love relationships, including marriage and family; experiences of the body (health, illness, growth, decline); leisure, recreation, and use of solitude; memberships and roles in many social settings. Each relationship is like a thread in a tapestry: the meaning of a thread depends on its place in the total design. (Levinson 1980, 278)

Related to Kurt Lewin's concept of 'life space' (Lewin 1997), *life structure* refers to a totality, including a small number of elements demanding the central place (most often, 'work' and 'love' (Levinson 1980, 278). Beyond these *central components*, which generally shape various phases of restructuring one's life structure, the constant modification (for example, in intensity) of *peripheral components* (such as leisure activities and participation in social movements) may significantly alter the overall pattern. Finally, *unfilled components* may become highly influential: '*A person urgently wants but does not have a meaningful occupation, a marriage, a family; and this absent component plays a major part in the life structure*' (Levinson & Levinson 1996, 23). The person may attempt to fill the void or compensate for something that the individual does not dare to hope for any longer because of fear from unforeseen consequences.

The concept of the life structure aims to overcome unproductive dichotomies between the 'inner' versus the 'outer' world, 'the individual psychological' versus the 'social'. '*Theoretically, the life structure forms a bridge between personality structure and social structure.*' (Levinson 1980, 288).

> The life structure as a whole, and every component in it, has both external and internal aspects. [...] The life structure stems from the engagement of self with the world. To be truly engaged with the world, one must invest important parts of the self in it and, equally, must take the world into the self and be enriched, depleted, and corrupted by it. In countless ways, we put ourselves into the world and take the world into ourselves. Adult development is the story of the evolving process of mutual interpenetration of self and world. (Levinson 1980, 278).

Acting socially requires strong psychic involvement – *Besetzung* (in English, *cathexis*; in French, *investissement* (Laplanche & Pontalis 1973, 62)), lies at the core of any concept of mental health and neurotic inhabitation; however, social theory rarely explores it. The barely stable life structure constantly changes in a '*series of structure-building and structure-changing (transitional) periods.*' (Levinson 1980, 279). Periods of structure building take about seven to ten years. Individuals change their life structures for up to a third of their life. The basic fabric of adult life involves sequences of structure building and constant changing over the phases of adulthood, making up for the cyclic nature of the life course. The social environment with age-grading and age-graded social institution, together with biological ageing, contribute to a staged model of adulthood with particular stages and tasks to be mastered. However, the dynamic of structure-building and structure-changing enforces sudden breaks and restarts throughout life, allowing for – speaking of their socio-psychic state – quite old twenty-somethings and quite young fifty-plus. The cyclic nature of phases of restructuring is at the core of Levinson's model, not so much the overall structure of Levinson's endlessly reproduced graphical representation of the life cycle (for a critique Sugarman 2001, 115ff.).

While crises that are expected (such as transition when thirty years old, the death of the parents) or unexpected (such as sudden breakup of a relationship or the loss of a workplace thought to be safe) contribute to the dynamic of life structure-building and changing, the dynamic has also important *intra-psychic* sources. Levinson's approach resonates well with Eric H. Erikson's model of psychic development in adulthood and development tasks arising later in life, where any stage could be completed only by making considerable – ineluctable neurotic – compromises. Any successful compromise between the desired and the available, being a good-enough, creative solution in the first place, becomes a burden, heavily felt over time and providing momentum for further change.

> No matter how satisfying a life structure is, in time, its utility declines and its flaws generate conflict ... no life structure can permit the living out of all aspects of self ... The primary tasks of every transitional period are to question and reappraise

> the existing structure, to explore various possibilities for change in the self and the world, and to move toward commitment to the crucial choices that form the basis for a new life structure (Levinson et al. 1978, cited by Wolfe et al. 1990, 957).

The research of Fleischer et al. (2010) on adult education suggests the following propositions. Participation in adult education – notably formal adult education – could be understood best as a move within a structure-building process, which has to be – in any case – embedded in an existing life structure that requires substantial change. Entire life stages become the recommended period for observation, lasting between approximately five to ten years. The life structure and all its components provide and restrict opportunities for learning. Formal adult education supplements these learning opportunities through coursework, by its hidden curriculum or by participation in its social communities. Motivation for participation arises when building up or changing the life-structure; barriers come from the external social environment or psychic inhabitations. Educational activities can be one among various ways to achieve goals: it becomes important to understand potentially more effective alternatives (such as seeking a more learning-conducive workplace instead of taking a course). Observing and analysing the individual urge to build up and restructure the life structure thereby becomes a new basis for understanding and explaining participation and non-participation in adult education.

Ongoing, cyclic change within individual life structure *generates* potential use for and interest in educational activities, bound and embedded in a particular developmental frame. Today's 35-year-old participant may, ten years earlier, have had no interest in participation. Structure-building and structure-changing activities are lifelong sources of motivation for participation in organised learning. A life-structure-informed perspective differs from rational-choice, human-capital approaches by offering far more possible reasons, beyond increasing wages or securing workplaces, for participating in specific educational activities (individuals make choices according to their life dreams, not the choice promising the highest return of investment). While human-capital perspectives find it hard to explain why formal education should become 'delayed' to adulthood (Loewenstein & Spletze 1997), a life-structure approach explains why interest in formal education may arise later in life. Finally, continuing restructuring of the individual life structure inspires participation in formal adult education.

Levinson's stage models have been strongly and convincingly criticised for being decontextualised and ahistorical instead of revealing universal aspects: it make no sense to study individual pathways through an ahistorical stage model, where history explains only some variations. Elder and Shanahan argue that individual adult development evolves within a structure irrevocably constituted by history and the dominance of existing institutionalised life-course patterns (Elder & Shanahan 2006, 670). More recent life-course research risks forgetting Levinson's core insight, taken from C.G. Jung and Erikson, that maturation process changes developmental dynamics; this leads to new needs, aims and interests and provides an inner psychic motor for change, transitions, development, learning and the desire to 'return to education'. The new and particular interests in (formal) adult education, not driven by external forces, also depend on available opportunities. As a paradigm discontinued and subverted by some of its own hypotheses, it awaits a systematic review, which could secure its potential for future research of participation in adult education over the life course.

4.3 Exploring the expected features of participants in formal adult education

In the following section, I sum up my assumptions for the characteristics of participants.

They have irrevocably terminated initial education: Their programmes form a new starting point in a clearly distinct segment in their educational and learning career. Participants purposefully chose to enter their adult education. They should be able to explain their decisions. They also share experiences of life and work outside school, so their abilities to reflect on their participation in education differ from pupils or students with uninterrupted education.

They engage in a clearly defined period of highly intensified learning activities that form a life event: Given the workload of formal adult education, most participants must temporarily rearrange their 'life structure' for extended periods, usually for several years. They normally can not follow a formal programme in their 'spare time' or by exchanging one minor leisure activity for another. For the individual, taking up formal adult education becomes thereby a life event, comparable to getting involved in an intensified intimate relationship, raising a child, becoming an elected representative in a civic organisation or providing care for a demanding family member. The individual will likely notice the start of the engagement (intense need to rearrange obligations) and the end of the programme (suddenly a significant amount of time becomes available again). When presenting their life history, individuals often have difficulties recalling any details of participating in non-formal courses and training; however, they generally remember participation in formal adult education.

They combine learning activities with other responsibilities such as work, family obligations or other activities: After finishing their initial adult education, adults generally have a 'life structure' with one, two or even more focal elements such as work, family obligations or civic engagement. In contrast to initial education and most non-formal courses, formal adult education has to be embedded as a central component in an already filled life structure. Therefore, not only finding enough time, but also building up a strong enough attachment to the demanding programme may become challenging.

They find challenging (at least some) tasks involved in the programmes: The demanding nature of broad formal adult education programmes requires participants to deal with the feelings of being challenged. The programmes have at least some requirements (for example, mastering tasks in mathematics, reading and writing in a foreign language, providing long essays or demanding projects, etc.) difficult to master ('I was never strong in …'). Individuals may experience again strong feelings of uncertainty and they must do without the confidence achieved in other spheres of their adult life. They may be confronted with individual weaknesses and *failure* on various levels. They may experience moments where they almost give up. Furthermore, they have to give up their dreams to master the various tasks perfectly and without any strain and difficulty.

They pursue significant personal goals of vital importance: Given the demanding nature of formal educational programmes, individuals likely connect their decision to participate with important personal goals – both specific ones yet also unconscious fantasies about their future lives. Fantasies about and actual participation in the programmes become part of their individual identities. While it would be useless to ask for deeper motivations in the case of 'non-formal adult education', in formal adult education, decisions are likely to be founded in the personal development history. However, individuals may not be aware of the more complex and deeper roots of their desires and may prefer to present socially accepted, but impersonal justification for their decisions. Finally, hopes and expectations connected to formal adult education could also be illusionary. From an external perspective, participation could also hinder individual development through regressive fantasies. However, it makes sense to ask about the developmental significance of formal adult education – which is not true for many short courses and trainings.

They seriously consider whether or not to seek substantial changes in career (and/or other fields of the life structure): Because completing a programme expands opportunities for social mobility, participants likely reflect on possible changes, at least at some stages of their programme. Also playing a role is the need to reorganise the life structure in order to participate and the personal significance of educational goals. Even when an individual's reflections finally confirm their chosen pathways and their programme seems to have no consequence for their life course, the intensified process of considering one's future forms an important side element of formal adult education.

Overview 12: Features of participants in formal adult education

Participants in formal adult education
i. have irrevocably terminated initial education
ii. engage in a clearly defined period of highly intensified learning activities forming a life event (not a continuous process) dividing time in before/after
iii. combine learning activities with other responsibilities such as employment, family obligations or civic engagement – must adapt their way of living temporarily for balancing the requirements of the programme and other obligations/interests
iv. find challenging (at least some) tasks involved in the programmes
v. pursue significant personal goals of vital importance
vi. seriously consider whether or not to seek substantial changes in career (and/or other fields of the life structure)

Source: Own Description

All characteristics chosen for our ideal type of participants in formal adult education refer to the lifecycle. A person's age when finishing formal education makes a difference. Late adolescents normally have much more flexible life structures than adults in their early 30s, who also experience their future prospects differently than those in their late 40s. In the same way, adults in their early 20s, in their 30s or their late 40s will use formal adult education to support different developmental tasks.

4.4 A new typology of participation patterns in formal adult education

Researchers generally explain participation through an individual's attributes (such as belonging to a social milieu) and personal motives (such as work versus leisure). A meaningful typology for adults in formal programmes related both to their prior education and present and future occupation requires a much more complex approach.

These examples from our case studies illustrate *patterns* and prepare for a discussion of my typology (for an overview on the material and methodology, see Annex 8.1):

Borjana[16] from Bulgaria, in her late twenties, started to work for a chemical company with approximately 250 employees. Her work involves advanced information technology. She has continued her history studies and was hired on the condition that she was actually a full-time student; however, some compromises were made later. She needs her job to support herself, but her studies, her career intentions and her current job are not related. (Based on Ilieva 2008)

Kristina from Estonia, in her late twenties, works in the chemical industry for an enterprise with approximately 100 employees. She dropped out of technical education when she was much younger and has worked at various jobs that require no qualifications before starting at a business school on the lower secondary level. During her studies, she started her current job, having worked during a school internship in the same company. Since then, she has worked as a secretary, but she later decided to start a university course in business administration to gain a new starting point for her career. (Based on Tamm 2008a)

James from Ireland, in his early twenties, has just completed a programme leading to a degree at ISCED 5 level in printing. He has worked as a trained printer for the same highly specialised, but declining, printing company before, during and after his education. Even though his current job does not require the qualification, his employer encouraged him to attend the programme and improve his skills for future activities. (Based on Team EDC/CSHD Sp4 Project 2008)

16 Pseudonyms have been used for all interviewees and enterprises.

Peter from Austria, almost 40 years old and with no family obligations, was hired, after a longer spell of unemployment, as an unskilled worker for a chemicals manufacturer, two years ago. He was trained as an electrician, but has worked for several years as a self-employed driver. He was attracted by the high wages for shift work in the chemical industry. His employer has invited him to participate in an eighteen-month course in chemistry, leading to a certificate on ISCED 3 level. After passing the examination, he will be acknowledged as a skilled worker and will enjoy a statutory wage increase – based on a collective agreement. (Hefler & Bacher 2008a)

A common way in classifying such cases would be to refer to gender, age, educational background, migration experiences or ethnic minority status, occupational position or job seniority and characteristics of the employer. Furthermore, one could look for motives such as whether an autonomous decision was made to participate, whether the employer explicitly encouraged participation, whether the individual intended to stay with the same employer, and so forth. In the following section, I provide a more integrative approach, tailored for formal adult education.

A typology of patterns of participation

The typology uses three dimensions:

1. Formal adult education as a life event in the lifecycle

As discussed earlier, formal adult education is seen as a *life event*, which requires a significant temporary change of an individual's way of living and which involves significant developments in personality, self-awareness, cognitive abilities and vocational/professional development. In contrast to various other educational endeavours, participation in formal adult education should occur rarely and be related to significant developmental issues in the individual's lifecycle. Consequently, I use the supposed significance for the life course as the main dimension of our typology. I discern five main types:

(I) *Working while completing formal education (Completing)*: We expect education and work to overlap in the phases 'late adolescence' (15–24 years), 'first transformation/crises' (25–34 years), and also in any other life stage, when an individual focuses again on education and development. Work may provide required resources and may become an additional source of learning and development. However, the focus remains on continuing and completing the educational programme, so that if the job conflicts with the educational pathway, then the person will likely change jobs, so that the programme could be completed.

(II) *Returning to education and revising a temporary transition from learning to work (Returning):* In 'late adolescence' and sometimes later, individuals may decide to stop their education and start working on a full-time basis. A person may leave educational programmes because of the 'pull effects' of the labour market ('becoming contrary to initial intentions more and more absorbed by a job taken only to support the living costs while in education'), unsolved personal conflicts with the educational institutions or other personal developments. This could happen at a foreseen transition point or by dropping out of an already started programme. Tensions between parenting (including a need for more income when supporting a family) and the study requirements of educational programmes are another important factor in terminating a formal educational programme. However, a significant number of people only temporarily stop their initial educational programme. Their developmental steps indicate the desire 'to return to school' and take up studies again. Moreover, institutions could foresee 'returning' to education in cases such as returning to full-time professional education based on some years of working experience.

(III) *Transformation of the existing career pathway and/or individual development (Transforming):* Formal adult education may provide the basis for a significant break with the existing career pathway and life style. This will be more relevant in later stages of the lifecycle, where previous decisions have already contributed to a stable professional identity and social position. Motivations for change could come from the environment (worsening labour-market prospects in declining industries), the dynamics of career couples and the family lifecycle, but also from personal developmental issues in activities that build and change life structures ('pursuing a long-suspended youthful dream when facing social pressures').

(IV) *Reinforcing an existing career pathway (Reinforcing)*: At any career stage, individuals could use available opportunities in formal adult education to solve actual developmental issues or to support progress within their chosen line of occupational or professional development. However, this option exists only with sufficiently satisfying and stable career pathways. I expect this movement within the lifecycle to become the central factor for analysing employee-employer relations. Acquired and actual work experiences provide an exceptional basis for studies not available in initial adult education or for newcomers in an occupational field. The employee and the employer could be interested in reinforcing a chosen career pathway. However, education could also prepare for changing employers and realising the newly acquired competences in a new workplace.

(V) *Compensation for shortcomings of an existing career pathway (Compensating):* Any career, although appreciated and satisfying in principle, may not completely satisfy an individual's personal requirements and desires. Formal adult education may compensate for these shortcomings. Here, learning opportunities available by the formal programme contribute little to the current workplace. Benefits are mainly expected on a personal level. However, spin offs for the professional career could substantially support the often-fragile balance necessary to 'deal with a job'. As a compensatory strategy, alongside the continuation of an established career pathway, participation in formal adult education is much less significant than in the other four types; partially because programme completion has little importance. Compensatory strategies may be useful at any stage of a person's life, but they will be most significant in later phases, when reinforcement and change of a chosen pathway are no longer easily available or desirable.

Workplace tasks, work experience and formal adult education

Because work and life experience serve as important resources in adult education, the second dimension of our typology involves the relationship of current or previous employment and a programme's content and tasks. We include the following dimensions in our analysis:

- *Relation of the content of the programme and the actual work tasks:* I distinguish between whether a programme intends to support an actual task (for example, engineering education for a skilled worker maintaining production lines or a course in nursing practice for assistant nurses) or whether it covers a clearly separate area (for example, legal studies for an information-technology administrator or social work for a sales manager). The relationship shapes both current employment and the opportunities to build on actual work experience. Moreover, the relationship influences the range of the employer's expected support for the participation.
- *Time order of starting the current position and formal education:* Considering whether the educational programme was started before or while working in the current position helps to assess the interdependency between the work assignment and the educational programme.

Relation to the initial educational system and the hierarchy of qualifications

The social significance of formal adult education depends on the degree to which acquired qualifications open further career prospects beyond qualifications acquired in initial education. Therefore, the typology's third dimension compares the level of the qualification from an adult education programme to the hierarchy of qualifications. I restrict my analysis to the following points:

- *Progress or no progress on the educational ladder:* I consider whether participation in a formal programme leads to a next step on the educational ladder. This depends both on an individual's prior educational achievement and the qualification offered by the programme. For some types, I define the progress on the educational ladder as substantial; for other types, it is of little relevance.
- *Same or different programmes of initial and continuing education:* I differentiate between educational programmes designed exclusively for adults and those where adults use the same programmes as 'traditional students'. In many countries,

adult learners join the programmes of (sometime much younger) 'traditional' students. Part-time studies may not differ from full-time programmes, except in the overall duration of the programme.
- *Dependence or independence from the initial educational system:* An adult education programme reflects the strengths and shortcomings of the (mainly) state's provision of initial education. Finishing the initial or the adult learning programme involves comparable tasks and leads to comparable rights (for example, access to higher education or to work in a profession) and positions. However, many countries have formal adult education programmes that have no equivalent in the initial educational system. These programmes either require work experience in a certain field or are open to all adults holding a certain level of qualification (for example, university matriculation).
- *Requirement for professional and/or life experience*: Among the formal educational programmes available only for adults, many limit entrance to those with experience and/or a qualified position in a certain occupational field. Often, these programmes could be regarded as continuing education for certain professional groups. The qualifications achieved are of value mainly within the restricted professional field and have little relevance outside the particular professional communities.

Overview 13 summaries the typology with the main dimension as the significance of the formal adult education in the life course. Because the significance of career in a person's life course strongly connects to the relationship of formal adult education with the workplace, I use the workplace only as a subordinate dimension (to exclude cases that do not meet the assumed logic of a type). Our main dimensions include the expected combinations of formal adult education and the workplace. We attributed a type to an observed case only when the significance in the life course and the relation to the workplace fits our expectations. Overview 13 provides the relations of the content of the formal adult education and the workplace that we would subsume under the patterns. Finally, I use the relationship to the formal adult education system only to differentiate the most important patterns.

The typology focuses – for pragmatic reasons only – *at one moment of time* on the pattern 'life course/ educational programme / occupation / achieved level of education / existing educational ladder'. Clearly, with the ongoing participation, patterns may change: in which case, so the classification according to our typology. This may be particularly the case, when people change their workplace while participating in a programme. Moreover, the types 'Returning', 'Completing' and 'Transforming' are also connected logically. Employees, who change their priorities from work to education, will frequently be seen later on in the pattern 'Returning'. Someone who starts an education in a field different from their former occupation will probably enter her or his new field before completing the educational programme; again, we would classify the new pattern as 'Completing'.

Overview 13: Patterns of participation events in adult education

Lifecycle				**Expected relation of formal programme to work assignment**		**Relation to initial vocational system**	
Focus	Main Types	Sub-types	Description	Relation of contents/tasks	Start of programme before/after joining the current employer	Dependence/ Independence	Step ahead in relation to individual educational achievement
Education	I Completing	Ia Finishing	Working while studying without particular connection of work and education	Insignificant	Before	Dependence	One step ahead
		Ib Entering	Being hired in late phases by an employer in need of graduates	Strong, clearly visible relation	Before	Dependence	One step ahead
	II Returning		Returning to education and overruling a temporary transition to work	Insignificant	After	Dependence	One step ahead
	III Transforming		General transformation using education as a basis	No relation	After	Dependence	No requirement
Work	IV Reinforcing	IVa Progressing	Progressing in the current field by at least one step on the educational adder	Strong, clearly visible relation	After (exceptional: before)	Dependence	One step ahead
		IVb Adapting	Making one step in the current field, in parallel to an existing one not relevant in the field	Strong, clearly visible relation	After	Dependence	Step ahead only in relation to qualifications relevant for the current job
		IVc Specialising	Completing programme as a specialisation	Strong, clearly visible relation	After	Dependence	No requirement
		IVd Peaking	Completing a formal programme designed for experienced professionals in the field	Strong, clearly visible relation	After	Independent, one level ahead, fixed requirements	One step ahead (often ISECD 6)
	V Compensating		Compensating for the restriction of an existing pathway	Insignificant	After	No restriction	No requirement

Source: own description

Discussion of types of participation patterns

In the following discussion of the various patterns, I only rely upon some selected cases to illustrate our argument. We focus on those patterns most relevant for our further research (that is 'Reinforcing', Type IV, and its respective subtypes). We only briefly discuss other patterns.

Type I 'Completing' – Completion of a step within (initial) formal education and its variation 'Finishing' and 'Entering'

Many adult learners combine studying and working for economic reasons and for reasons of learning and experience. The work assignments frequently increase gradually so that any clear turning point is difficult to identify. The educational programme started *before* any current job activity and the individual's focus remains on completing the educational programme. The participants regard themselves as students who also work. No matter how satisfying, the chosen job is regarded as temporary. The job supports the educational endeavour, not the other way round. Workplaces are chosen according to requirements of ongoing studies; therefore, when job responsibilities become excessive, students normally look for another job better suited to combining with the ongoing studies. With regard to their life courses, they have not yet finished their education or they have not completed a later period devoted mainly to learning. Because we expect this to be one of the biggest groups, we further divide this pattern into those cases with an insignificant relation to workplace and those with a strong relation to the works tasks. The *'Entering'* category often becomes a way to 'enter' into a position longer than the educational programme. *Borjana* (see above) illustrates this type of *'Finishing'* in almost all dimensions.

Type II 'Returning' – Re-entry in the initial (vocational) education pathway

Many younger adults change an earlier decision to leave the educational system. After working for some years, they decide to take up education again, as in the case of *Kristina* (see above). The degree of career engagement could be very different, from occasional work when one needs money to high commitment in jobs where youthful flexibility is of particular value (as in tourism or advertising that require working long hours). In any case, career decisions remain temporary. Unlike more mature adults, they perceive themselves as 'returnees', who follow an educational pathway missed earlier, and not as adult learners, who combine work and learning while interrupting or changing a developed occupational career. When deciding to start formal adult education, they shift their focus from work to education. When the actual job and the intended education can not be combined, the participants will likely leave their jobs. The employer has to face the reality that the employees will leave the company and start in fulltime studies or find a job more supportive of their new educational goals.

III 'Transformation' – Taking up formal adult education to prepare a change of the occupational field

Some adults choose formal adult education to foster a fundamental change in their occupational career. The wish to leave a particular occupational field and (or) to enter a different field – with little or no connection to the present one – drives the educational engagement. They definitely regard their actual employment as temporary and will leave when a satisfying position becomes available in the intended new field. In other cases, participants stop working and concentrate exclusively on their educational project, at least for a certain period. They choose formal education according to its expected contribution for entering the new occupational field, regardless of whether this requires mastering additional steps on the educational ladder.

Type IV – Basic Type Reinforcement – Entering formal education for a higher level of qualification compared to what the individual has previously achieved

In our research within the LLL2010 project, we are especially interested in the employer-employee relationship when it comes to participation in formal adult education. I therefore focus on the *'Reinforcement'* type, because here I presuppose a strongly shared interest by both the employee and employer. I further differentiate the main type in the following four subtypes: *'Progressing', 'Adapting', 'Specialising', 'Peaking',* among which the first is most common.

For adults established in their occupational field and intending to further pursue their chosen career, formal adult education can improve the basis for their continued development, either with the present employer or elsewhere with similar occupational responsibilities. Work clearly remains the focus and educational offers are chosen so that they do not interfere with current work assignments. They select formal adult education with respect to its possible impact on the chosen career: the education could be based on actual work experience in the field and may expand professional competences relevant to the occupational field.

The chosen formal programmes are vocational; they engage in general education only when required for access to the intended final programme. Normally, the vocational programmes directly connect to the occupational field. Moreover, the programmes mirror the structure of vocational educational programmes available in initial vocational education. Because the participant already works in the chosen occupational area, parts of the programmes may become redundant. We can find all of these characteristics in the case of Emese.

> *Emese, in her early forties, has worked for a medium-sized printing company, for almost a decade. She used to work in the textile industry as an unskilled sewer, but after her parental leave, she joined her current employer and become engaged in logistics, taking on increasing responsibility year by year. The company trusts her abilities and, in the near future, she should assume the responsibilities for the logistics. The management has encouraged her to pursue a basic qualification in logistics. She follows a seven-month programme offered by a private for-profit provider, leading to a qua-*

> *lification on logistics on ISCED 3 level. While she participates in the course mainly in her spare time, tuition fees were covered fully by available public co-funding offers.* (Based on Szöllösi 2008)

Peter and James (see above) also illustrate these characteristics.

'Progressing' is among the most significant types of participation patterns. Because educational offers on the different levels of formal adult education could be highly different and because the actual work situation is highly influenced by educational level previously achieved, the level of education differentiates participants within this type into rather distinct subgroups.

'Adapting' is an important variation of the type *'Progressing'*. *'Adapting'* differs from *'Progressing'* only in that the participant may already have achieved a qualification at the same or even a higher level in a different field. Alternatively, the achieved qualification may not be valued in the present situation (for example, because it is a vocational qualification for a different occupational field or was attained abroad and is not valued within the local system).

Despite only one different criterion, *'Adapting'* has very different participation events than *'Progressing'*. The participants have either chosen an occupational field not related to their formal education or share a migrant background (or both). Moreover, the certifying aspect of the chosen formal adult education is often more important than in the type *'Progressing'*. The formal adult education completes a process of acquiring an occupational/professional competence, which has started much earlier and which is grounded in educational experiences and workplace learning, as illustrated in the case of Darja:

> *Darja from Estonia, in her late forties, holds a university degree in humanities, and has worked as a project manager for a long period and for more than 10 years for the current employer. Foreign investors bought the small service provider and established a new management in 2004. Without a formal qualification in her present field, she has felt threatened by the prospect of redundancy and despite her long-term experience, she has suffered from low self-esteem 'It seems to me that if one had started to revolutionise the company matters I would have been one of those whom one would not have wanted to see here. (…) I felt low, because my self-pride had been … I really felt incompetent.' Therefore, she has chosen a part-time master programme in economics, which seems most appropriate to back up her professionalism. However, her employer did not support her.* (Based on Tamm 2008b)

'Specialising' is also a variation of *'Progressing'*. Here, the chosen programme does not lead to any progress on the educational ladder. However, with regards to the formal education, *'Specialising'* duplicates an already achieved qualification, but with a different focus of specialisation. The decision to follow the educational offer is made only with respect to the specialised knowledge available within the programme. This knowledge should complete the competences already achieved by related education-

al programmes on the same or even a higher level or by workplace learning (as in the case of Judith below). Nonformal programmes – when equal in reputation – would also fulfil this role: therefore, in the pattern *'Specialising'*, the availability of formal offerings and their relative advantages compared to nonformal offerings become the main dimension of explanation.

> *Judith from Austria, about 30 and a mother, holds a degree in business administration (ISCED 5) and works for a business consultancy firm. She has followed a three year part-time university programme of applied science in knowledge management, which should support her specialisation in this field and could be valued by not only the present employer but also by a wide range of other organisations.* (Based on Hefler & Bacher 2008c)

The type *'Peaking'* forms another variation of reinforcement. Educational institutions – mainly in the higher education sector – offer formal programmes for experienced practitioners or professionals in a certain field. Professional experience in a certain position is an admission requirement: by definition, such programmes cannot be available within initial education. Often, a minimum level of formal qualification is also required to attend the programme. The offerings should provide professionals with updates in various fields of knowledge and improve their professional competence. The learning opportunities generally include working and learning within a group of a comparable professional status and background. Bela represents such a case:

> *Bela from Hungary, in his forties and a father, has worked for approximately ten years as a sales and quality manager in a small wholesale company. As an adult, he has already completed a university degree in management studies, paid for by the company. Actually, he participates in a part-time Master of Business Administration programme, open only for graduates in an appropriate position with three years of professional experience. To preserve his independence, he pays for the programme privately.* (Based on Józan 2008).

Offerings of this type are rather similar to nonformal educational offering for professionals, even when they lead to a formal degree at ISCED level 5 or 6. However, society and the labour market often do not acknowledge these degrees in the same way as degrees obtained in the initial educational system. The degree frequently duplicates an existing degree on the same ISCED level. The prestige of the institution or the programme frequently shapes the programme's value in the labour market. Because an institution's reputation is often a local phenomenon, the degree may be more valued locally. Participants without a comparable qualification could not assume that their degree would be generally accepted as a sign of progress on the educational ladder. Sometimes, the degrees are explicitly exempted from a more formal acknowledgement in some areas (such as in public administration).

V 'Compensation' – Formal adult education as an arena for meeting individual aims not covered by the occupation

While Types I–IV mark significant steps within the life course, either restarting or completing an educational pathway for changing or reinforcing an existing occupational career, the participation pattern in Type V, *'Compensation'*, does not connect to any significant change of the life course. Participation in formal adult education offers a personal fulfilment not available in the workplace. Even when a particular educational programme likely will have a positive impact on career advancement, this is seen only as a side effect. The individual continues to focus on work and the educational programme does not restrict professional advancement in any way. The case study of Luna provides an example:

> *Luna from Flanders (Belgium), in her thirties, has recently started a study of sociology years after completing university studies in Romance languages and anthropology. For eight years, she has worked as a project manager for a small private consultancy firm with approximately 40 employees in the field of occupational safety and health. Even when she emphasises that some elements of her study programme such as statistics could be of some use for her current job, her choice of a programme is not linked to her work: 'I follow this course in sociology because it really interests me. It is my own choice'.* (Based on Vermeersch & De Rick 2008a).

Clearly, this kind of compensation could be achieved also by nonformal education offers. Availability and criteria for access (for example, low, or even no, tuition fees) are seen as pull-factors, leading to the decision to choose formal instead of comparable nonformal offers. However, the prestige of certain educational opportunities (higher secondary education, higher education) could significantly improve personal satisfaction with a programme, even when a person does not expect the achieved 'title' to influence the professional career.

4.5 Outlook: Explaining individual decisions to participate in formal adult education: towards a new framework building on typologies

The participation patterns in formal adult education focus on the place of a programme within an individual's occupational careers. The nine types express 'social functions' of the programme as understood from the subjective individual vantage point. They also expand the basis for studying the 'objective', structural and institutional meaning of participation in formal adult education. While a valuable step in its own right, the typology of participation patterns does not completely explain participation in formal adult education. Obviously, the typology reflects my other proposals in Chapters 3 and 4. By shortly discussing how the previously introduced typologies relate to my typology on participation patterns, I outline a framework for future research.

Integrated or independent part of the life structure: While formal adult education often forms an independent part of the life structure, participation patterns differ clearly in this respect. When the focus is either on education (Patterns I–III) or '*Compensation*' (Pattern V), participation forms often temporarily a new, independent area of the life structure. In the case of '*Reinforcing*', we find both cases where participation forms a new area of the life structure, and cases, where formal adult education is widely embedded within the current job and therefore – as nonformal company training – requires little adaptation of the life structure.

Programmes oriented towards participation or outcomes: Participation patterns are not linked to either of the two dominant programme orientations. When returning to education or seeking personal transformation, individuals may prefer (at least, for a while) programmes that do not reject participants at an early stage. Participation may start without any intention to complete a programme. Those participants focusing on their occupations may prefer programmes oriented towards clear outcomes that build credentials valuable later in their career. Among programmes used for '*Reinforcing*', we clearly find more outcome-oriented programmes; however, some participation-oriented programmes also exist, particularly when formal programmes support individuals in already acquired new roles.

Participation as institutionally foreseen or individually arranged: Participation patterns clearly relate to the proportion of institutionally prescribed and individually arranged participation events. '*Finishing*' is – per se – institutionally foreseen as students are expected to finish their programmes however, it leaves undecided if the enrolment in a programme has been institutionally prescribed or not. '*Returning*' to education could be both an institutionally supported and a highly individualised decision, depending mainly on the timing and the overall societal institutionalisation of work-to-school transitions. '*Transforming*' somewhat implicitly connects to an individualised and *not* an institutionally supported decision. The pattern of reinforcing more likely refers to institutionalised patterns of various types of careers (see the next point). Only when individuals resist their exclusion from particular career steps, do we usually find individual participation in not institutionalised pathways. '*Compensating*' reflects always a personal decision, not an institutionalised prescription.

Strong/loose institutionalisation of participation within career patterns: While formal credentials are somewhat acknowledged in any career pattern, participation in formal adult education could be either firmly or hardly established within a certain career. Organisational, occupational and professional careers and their institutionalised links to formal adult education interact with the outlined participation patterns. '*Finishing*', '*Returning*' and '*Transforming*' could lead to new starting points for any type of career. However, a cross-country comparison (Chapter 6) will show that societies differ in the extent that they provide the opportunity for an 'alternative', 'non-standard' starting point for 'late bloomers'. *'Reinforcing'* is also well linked to all three types of institutionalised careers; while formal education could be purposefully incorporated or not for organisational careers, formal education is often foreseen for occupational and professional careers. Even without the support of their employer, individuals may follow well-marked lines within occupational and professional career frameworks. Beyond the most frequent pathways, individuals may opt for experimentation and *bricolage*, choosing programmes not established for a particular career. Finally, the pattern *'Compensating'* does not link to any institutionalised career opportunities.

Type and organisational field of formal education: The participation patterns are also linked to the seven types (I–VII) of formal adult education, respectively the seven related organisational fields outlined in section 3.6. Because participation patterns in this section are designed for the employed, we find a link to the type 'Customised Programmes' (V), per definition provided by employers for their staff. In contrast, the type 'Retraining' (IV) plays no role, except for active labour-market programmes that pay enterprises for formal training and integration of former (long-term) unemployed. Among 'Finishing', we predominantly find links to the type III 'Higher Education Programmes accessible for Adults' and to type VII 'Continuing Professional Education'. For 'Returning', we see a clear leaning towards both type II 'Second Chance Education' and again for type III. 'Reinforcing' is linked mainly to type VI 'Continuing Higher Education' and type VII 'Continuing Professional Education', but also to type III. As 'Basic skills and remedy programmes' (Type I) address firms as a platform for reaching out to various vulnerable groups, we find a link between 'Progressing' and 'Adapting' for formally low qualified employees and this type of formal adult education. 'Transforming' and 'Compensating' have less clear links to any of the seven described types of adult educaiton.

My short review demonstrates that progress could be made by integrating these proposed typologies and by expanding the analysis to all participation cases, beyond adults combining gainful work and study. However, we would need to take a life-course perspective – encompassing the subjective-biographical, the lifespan-developmental and the objective-structural dimensions – for developing a full understanding of individual participation decisions. Identical participation patterns may represent different kinds of experience, depending on whether the person started at 25 or 40 years (social time), in 'early adulthood' or in 'midlife transition' (developmental time) or in 1990, 2000 or 2010 (historical time). Some may easily integrate educational programmes in the life structure, others may have increased stress, and others may find that it provides a safe haven, a retreat and secure starting point for rebuilding a life structure found unbearable. Quantitative longitudinal studies covering the whole life provide important insight in expected and quite unexpected patterns of participation in formal adult education.[17] Biographical qualitative studies reveal the subjective significance for participants' identity and further development. They reveal the staged nature of participation over long time spans – for example, a trajectory leading from traditional second-chance education to full-time university study that spans more than a decade (Siaria 1986). This does not only consist of work-to-school and school-to-work transitions, but many developments over a period spanning more than one development stage.

Let's return to Rita, exploring what makes her into a prototype heroine. She definitely follows the 'transforming' pattern, as nothing in her hairdresser career prepares her for studying 'English literature'. She independently crafts her return to education, which is not institutionally foreseen for her, although the 'open university' of the 1970s encouraged radical personal projects. She is an outsider, not because of her age but because of her working-class background. Step by step, she makes education central to her life structure, first following TV programmes, then contacting her tutor and later intensifying her study. She postpones motherhood, leaves her non-supportive boyfriend, quits her vocation for jobbing as a waitress and changes her working class neighbourhood for a sublease in an upper-class student milieu. She virtually reinvents herself, constructing a new identity. We do not know about her future fate; however, we expect higher education to offer her a new professional start, given Great Britain, the late 1970s and her outstanding gains in confidence and competence.

However, the majority of biographical vignettes studied in this chapter imply less dramatic developments that rely much more on institutionalised patterns for participating in and gaining from formal adult education. Therefore, the institutionalisation as part of career patterns and likely outcomes of formal adult education make participation more accessible and less demanding; yet at the same time, more predictable and less a mechanism for social change and individual emancipation. Within a framework sensitive to institutional qualities of formal adult education, the whole spectrum can become the object of further research.

17 Studies are not restricted to 'formal adult education', yet cover 'credit courses' or similar proxies for formal adult education. For the United States, see Elman & O'Rand (2007) which reveals that women participants more often have multiple burdens from employment and family work.

Chapter 5: The qualification providing enterprise? – Learning, training and formal adult education in small and medium enterprises

5.0 Introduction

For-profit enterprises together with non-profit organisations of all kinds play a key role for lifelong learning – as they do for nearly any area of social life in modern societies (Drori et. al. 2006a, 2006b). They employ graduates of both initial education and further education. They open up different opportunities for everyday learning in the workplace, supported or not by continuing education and training, nonformal or formal. Yet, organisations are far from neutral agents. They apply their policies and pursue their politics, shaped by their institutional environments and purposefully adjusted to their strategic interests. Organisations' decisions on hiring and firing, on channelling employees into jobs and careers, on promoting and supporting employees by further education turn them into gatekeepers for individual career development and key players in social stratification. As we have seen, employers' trust in credentials potentially endows any type of educational programme's social charter: consequently, we have to consider the role of the employing organisations when studying formal adult education.

Nonformal training initiated and funded by enterprises makes up the majority of educational activities in most European countries. Employers' engagement in or reluctance towards training is the single most important factor shaping the European Union's structural indicator on lifelong learning. However, beyond the fact that most participants in formal adult education are employed, the formal/nonformal distinction apparently plays no role for company training; training is expected to be mainly nonformal. Formal adult education as a discrete component has been therefore almost neglected by both theories and empirical research on company training. However, in this chapter, I will demonstrate that formal adult education needs careful consideration as part of the companies' human resource management and development policies.

Diagram 6: Participation in formal adult education of employed persons and proportion of employees with (some) support by the enterprise

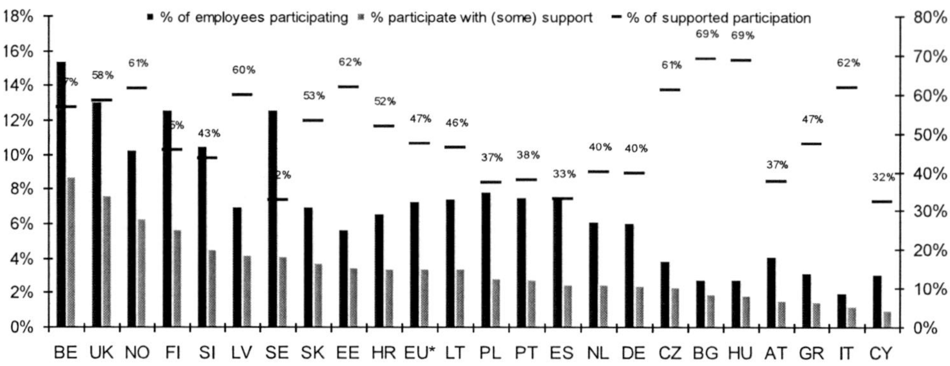

Source: First reported formal activity, Micro data set AES 2005–2007, own calculation

For organisations, it is not exceptional to see their employees participating in formal adult education. In countries for which formal adult education implies participation in multi-year, time-demanding programmes – such as in Austria, Bulgaria or Estonia, participation rates are between two and four percent in the average but clearly above that level (6–12 percent) for the younger and mid-career staff. From the standpoint of life-cycle-oriented personnel management (Schein 1978; Graf 2002), many workers could be expected to participate in extended spells of formal adult education programmes at one moment in their career (although data are missing and estimates available are notoriously vague). Expectancies for participation over a lifetime are above 20 percent in all countries (the smallest in Bulgaria, the highest in Norway, England and Scotland, see Hefler et al. 2011, 47ff). For highly skilled employees and firmly institutionalised formal adult education within organisational careers (for example, preparation for craft mastership in Austria or Germany), the expected participation rates may even be much higher. As a life event for the individual worker, formal adult education is therefore as frequent as parental leave.

The Continuing Vocational Training Survey (CEDEFOP 2010) defines formal adult education of staff as corporate training when the company either contributes to the costs or allows paid workingtime to be used for some of a programme's workload. The Adult Education Survey indicates that roughly three percent of all employees are engaged, at any given time, in company-supported formal adult education and half of all formal learning activities would count as corporate training. The substantial country differences reflect the previously stated differences in the understanding of formal adult education. In Belgium, the UK, the Nordic countries and Croatia, between four and eight percent of the staff participate in corporate-supported formal adult education. On the bottom end of the table, in ten countries, less than two percent of the staff participate with some support of their employer company (see Diagram 6). However, participation rates do not reveal the level of enterprises' support for formal adult education. Some countries with comparatively high participation rates have considerably low support rates, such as in Sweden or Slovenia. In some countries with comparatively low participation rates, such as Hungary, Bulgaria or Estonia, enterprises support the vast majority of all reported formal learning activities; this partially reflects the existing individual employee rights. While in some countries (for example, Latvia, Norway, Estonia, Finland, Bulgaria, the UK and Hungary), enterprises more frequently support shorter courses; most countries have considerably low differences in support for short and extended programmes (+/- 10 percent).

In this chapter, I will consider formal adult education in enterprises against the backdrop of theoretical frameworks and empirical research on training in enterprises. I outline (Section 5.2) four frameworks for explaining enterprises' training behaviour and explore their assertions on formal adult education. In Section 5.3, I propose to focus on *training cultures* as crucial variable and outline an integrative framework. In Section 5.4, I develop a typology of training cultures and connect it with my case-study material. In Section 5.6, I analyse the place of formal adult education within companies' training cultures by investigating support patterns. In the outlook (Section 5.6), I ask about the relative dependence or independence between training cultures and support patterns for formal adult education.

5.1 Theories of training in enterprise and the position of formal adult education

Any theory of company training implies a theory of organisational agency. Observed training behaviour may reflect mere environmental conditions or genuine organisational decisions. When environments provide powerful explanations for training behaviour, it is sufficient to know about and measure the causes for emerging patterns. By comparative cross-sectional and longitudinal statistical analysis, we learn about likely environmental effects on training activities. However, when the key factor is the companies' voluntary decisions, then we need to know about individual organisations in more detail. Qualitative methods for understanding 'organisational biographies' become irreplaceable. The methods used to study organisational behaviour, consequently, result from theories on organisational agency (Ouchi & Wilkins 1985).

Given the outstanding differences in levels of training activity, both between similar enterprises (same size, sector, technology) in one country and aggregates of enterprise between countries (Hefler & Markowitsch 2008), our thoughts about organisational agency become decisive. Organisational research struggles with competing questions: 'Why are organisations so similar?' versus 'Why are there so many different organisations?' Focusing more on organisational behaviour, the opposite approach considers, 'Why do organisations *behave* so similar?' as opposed to 'Why do organisations *behave* so differently?' However, the two pairs of questions overlap; they do not replace each other. Some theoretical frameworks (such as organisational ecology, Baum 1999, Baum & Shipilov 2006) demonstrate that organisations could be very different despite behaving quite similarly or could be very similar, despite behaving very differently.

Theoretical frameworks playing down organisational agency have been dominant for a long time and remain powerful in research on training in enterprises. They include functional theories, technological theories, and neo-marginalist economic theories of the firm (including institutional economics). Since the 1970s, organisational ecology, so-called *rational choice institutionalism* and early contributions of *organisational institutionalism* have been developed in opposition to 'one best way', rational choice frameworks for explaining growing *similarities* in organisational behaviour. All three approaches have little interest in organisational agency, yet explain similarities in behaviour without converging towards one best fit. All theories together explain differences in observed behaviour resulting from difference in the environments of enterprises.

Theoretical frameworks taking a particular interest in organisational agency are diverse. They include the *resource-based view of the firm* (Barney 1991, Barney & Hesterly 1999), anthropological studies of organisational behaviour, organisational psychology and more sociological organisational research based on theories of *organisational cultures* (Martin 2002), various strands of *historical institutionalism*, younger (starting from the middle of the 1980s) contributions of *organisational institutionalism* that focus on the interplay between institutional processes and organisational processes, reflecting organisations' strategic choice and organisations' roles as institutional entrepreneurs (Battilana et. al 2009).

Theoretical frameworks linking education and the economy typically focus on school-to-work transitions or on the firms' behaviour in providing training. Formal adult education fits in neither of these lines of research and remains therefore a marginal topic. Since the early 1980s, the sociological paradigms linking the worlds of education and work have been classified by handbooks and literature reviews into three (Fuller & Rubinson 1992, Rubinson & Browne 1994) or four paradigms (such as Luo 2002). I focus on the organisation's role in training and build my overview on Luo's approach; however, I change wording and emphasis. I discuss (1) human capital theories, (2) technological approaches, (3) organisational structure and culture theories and (4) organisational institutionalism. Paradigms (1) and (2) could be labelled together as functionalist approaches, (3) and (4) as cultural and power conflict approaches. I focus on the expectations for the role of formal adult education deriving from the frameworks.

Overview 14: Characteristics of frameworks for explaining observed (measured) levels of training activity

Framework	Time-Frame	Level of events explaining training incidence	Interest in organisational agency	Main interpretation of observed (aggregated) behaviour	Interpretation strategies for observed differences in aggregates (between size classes, sectors, countries)
Human Capital & Rational Choice	short-cycled	organisation	low* (enterprises behave similar in similar environments)	Investment function in a given market environment	Differences in functions – for example, by scale effects; institutions or the like
Technological Approaches	short-cycled	sectors & societies	low (choosing between a limited number of packages)	Impact of 'hard' and 'soft' technologies, expansion/restriction of competition	Differences in diffusion of technologies and institutional frameworks in favour/opposing certain packages
Organisational Culture	long-cycled	individual Organisation	very high (= focus)	Structuration by sediments of past micro-processes ('freezing'); power differences within the organisations	Pattering within organisational life cycle; presence/absence of moderating influences on organisational level processes ('chocks' etc.)
Organisational Institutionalism	long-cycled	organisational fields, societal sectors	high (different reactions to pressures and opportunities, institutional entrepreneurship)	Impact of institutional pressures and opportunities, moderated by organisational behaviour, power of dominating organisations (within organisational fields)	Differences in institutional processes and their consequences in organisational fields; differences in relative impact of institutional processes compared to other ('technical') processes

Source: Own Description; * With the exception of the resource-based view of the firm

Human Capital and Rational Choice Approaches

Human capital theory and related rational choice approaches explain the take-up of education and training by the expected outcome for the firm or the individual. Educational activities – understood as an investment, calculable in money – are expected to lead to improved capabilities, which become translated into improved performance, so that benefits achieved could be distributed among the firm and the employees. As long as returns on investments exceed benefits of alternative uses of resources (including consumption), rational agents invest in education and training. Under perfect market conditions, however, employers or employees monopolise returns, depending on the type of training. Firms are expected to invest in firm-specific, non-transferable skills, useless outside the organisation, because they could claim most of the benefits of improved performance, since the employees – deprived of an exit option – could not press for higher wages. Formal education – no matter whether for the young or for adults – provides general, transferable skills, useful in any workplace, so that – in the absence of any institutions – employers have no reason to invest in this type of training, because they have to fully reimburse the individual for improved performance, otherwise the person might work for another firm ready to reward fully the newly acquired skills. A firm's investment in transferable skills and therefore formal adult education could be explained only by considering imperfections of the markets and transaction costs (allowing payment below individual productivity) or the strategic resources of a firm (allowing payment above individual productivity). Rational market participants are deprived of any individual characteristics (see Maurice et al. 1986, 9f), so any aggregated difference in human capital investment is understood as the outcome of either different levels of market failure or the benevolent consequences of institutional arrangements, in short, as environmental issues.

Human capital theory does not distinguish between 'formal' and 'nonformal' education; however, the difference relates to the distinction between general and firm-specific training. 'Formal' education is by definition 'general', because it is transferable; only 'nonformal' training offers the alternative of not being transferable. Moreover, human capital theory refers to comparably extended units of learning, typically measured in additional years of education. 'General' or 'firm-specific' refer not actually to the content of education, but to its transferability with given institutional conditions in an economic sector[18]. 'General' education equals to the presence of exit options for employees, who may seek for better pay for their new qualification elsewhere, 'firm-specific' to the absence of option to use the skill with a new employer. However, 'post-Beckerian' variants of economics of education, starting with Bishop (1988), explain why firms may invest in 'general' training. These approaches highlight the value of unique packages of firm-specific experience and general (formal) education. By combining firm-specific experience and formal (general) training, firms may unleash their employees' genuine, situated and thereby firm-bound potentials that are hard to copy; this allows for a market premium high enough to pay wages substantially above market level. Staff participating in formal adult education could not expect to receive higher wages for their newly acquired qualification elsewhere, because their present pay already is above market level for the newly achieved formal qualification (for more studies, see Bishop & Kang 1996; Loewenstein & Spletzer 1997; Acemoglu & Pischke 1999; Backes-Gellner 2005).

For a human capital (or rational choice) framework, an organisation's total training activity represents the sum of recent 'case-by-case' training decisions, reflecting the situation in the various subunits of the enterprise, the expected outcomes of particular training interventions and the availability of alternatives to training. However, any enterprise in a comparable situation is expected to show a similar behaviour; therefore, rational behaviour is considered a constant, not the individual behaviour of the firms and we study an *investment function* in a given market environment. Therefore, differences

18 Any education useful by all employers could become 'non-transferable' and thereby 'firm-specific', when mechanisms block employees exit strategies, as underlined by Streeck (2011) with the example of skilled workers in the Japanese automobile industry: companies massively invest in – speaking of its content – highly 'transferable' skills of their employees, because a firmly enforced rule of never employing former employees of competitors blocks individual exit strategies and therefore transferability of training on the sector level.

between aggregates of enterprises (such as sizes, classes and countries) are interpreted as differences in the input for that function. Examples include economies of scale for explaining differences in training behaviour between small and large enterprises, differences in labour supply on local markets or differences in institutional frameworks as strictness of employment protection or availability of payback clauses for training.

Technological Approaches

Technology based theories stress the raising complexities of production processes, requiring ever-increasing levels of specialisation and division of labour between emerging expert groups. Constant change, driven by technological innovation on a societal level, adds to these complexities and requires short-cycled adaptations. Expertise could be dispersed differently among groups of employees, depending on the social technologies applied to control and govern the transformation of individual capabilities into organisational performance. Modes of organising work – Taylorism, Fordism, lean management, high-performance work systems – are interpreted as more or less efficient social technologies, to be chosen based on their effectiveness and efficiency for a chosen technological infrastructure. Combined with competition on liberalised markets, newly arriving technological solutions are expected to become universally required. The paradigm's strongly criticised determinism prevails even after modifying the assumptions: Choices are thought to be limited to a defined number of complementary combinations of 'hard' and 'soft' technologies. Increasing complexities and technological change – moderated by social technologies applied to work organisation – define training needs for companies.

This has mixed implications for formal (adult) education: More professional education is required for an ever-increasing number of expert roles and more general education is claimed to be required for securing high levels of flexibility and trainability in quickly changing environments. Levels of formal qualifications required for new entrants are expected to increase. However, reorganisation of work and the organisations' desire for tighter control may lead to severe deskilling of large segments of the workforce. Socio-technological change is expected to lead to skills obsolesce, breaking with the institutionalised promises of lifelong validity of educational credentials. Organisations are seen as free to decide how they meet their demand for up-to-date, cutting-edge skills, either by recent graduates replacing employees with outdated skills or by updating skills of the existing workforce. By definition, firm-specific know-how is not available on the labour market and typically costs more to transmit; therefore, further education for existing personnel is expected to play an important role for meeting increasing skill demands. However, there is principally no preference for formal or nonformal training beyond possible legal requirements to only employ 'licensed' personnel for certain tasks.

For a technological approach, an organisation's total training activity indicates the intensity of technological and competitive pressures, modified by applied social techniques to organise and control work. Organisational agency is of minor interest, because only a few 'package solutions' are expected to be available. Today's training activity is interpreted as the result of *recent* changes in technology or competitive pressure. Aggregated training volumes are consequently interpreted as a measure for change and competitive pressure within a particular sector, not as the outcome of enterprises' agency.

Organisational Culture Approaches

Concepts of organisational cultures focus on organisational agency. Organisations develop idiosyncratic patterns of organising work and shape social relations within the workplaces. They create stable structures and organisational cultures.[19] Patterns emerge in career pathways and segmented internal labour markets, codes of conducts and flows of exchange. Firms within one sector or size and comparable hard and soft technologies develop nevertheless different organisational cultures; one organisation may host various cultures. Informal communication develops differently within organisational units; this allows for openly expressing or silencing conflicts. The attitudes of leaders and the founding generations may imprint organisational cultures. Cultures are driven by internal processes and more influenced by the shared past of an organisation's members and the outcomes of previous decisions made than by the contemporary environments. Highly different organisations meet the required minimal fit for survival. Because of buffering of any environmental feedback, rationality remains strictly situated within the idiosyncratic norms of the organisation. The considerable levels of deviation and misbehaviour that emerge become accepted and naturalised as 'the way things are done here'. Employees adapt to how education and training is implemented within the company and internalise beliefs.

Patterns develop that, for example, make it appropriate to offer training in case of a promotion or to apply for a course at least every second year. Levels and types of formal education become desirable for various social positions and the relation between groups – such as between team leaders and their group members; this shapes the behaviour of management and promotion-seeking employees. Therefore, for a cultural approach, any organisation develops a use of formal education and nonformal training that cannot be explained by rational choice arguments alone, but has to be reconstructed in the context of the organisations' conflict ridden history.

Organisational culture approaches interpret a given training activity – preferably measured for a number of years, not only for one – as an outcome of various underlying *time-spanning* social processes within a *single* organisation. It focuses on developments within one organisation and relates processes emerging over time with current

---

19 Various groups of researchers and practitioners claim expertise for organisational cultures. Research-inspired approaches such as in organisational anthropology or organisational theory compete with clearly normative or interventionist approaches from management research and organisational development. The 'organisational culture wars' (Martin 2002, Chapter 2) could be understood better as a struggle for legitimacy and resources of professional expert groups than alone as a conflict between paradigms within social research.

training activities: the reason for a single training activity could not be traced back to isolated causes, because whole cultural patterns make their impact. Major changes in training activities are therefore explained as changes in cultural patterns, which may occur as results of internal processes (such as power struggles, changes in generations of employees) or external shocks (such as a takeover). The actual reason for changes in levels of training activity could not be identified before empirically examining historically and locally situated organisations.

Organisational Institutionalism Approaches

Organisational institutionalism explores the ways that belief systems are spread across organisations, become shared by the organisations' members and exert influence on the organisations. Relevant institutional processes arise on the local, organisational field level and shape organisational processes of the individual organisation. Typically, institutional processes combine cohesive (such as rules), normative (such as standards of professional conduct) and cognitive (as hegemonic theoretical assumptions) elements for constructing the 'social facts' that individual members of an organisations, irrespective of their social role, take for granted. Organisations may fully or symbolically comply ('decoupling'; Meyer & Rowan 1977) with, openly oppose or actively subvert institutional pressure (Oliver 1991). Because organisations often belong to several organisational fields, they face competing institutional claims on their organisational processes.

The use of formal credentials by employers is highly institutionalised on a societal level and formal adult education subscribes – as outlined in Chapter 3 – to the institutionalised belief in education. The use of training is institutionalised on the organisational field level and on the level of various professions (for example, human resource management). The high legitimacy of formal education makes it attractive to search for 'formalisation' of nonformal programmes. The use of training becomes thereby a ready-made, institutional building block, applied prior to any reflection in given situations. Training becomes the cure to any woes: restructuring requirements, introduction of new software, vacancies of middle-management positions, and reports on bullying or bossing or sexual harassment. After institutionalisation, critical evaluation may occur, yet even disappointing results do not change or alter fundamental beliefs (Hefler 2010b).

Measured accumulated training activity is taken as representation of organisation's answers to established institutionalised expectations. Observed differences between average training activities are traced back to differences in institutional processes in various organisational fields. However, this approach requires additional information on the strategic behaviour of the organisations, even when organisational agency is certainly not as important as in the approaches linked to organisational culture.

I strongly support the call for an integrative approach that considers investment motives, technological underpinnings, evolving cultural patterns and the impact of institutional processes. I find it particular fruitful, as Pedersen & Dobbin (2006) advocate, to combine an organisational culture approach that highlights the importance of organisational agency, and an organisational institutionalism approach that highlights the importance of cognitive frames evolving on organisational field level. In my next section, I will explore this interaction between organisational agency and limiting and enabling 'social spaces'.

5.2 Reasoning the emergence of stable training patterns on company level: Training cultures

I propose – following an approach developed together with Jörg Markowitsch (Hefler & Markowitsch 2008) – to interpret the typical data available on enterprises' training activities as a representation of an *evolved*, considerable *stable pattern*, of how companies use training. We have decided to call *metaphorically* this overall pattern *training culture*; we argued for the existence of *types* of different training cultures, which help us to understand the behaviour of enterprises towards training but also towards other aspects such as towards existing public-support schemes or their readiness to support formal adult education. Instead of understanding indicators, such as 'number of hours in training per employee', as resulting from a series of training decisions driven by contemporary factors, I propose to treat them as a representation of stable cultures.

We propose to differ between 'reactive' and 'expansive' training cultures: Overview 15 presents the basic opposition between the two patterns. The cultures differ in their overall attitudes towards training. The cultures understand it as a cost factor or an investment and differ in the level and range of training activities, in the development of the overall use of training, the dependence of environmental factors ('drivers', 'barriers') and the diffusion of training activities in a given workforce.

Overview 15: Reactive versus Expansive Training Cultures – Defining characteristics

Reactive Training Cultures	Expansive Training Cultures
Training mainly seen as a cost factor and therefore minimised	Training is understood as an investment with significant value added
The average training activity (over a multi-year period) is comparatively low	The training activity is high and tends to make full use of the potential to support workplace learning
Experiences with and competences about the use of training are restricted to smaller groups of employees	Experiences with and competences about the use of training are widely diffused within the organisation, providing a framework for further improvements
Training mainly reacts to a need, the training volume depends on the increase/decrease of this needs	Within an existing potential (training potential), the use of training and other opportunities to support learning at the workplace are optimised; changes in external requirements influence only the composition of the range of training activities, not the level of activity
Changes in external factors may lead directly to more/less training	Changes in external factors have little effect on the level of training activities

Sources: Adapted from (Hefler & Markowitsch 2008, 40).

We have argued (Hefler & Markowitsch 2008, 41ff) that unlike the typical expectations for 'investment goods', training is not unconditionally available for all issues in an organisation. Setting aside particular situations (for example, fundamental changes in technologies), employees could reasonably undertake only a limited number of training activities in a year. Learning and development often require a step-by-step approach: Simply providing more hours of instruction in the same period does not directly translate into more learning. Therefore, reflecting the progressive, step-by-step nature of learning processes and after already having a high level of training activity, organisations could not easily compensate in one period for training activities not accomplished in previous periods. Therefore, an organisation may judge itself against the degree of having annually used its *training potential*[20] (Hefler & Markowitsch 2009).

By speaking of training cultures, I link my argument to the vast and contested field of the study of 'organisational cultures'. I take Joanne Martin's mapping of the terrain (Martin 2002) as my preferred guide.

To speak of 'training culture' evokes the multiple components of 'organisational culture' as formal structures, rules, regulations, but also stories, rituals, jargon and physical arrangements and many more.[21] The most frequently studied outcomes of 'organisational culture' include openness for or resistance to organisational change or organisational learning. Features of organisational cultures found most important ('valuing people', 'organisational learning') are understood as both basic components of 'organisational cultures' and their vital outcomes. Moreover, organisational cultures reflect their societal environments, brought into the organisations by the employees, the suppliers, the customers, the share- or stakeholders or regulative authorities (Hofstede & Hofstede 2005).

'Training cultures' are thought to be relative autonomous from more general accounts and dimensions of 'organisational culture'. Organisations with one single type of organisational culture could have different types of training cultures. For

20 The idea of training potential is introduced as a vague guideline, as it is impossible to state a level applicable for all types of organisations or groups of employees. To assess the use of training potential, we have proposed a crude proxy elsewhere: the organisational training potential of the average of employees (not for an individual employee!) on ISCED 0–2 is at least 40 hours per years, for the average of ISCED 3–4 at least 50 hours and for the average of ISCED 5–6 at least 60 hours (see also Hefler & Markowitsch 2008). These are only roughly estimates for gauging the likelihood that an organisation makes a high use of its training potential. Organisations – in certain sectors, using certain ways to organise their work and to outsource activities – may have a considerable higher training potential (demonstrated by much higher levels of average training activities).

21 Organisational cultures matter for important dimensions such as the gendered or degendered nature of work and organisational decisions (Ely & Meyerson 2000, Ely & Meyerson 2010), the dignity of work (Hodson 2001), the presences or absence of fear and obstructive behaviour among co-workers (Kish-Gephart et al. 2009) and the encouragement of expressing or silencing of conflicts (Perlowa & Repenning 2009).

example, organisations with highly gender-stereotyped work organisations can be either weakly or strongly involved in training. However, various cultural aspects of organisations are nonetheless expected to interact with training cultures. When organisational cultures focus on control within a low trust climate, accompanied by high rates of turnover, more expanded training cultures could not be expected to evolve. The interaction of features of organisational cultures and particular training cultures is a field for future work and hardly considered in the following account.

Martin (2002, Chapter 4) proposes to discern between an *integration perspective*, supposing one dominating organisational culture, a *differentiation perspective*, assuming conflicting sub-cultures within one organisation and a *fragmentation perspective*, challenging the assumption to see more common, more stable patterns to arise. As a starting point, I take an *integration* perspective, expecting one training culture to dominate an organisation. However, what appears as a homogenous culture may be a composition of diverging training cultures in various organisational units and their particular subcultures. Within organisations, training activity in otherwise highly similar units may be different. Consequently, the study of training cultures could and should be extended to *differentiation* perspectives. Finally, guiding assumptions of the 'training culture' approach seems not compatible with the fragmentation perspective: demonstrating high levels of fragmentation imply the rejection of the idea that 'training cultures' play any substantial role.

In the following, I develop a framework, stressing eleven interrelated assertions, explaining the rise of training cultures.

The core: 'training cultures' as a compromise between 'work organisation', 'institutional claims' and 'organisational cultures'

In my explanation, I define 'training cultures' as the comparatively stable organisational patterns to *support individual and organisational learning* in the workplace by appropriate interventions. Beyond formal or nonformal off-the-job training, available support mechanisms include on-the-job training, time for self study (with traditional or new media), learning projects and deliberate practices (Ericsson et al. 1993, Ericsson 2009), various forms of group discussion, coaching and mentoring and many more (see CEDEFOP 2010m for a typology of the so-called 'other forms' of training). Ways to support learning complement and partly replace each other: However, for characterising a training culture, the overall frequency and intensity of interventions for supporting learning is crucial, not the mix of instruments used.

The development of 'training cultures' is shaped predominately by three complexes, building together the core of the explanatory framework (Diagram 7).

Diagram 7: Explanatory framework of factors shaping 'training cultures' – Propositions 1–3

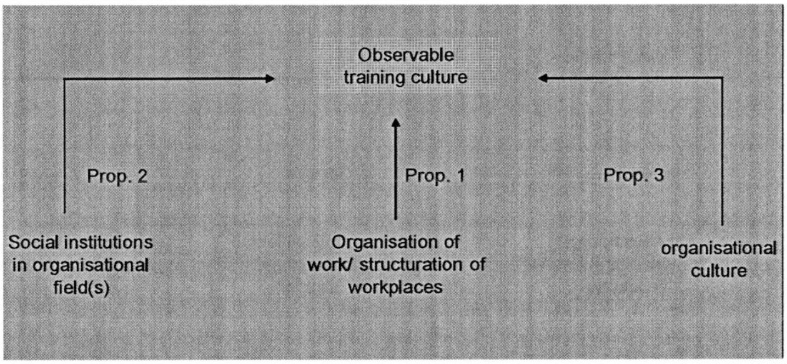

Source: Own description

- *Proposition 1: The organisation of work defines the range of opportunities for intervening in favour of learning; consequently, it predetermines the space for training cultures to evolve*

Although economic activities exert some influence, the way how work is organised into sets of workplaces defines an organisation's requirements for skills and competences. For a comparable product, work could be organised so that fewer of the workplaces require high skills, while the vast majority of workplaces have low skill requirements. In contrast, producers of the same product may have high skill requirements for most workplaces. In the former case, only a minority of workplaces requires and allows for high levels of individual workplace learning; in the latter, learning requirements and extended learning opportunities characterise most workplaces.

In organisations with few workplaces demanding high skills, the organisation has little support for learning for most employees because it purposely has low learning requirements for workplaces: consequently, little space exists to develop expansive training cultures. When most workplaces require high skills and allows for their use, it makes sense to develop more expansive training cultures; however, vast opportunity for training does not automatically lead to more training.

Since the early 1980s, various strands of research have broadly discussed the central role of work organisation for training (management Koike & Inoki 1990, Koike 1994; political economy Leoni & Gaj 2009, Cristini et al. 2008, Cristini et al. 2003, Leoni et al. 2001, Arundel et. al. 2007). Organisations could be described by the distribution of workplaces with particular characteristics within their workforces (Mintzberg 1979). One product or service could be produced successfully by different strategies to organise work. The division of labour between organisations creates 'expert' or 'professional' organisations, which predominately employ professionals and have almost exclusively workplaces with high skills demand.

To sum up, the lower the proportion of workplaces with low skill demands and little opportunity for applying newly acquired skills, the larger is the space for developing more expansive training cultures. The proportion of workplaces with high skill demand is expected to be the single most important predictor of an organisations' type of training culture.

The way work is organised – leading to upskilling or deskilling for some of the workforce – is consequently the key to understanding the formation of training cultures. Yet, it is also decisive for creating the demand for formal qualification and the institutionalisation of occupational careers. Therefore, whatever changes the organisation of work is of vital interest for understanding training and the importance of formal qualification – as I will discuss later on (Propositions 4–6).

■ *Proposition 2: Institutionalised expectations and taken-for-granted assumptions on training & development, present on the level of organisational field(s) imprint organisational 'training cultures'*

Within organisational fields, societal or even global institutional expectations become revised for the local level. Institutions are frequently considered as a reason for training. However, studies are mainly done on the societal level of proxy indicators representing formal institutions (such as strictness of employment protection, strength of trade unions), (see Brunello et al. 2007). Other considerations include laws directly relating to training (such as professional standards, individual rights for training established in collective agreements). However, the influence of legal institutions on training is typically conceptualised in a direct way: the presence/non-presence of an institution is expected to trigger training activities. Here, I argue that formal and informal institutions (such as cognitive schemes, etc.) alike influence the development of training cultures: an institution's impact on present training activity and its influence on the development of training cultures could be different and should be distinguished.

Using arguments present within organisational institutionalism (Scott & Meyer 1994, Monahan et al. 1994, Dobbin et al. 1994, DiMaggio & Powell 1983, Dobbin 2009, Luo 2002, Luo 2006), I stress the importance of including more institutions that are informal. This would include the impact of professions and their standards communicated in professional education (for example, personnel management standards diffused in programmes on business administration, human resource development standards diffused in personnel and training managers' programmes) or beliefs on the value of education and training established in the wider society. The institutionalised claim that an organisation of a certain size has to have a 'training and development department' or a 'training plan', turns specific elements into natural building blocks of organisations. Institutionalised beliefs and values on a societal level could also make their impact on the beliefs of what has to be done in the field of training and development (Luo 2007).

Beyond the inclusion of more informal institutions, the focus on more local orders is crucial for a more appropriate understanding of the impact of institutions on training cultures. Within organisational fields, the cohesive, normative and cognitive layers of institutions are interpreted and revised in their significance for the members of the field. Only by considering the relative autonomy of organisational fields in reinterpreting institutional claims can we understand the impact of institutions on 'training cultures'. Any country-wide formal institution (as a legal requirement for providing training) will certainly find a highly specific interpretation on the organisational field level, becoming relevant for the individual enterprise only in this modified version.

■ *Proposition 3: The idiosyncratic organisational culture of a given enterprise, representing the history of an organisation, shapes the 'training culture'*

Organisational cultures shape 'training cultures' by favouring ideas, values or norms that possibly support training initiatives. Similar designed training intervention could be perceived highly successful in one culture, yet worthless in others: Beliefs in the value of training are imprinted by the collective training experiences, which are shaped by the organisational culture (Bunch 2007). The social significance of training echoes more general features of organisational cultures: in organisations characterised by low levels of trust and high level of direct control, training may be perceived as a disciplinary measure, signifying a negative appraisal of individual performance. In organisations with a high-trust, responsible autonomy culture, training may be seen as a gratification earned for demonstrated efforts. Employees, who experience their workplaces as undermining their dignity, might learn a lot when participating in off-the-job training, yet withhold their new skills in reaction to the violation of their perceived membership rights. Organisations often have a long-term organisational memory and attitudes towards training result from historic practices, which may no longer be present: stories told on 'successful' or 'devastating' experiences with training could span decades of organisational experiences.[22]

Propositions 1–3 make up the core of the explanatory framework by integrating all four explanatory approaches for enterprise training. However, the three propositions include substantial potential for conflict and ambiguity: 'work organisation', 'institution present on organisational field level' and 'organisational cultures' could exert divergent impact on training cultures: where one level – such as 'institutions' – favours the development of 'expansive training cultures' – other levels – such as the work organisation chosen – may provide little justification for any expanded training activity. 'Training cultures' therefore mediate the impact of potentially divergent drivers; when impulses are contradicting, training cultures may remain instable. For

22 To study the interaction between organisational cultures and training, the former need to be classified on selected dimensions or according to one or several dominating features. Putting into operation the dimensions – for example, *goal, support, rules, or innovation orientation* (Van den Berg & Wilderom 2004) – have to be developed first, before studying the interrelation between culture and activity. However, I propose to look less on the interaction between such variables as 'organisational climate' and 'ongoing training' activity and more on 'training cultures'. More longitudinal studies are required on how the ups and downs in 'climates' have long-term effects on 'training cultures'.

example, enterprises may institutionalise compromises that respond 'ritually' to high institutional pressure for extended training activity (for example, by under using a large training budget).

Moreover, Propositions 1–3 imply that for stable expansive training cultures to arise, minimal requirements on the side of work organisation and on the side of organisational culture are indispensable. Institutional claims may further support the development of expansive training cultures, or – when neither work organisation, nor culture support training – evoke 'Potemkin villages' of training in the first place. However, even in the absence of any support by the work organisation and organisational culture, symbolic compliance to institutionalised expectations to provide training is far from being a negligible force (Scott 2008b, 171) and may become a driver for change in its own right later on.

Dynamics of 'work organisation' become central for 'training cultures'

Work organisation defines the proportion of employees requiring high skill levels and therefore finding opportunity for workplace learning and being empowered to use their learning in daily work. I have highlighted that the organisation of work is not determined by technological requirements or 'one best way' solutions, but by highly variable and a contested field of politics (Edwards & Wajcman 2005) within an organisation and in the wider society. Whatever provokes changes in work organisation is expected to have an impact on 'training cultures'. Many drivers (such as technological progress) typically tested for their impact on training may have an impact on work organisation and only a mediated impact on training. Three propositions try to grasp the effects of changing work organisations.

- *Proposition 4: 'Technical' requirements shape considerably broad parameters for organising work, effective and efficient enough for allowing organisational survival: Changes in technologies or competitive pressure broaden or narrow these parameters, yet, rarely enforce unconditionally change.*

The parameters for organising work are clearly shaped and changed by evolving 'technical environments'.[23] Many components of the 'technical' environments – such as the advent and development of new technologies, including the decreasing costs of their implementation; the supply of skills on local labour markets; the erosion of barriers for international trade – have been studied in relation to their impact on work organisation and training. In the long run, fundamental changes in technologies and competition – such as the diffusion of ICT – alter the way that work could potential-

23 Despite strong criticism (Lounsbury 2008), I find the opposition between 'technical' and 'institutional' requirements (Scott & Meyer 1991) *heuristically* useful, when interpreted in its original intention, while respecting that there is nothing like pure 'technical' requirement or process 'without' any 'institutional' components and hardly any 'institutional' requirement without any 'technical' justification.

Diagram 8: Explanatory framework of factors shaping 'training cultures' – Propositions 4–6

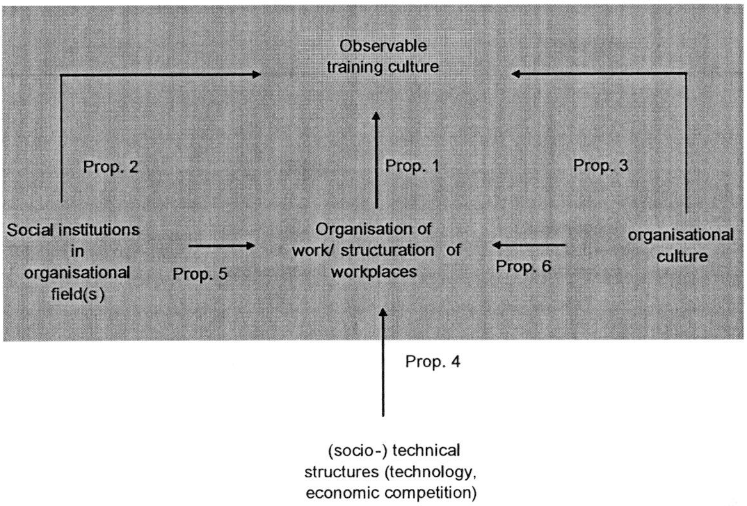

Source: Own description

ly be organised: they expand the opportunities, allowing for more variation or they single out particular now inefficient ways of organising work. However, 'technical' forces *only* alter parameters and are not 'deterministic' in any way. Moreover, changes in the intensity of competition or technology interact with institutional changes and modifications of organisational cultures.

- *Proposition 5: Institutional models and pressures on organisational field level shape the work organisation: Changes in dominant models alter the dominating ways of organising work.*

Organisations belonging to one field share institutionalised understandings of how work should be effectively organised, routed not only in legal regulations, but in shared professional models and cognitive beliefs. Models of organising work such as '(neo-)Taylorism' or 'high-performance, high-commitment work systems' are institutionally designed and present in variants on organisational field level. Occupations or professions provide 'building blocks' to legitimately achieve organisational goals with low levels of risk.

Even in absence of legal requirements, organisational fields contain wide-ranging expectations, such as in connection with institutionalised conceptualisation of 'organisational citizenship' (Monahan et al. 1994, Dobbin et al. 1994, Dobbin 2009). All relevant actors – managers, employees, customers, supervisors of regulatory bodies, judges in labour rights courts – may be convinced that there are some ways to do things right, while alternatives are clearly wrong, even without a binding regulation or any proof for their assumptions. Politics and consequent changes in the popularity and legitimacy of forms of organising work are therefore crucial for the development of work organisation.

- *Proposition 6: Organisational cultures shape the work organisation by informing choices between alternative technological solutions and non-/compliance to institutional claims*

Organisational cultures shape decisions within the parameters left by technological and institutional environments. For various types of organisational cultures – such as low- versus high-trust cultures, formalised versus informal cultures – different types of work organisation seem appropriate (for the impact of work organisation on culture, see below). High levels of formality hardly fit 'lean management', nor low levels of trust with 'project organisation'. The already established organisational cultures limit management's strategic choices between various ways of organising work; organisational cultures could turn out as difficult to change and limit the choice between technological and institutional alternatives.

Therefore, organisational cultures influence adapting or implementing concepts of work organisations: 'Organisational insiders' may have clear visions of the type of 'organisational innovation' that would fit into the organisational culture. Reforms not rooted in organisational culture may remain – at least, for a period – only symbolic. While an organisation symbolically embraces new practices, business remains practically unchanged.

Consequently, organisational cultures add to the path-dependences of the organisation of work. They increase the inertia moderating 'technical' and 'institutional' impulses towards change. Organisations could be expected to stay with their culture – and consequently, with ways to organise work – even when this limits their prospects or even long-term survival. According to organisational ecology (Baum & Shipilov 2006), organisations with highly divergent cultures and work organisations stay in the game and are – contrary to managerial ideology – more likely to live on their saved resources as long as possible rather than respond to changing environments.

To sum up, organisational cultures clearly limit managerial discretion and the impact of 'technical' change and institutional requirements on work organisation. In another words, suddenly changing work organisation actually implies a disruptive change of organisational culture, including any type of unintended side effects imaginable.

Interdependences between the components of the framework

'Work organisation', 'institutions', 'organisational cultures' and 'technical environments' are obviously interrelated; moreover, 'organisations are creatures of their institutional environments, but most modern organizations are constituted as active players, not passive pawns.' (Scott 2008b, 178). Propositions 7–12 highlights the interrelations that seem most important. Propositions 8–12 discuss the link between organisational level, organisational field level and societal level.

- *Proposition 7: Institutional expectations on the organisational field level influence organisational cultures, increasing the similarity between cultures within one sector.*

The influence of the organisational field increases convergence of organisational cultures of organisations (such as banks, mobile-phone providers or hotels). Members of any organisation interpret their organisation's behaviour based on experience in and with related organisations. Consequently, expectations formulated on a field level interact with beliefs stemming from the history of a particular organisation.

- *Proposition 8: Once established training cultures – mediating institutional, 'technical' and cultural issues – constantly influence organisational cultures.*

An established training culture intervenes with the organisational culture and contributes to the conditions required for its continuation. Expansive training cultures spread experience with training and support instruments throughout the organisations and contribute to their positive perception. Reactive training cultures will likely contribute to the cultural conditions required for their prolongation: as a self-fulfilling prophecy, they will poorly implement training innovations, leading to poor results and thus leave little space for justifying training activities in the future.

Diagram 9: Explanatory framework of factors shaping 'training cultures' – Propositions 8–11

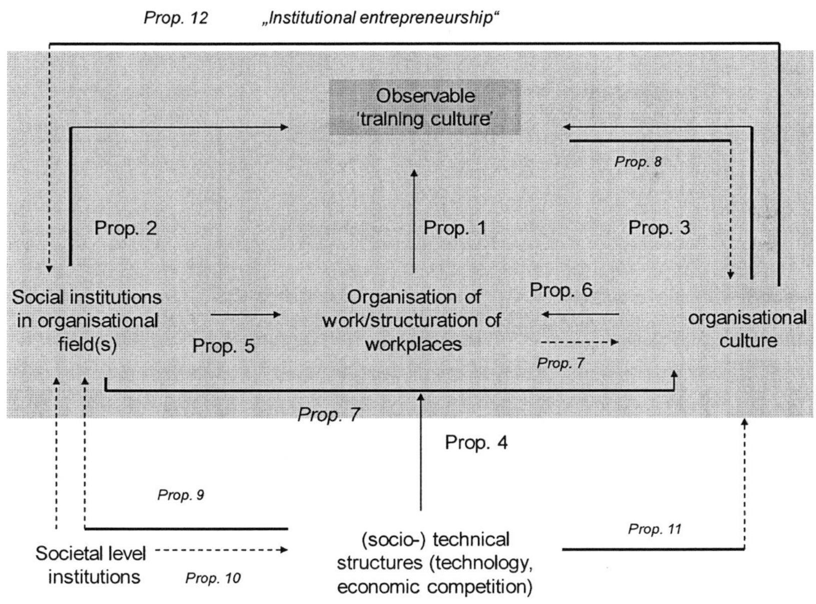

Source: Own description

- *Proposition 9: Changing technical requirements relevant for an organisational field trigger institutional change.*

Any organisational field could be described according to its technical and institutional requirements (Scott & Meyer 1991, Meyer et al. 1981). The landmark contributions of Meyer & Rowan (1977) stress the relative autonomy of institutional claims from technical requirements. More recent analysts also consider technical requirements as important drivers for change in processes of institutionalisation or de-institutionalisation (Scott 2008b, Chapters 5 to 7 for a review of literature.) Phases of increased competition could trigger institutional expectations (for example, cutting staff). Technologies could remain a 'must have' institutionally long after their technological justification has eroded.

- *Proposition 10: The impact of societal level institutions (such as welfare regimes; education systems, etc.) is mediated by the institutions and the technical requirements relevant on an organisational field level.*

Societal level institutions are not an independent source of influence, but the institutional and technical aspects of the organisational field filters and edit institutional pressure from outside the field. Societal institutions – for example, a strong occupational orientation of the labour market – may not influence a given organisational field, where almost all enterprises prefer to arrange their work according to internal principles and no strong trade union or other powerful actors limit their choice. However, it remains necessary to 'bring the society back in' (Friedland & Alford 1991), when working on the field level, as cognitive schemes of one society may be highly influential for both institutional processes and formation of organisational cultures. Luo (2007) explores the explanatory value of types of societies for explaining the preference for broad, growth-oriented training versus narrow task-oriented training and finds substantial support for society-level, cultural effects.

- *Proposition 11: Technical requirements set limits for the possible range of sustainable organisational cultures.*

While organisational cultures should not be taken as 'one best fit' solutions for adaptive requirements on technical or institutional requirements, technical requirements certainly limit the space for organisational idiosyncrasies. Substantial changes in technical requirements require changes in organisational cultures: otherwise organisations risk failing and disappearing. While in a certain way a truism on a societal level, Proposition 10 is important for country comparison, as societies are likely to differ in the space offered for organisational cultures to evolve. Competitive structures could limit the existence of certain types of organisational cultures (and types of work organisation) in some countries; these could still proliferate elsewhere, leading to important compositional effects, when comparing economies or economic sectors (for example, wood industry or textile industries are highly different across European countries). However, various processes of globalisation may reduce the number of competitive options for running, for example, a call centre, a hospital or a university.

- *Proposition 12: Dominating organisations or groups of organisations may prescribe their preferred practices on the level of organisational fields, functioning as 'institutional entrepreneurs'.*

The organisational culture of an individual organisation could become the model shaping institutional expectations valid in an organisational field. Organisations itself could adopt the role of *'institutional entrepreneurs'* (DiMaggio 1988), using their influence to set standards. Organisations may be perfectly in line with institutional requirements because they have played a leading role in their institutionalisation.

My twelve propositions outline an extended framework for future research, which clearly exceeds what I am able to do within my current bookproject. However, I would like to highlight three conclusions:

Firstly, the organisational field is clearly the most promising level for studying firms' training behaviour: the field level translates society-level institutions into the entities relevant for the organisations. Economic sectors are often poor proxies for organisational fields, as they subsume too many heterogeneous organisations under one sector and cut relations between clearly related organisations by positioning them into different sectors.

Secondly, it is indispensible to investigate an organisation's more stable pattern towards training, which represents the impact of technical and institutional drivers – past and present ones – modified by organisational agency.

Thirdly, by identifying an organisations' training culture, we actually learn about its likely future behaviour and its behaviour for more particular issues: in our case, the support provided for formal adult education.

Consequently, when analysing my organisational case studies on the support for formal adult education, I first identify the organisations' training cultures. For that issue, I develop a typology and explain it in Section 5.3.

5.3 A typology of training cultures in enterprises

To investigate the status of support for formal adult education within enterprises' training policies, we need to independently classify an organisation's approaches to corporate training and formal adult education. To analyse the training activities of the enterprises surveyed in the current project, I extend the typology of training cultures present in Section 5.2 to a typology of seven cultures: (1) *Suspended* Training Cultures, when previously existing training cultures are forcefully put temporarily out of order (2) *Minimizing* (3) *Streamlining* and (4) *Orienting* Training Cultures as subtypes of the Reactive Training Culture and (5) *Experimenting*, (6) *Elaborating* and (7) *Optimising* Training Cultures as subtypes of Expansive Training Cultures. I base my elaborated typology on nine dimensions, which are summarised in Overview 16.

Overview 16: Dimensions of training cultures

		Reactive Training Culture			Expansive Training Culture		
	(1) Suspended	(2) Minimizing	(3) Streamlining	(4) Orientating	(5) Experimenting	(6) Elaborating	(7) Optimising
[I] Level of commitment	(not decisive)	Low	Low to medium	High	Medium to High	High	High
[II] Level of activity	(Near to) zero	Low	Medium	Low or medium	Medium to high	Medium to High	High
[III] Proportion of training potential used	Suspended	Low	Low	Low	Medium	High	Nearly fully used
[IV] Constancy of use of training potential	Suspended	Constantly low	Constantly low	Low with unplanned peaks	Medium with spontaneous peaks	Constantly high	Constantly high
[V] Proportion of inevitable training	Suspended	High	High	Low	Low	Low	Low
[VI] Distributed experience and proportion of active participants	Low	Low	Medium	Low	Medium	Medium to high	High
[VII] Range of experience	Low	Low	Low	Low	Medium to high	Medium to high	High
[VIII] Dependency of volume of external drivers	Low	High	High	Low	Low	Low	Low
[IX] Momentum	Suspended	Towards a minimum required	Towards a minimum required	Towards a minimum required	Towards full potential	Towards full potential	Towards full potential

Source: Own description

[I] Level of commitment to training (such as a part of human resource development): Organisations express more or less commitment to human resource development and training in particular. I consider expressions of commitment firstly on the level of verbal (for example, in our interviews) and written statements (for example, mission statements; certification of HRD work such as Investors in People) representative for the organisation as such. Secondly, I interpret organisational procedures devoted to HRD and training as a proof of commitment, the latter would include a unit responsible for training activities, the existence of a (yearly) training plan or a training budget, the assessment of training needs (for example, within regular appraisal interviews), regulations on support for training or reward mechanisms for participation in training. Expressed support and supporting procedures together are used for tentative statements on whether the principle support for training in an organisation is likely to be high or not.

[II] Absolute level of activity in training: For a training culture, it is decisive if the total amount of training is significant or not. If an organisation must process many training activities, it inevitably builds up considerable experiences in the use of training. Moreover, the development of processes to deal with the related activities becomes a kind of necessity. I include therefore an assessment of whether the *absolute* training activity is considerably high or not (although the *relative* training activity may be different). Medium and large enterprises are likely to have considerable training activities, despite their overall negative approach to training. Small enterprises may have comparatively low training activities (a few number of courses a year), despite considerable high relative training activity. For empirical work, we have defined thresholds for identifying comparatively high or low absolute levels of training activities.[24]

[III] Proportion of training potential used: Enterprises uses a proportion of their training potential. Even when it is difficult to estimate the total available training potential of organisations, I build on the relation between an existing potential and the actual training activity. While enterprises with reactive training cultures use a low proportion of their training potential, for enterprises with expansive training cultures the opposite is decisive for my definition. Enterprises with a reactive training culture only use the smallest part of their training potential. Enterprises with an expansive training culture could be identified by the level of usage, showing a medium level of at least 10 %, while by definition, we expect to find enterprises that also nearly completely use their (postulated) training potential.

[IV] Constancy of use of training potential: Training activity – relative to an existing training potential – could either be preserved on an achieved level or not. In all enterprises, training activities may show some variety, with some ups and downs. However, in enterprises with expansive training culture, training activity stays significant throughout the years; while in reactive training cultures, training activities remain low in most of the years, even though there might be some peaks due to temporary factors.

[V] Proportion of inevitable training: Training may be made obligatory (for example, by health and safety regulations, training duties for professions) or required within technology related innovation projects (for example, introducing complex new machineries). Inevitable training activities are in place for all enterprises, no matter what kind of training cultures they have adopted. The absolute level of inevitable training

24 For assessing the absolute level of training activity of our SME sample, we have used a two-level approach. First, we have used the following threshold. For enterprises with less than 10 participants or less than 200 training hours (mostly estimated) per year, we have stated the level of training activity as ‘low’. For enterprises with a higher training activity than expressed, but still with no more than 30 participants a year and 600 training hours a year, we have stated a ‘medium’ level of training activity. For any organisation with a higher training activity, we have stated a ‘high’ training activity.

activities varies greatly with the sector and the way work is organised. However, when an organisation has developed an expansive approach to training, the training activities required lose importance relative to training activities voluntarily adopted. The proportion between required ('enforced') and deliberately provided training therefore varies between enterprises with different training cultures.

[VI] Distributed experience with training – proportion of active participants: Enterprises differ widely by the proportion of employees who have participated in training activities in previous years. Diffused experience is an important resource for further training activities. Moreover, the more people share experience with (satisfying) training activities, the stronger the support for further initiatives should be. For any expansive training culture, a significant proportion of the employees should share a personal experience with training. Aside from professional roles, a wider range of people should be in the position to advise on training and to promote training activities, based on their personal experience and professional understanding. The requirement for that kind of shared experience also explains why it is unlikely to develop an expansive training culture within a short period.

[VII] Range of experience with different types of training: Training could be used for unlimited goals, in a wide variety of fields and an infinite number of settings. However, organisations potentially have experience with a succession of alternatives ways to use training and invest in further development of the variety of training activities. The more different settings and approaches in the field of training an enterprise have experienced, the more likely it develops further approaches. Enterprises with little training activities often lack the experience to apply training to a variety of situations. The less experience, the more restricted is the range of opportunities visible to the members of an organisation.

[VIII] Dependency of training volume of drivers: The relative weight of inevitable training marks also the level, the training activity changes with the up and downs of particular drivers for training. In enterprises with expansive training cultures, therefore, the total training volume does not depend on the availability of external impulses as for example, public cofunding schemes. In enterprises with reactive training cultures, training volume is expected to vary with the up and downs of external drivers for training.

[IX] Momentum of growth of training activity: Current training activities could lead to both *reduced* training activity (for example, when narrowly defined goals are fulfilled) or *increased* training activity (for example, when promising results lead to more peer recommendations). For enterprises with reactive training cultures, by definition, current training activities do not lead to an increase in training activity for the next periods. Moreover, enterprises may even tend to reduce activities when possible. In enterprises with expansive training cultures, however, current training activities con-

tribute to an increase in training activities (as long as the available potential for training is not used).

In the following, I discuss the seven types of training cultures, based on examples from the case studies produced within the LLL2010 project.

(1) The Suspended Training Culture

In case of current severe external shocks, enterprises may lose temporarily any use of training activities. Typical shocks may include the hot phase for a final insolvency, extended interregnums in top management positions, phases before or after hostile takeovers or any fundamental change in organisational structures absorbing any available time resources of employees available. No matter, if a previous training culture was reactive or expansive, training activity comes to a halt, organisational support for training completely erodes and responsiveness to any external drivers as obligations or public support schemes fade completely. As long as the state of emergency lasts, training activity remains mostly suspended. However, even when organisations have finally survived, a former established expansive training culture might have fallen prey to the crises.

As organisations in crises do not typically participate in case-study exercises, no case for this particular culture has become available within the project. However, enterprises with *suspended training* cultures are likely to make up for a significant proportion of (in particular medium to large) enterprise, which report hardly any training activity in a year surveyed.[25]

(2) The Minimising Training Culture

Enterprises with a *minimising training culture* demonstrate little commitment to training (*Level of commitment: low*) and see it as a cost that should be limited as far as possible. Specific requirements (for example, legal obligations) or clearly defined goals (for example, efficiently using a new production tool) shape the decision on a particular training course. Most years have few training activities. (*Proportion of training potential used: low*; *Constancy of use of training potential: low).* Because little training activity evolves from enterprises' deliberate decisions, the proportion of required training activity is high: often we find only required training activities such as health and safety trainings. (*Proportion of inevitable training activities: high*). Therefore, both management and employees of enterprises with a minimizing training culture lack experience with most types of training opportunities. *(Distributed experience with*

25 Among enterprises with no reported training activity, there are – beyond enterprises with suspended training cultures – small enterprises with a 'minimizing' training culture, which has no training need in a particular year, yet not without the potential to use training and a propensity to turn for training, when particular events occur. However, there is also a fraction of (again mainly small) organisations, which start in highly precarious conditions and remain at the brink of bankruptcy throughout their existence, supported mainly by means provided by their founders. For this group, we would also apply the suspended training culture label.

training; Range of experience: low). Often, members of this type of organisation could hardly think about any additional training activity they would like to do, because they share so little positive experience with organised learning. This lack of experience and therefore imagination marks one of the strongest barriers for any increase in training activity, even when public funds available would cover full costs. However, even when drivers may increase training activity in the short term (*Dependency of volume for external drivers: high*) the overall tendency remains that training – as a cost factor – should be limited as far as possible (*Momentum: towards a minimum*).

Organisational case study 1: XY Service Estonia (10–19 employees)

The company provides business-to-business services on a project basis. Aside from the owner, it employs four project managers and around ten contributors on a contractual basis according to the changing demands of completing ongoing projects. Most employees are highly skilled or have at least upper secondary education. The company has gone through difficult years, but has recently become profitable. Skills and qualification are understood as a requirement for employment. The company regularly employs students who continue their studies while working and who may join the enterprise later, when they have the required abilities. Management's attitudes towards training are generally positive. Regularly, the company pays for external courses (five courses within the last year, mainly in project management). However, shorter courses from training providers were found useless and a waste of money and time. The considerably high training budget (approximately 500 Euros per employee) was not completely used during the previous years. Opportunities for public co-funding are well known but not used so far. Employees are invited to propose training courses, but their reluctance to select and attend courses does not result in any management reaction. In-house trainings were considered but found less useful and too distracting from the core work.

Source: Own summary based on Tamm 2008b

(3) The Streamlining Training Culture

Enterprises with a *streamlining* training cultures share most characteristics described for the subtype *minimising*. They use only a minor proportion of their potential for training (*Proportion of training potential used: low*) and their overall training activity is low over the years (*Constancy of use of training potential: low*). Again, most training activities present could not be avoided (*Proportion of inevitable training: high*), which also leads to a similar dependency on external drivers determining the quantity of training activity (*Dependency of volume of external drivers: high*). The decisive difference between the subtypes *minimising* and *streamlining* is the volume of training activity, which is substantial for the *streamlining* type. 'Inevitable training' activities sum up an important package of activities, in particular in medium enterprises with 100 and more employees. (*Level of activity: medium*) Legal obligations, requirements of quality management systems, training required in the course of technological improvements, project-based training activities in the course of process redesign and innovation; these and similar training activities lead to a total training volume that already requires some professional management and budgetary foresight. Quantities of 60 and more days of off-the-job training and budgets of 15,000 Euros and more are quite usual for companies with 100 employees. While the *relative* training activity remains low by any standards, training become at least a subject on the management's agenda. Overall, representative statements on trainings show a low commitment. Alternatively, a more progressive approach towards training is balanced by a list of reservations. (*Level of commitment: low or medium*) Training is still clearly understood as a cost, most managers seek to limit this cost. Naturally, publicly supported offers become a more important topic, as the volume of inevitable training become substantial, so that co-funding may lead to considerable rebates, but rarely to any increase in the training activity. Range of experience with training is low. However, significant parts of the workforce are included at least in some organised learning activity (for example, in health and safety) (*Distributed experience with training – proportion of active participants: medium*). The general tendency in the use of training is still oriented towards the required minimum. (*Momentum: towards a minimum*).

Organisational case study 2: XY Packaging Ireland (20–49 employees)

The enterprise is engaged in a niche market of the printing sector and limits training to that required by regulations and short-term needs in particular workplaces. The HR is described, ' it's as is or as needs insist'. Nearly any activity around organising training and workplace learning is informal and not regulated. Training-needs analyses are performed in order to meet quality management criteria. Available training includes courses for computer applications and for newly acquired printing facilities. Recently, within a lean management project, regular training activities were introduced to increase productivity-training activities. Training is clearly understood as a cost factor – even when fees are covered by public funds, the lost of working time is seen as serious handicap. The management is quite sceptical on the short-range returns of investments in training. Overall training activity is significant, but the use of the assumed training potential is clearly low. Learning on the job was clearly the most favoured way of acquiring new skills. Opportunities for workplace learning are somewhat restricted, given the stable production in a mature niche market. Because of the importance of optimising a given way of production, the workplace-learning regime seems more restrictive. Levels of organisational learning could be regarded as low to medium, but mainly focussed on competing on costs in a mature and shrinking market.

Source: Own summary based Team EDC/CSHD Sp4 Project (2008)

(4) The Orientating Training Culture

Enterprises with an *orientating* training culture share most features of the other subtypes of reactive training culture. However, they have a considerable high commitment level in the field of training – as well as in the fields of HRD, workplace learning and organisational learning. One could easily find an enterprise representative who clearly describes the existing level of training activities as insufficient and below the management's expectations for the future *(Level of commitment: high)*. Training is understood – in principle – as an investment. However, with little available experience with the return on investments in training, costs remain the most important concern on training. A vivid interest in further developing the training activity clearly conflicts with the overall low to medium level of current training activity *(Level of activity: low to medium).* Representatives acknowledge that the enterprise uses little of its training potential *(Use of training potential: low).* While the training activity is low on average, project-based training activities frequently have led to some significant increases in training activity. *(Constancy of use of training potential: low with spontaneous peaks).* The lack of experience with possible ways to use training combined with unequal experience with training among the workforce *(Distributed experience and range of experience: low)* clearly results in perceived disadvantages and blocks for further developments. However, any public policy in favour of training activity will find here a group of companies ready to take advantage of any support for long-term improvements of their training activities. The existing training activity is more defined by the voluntary attempts to use training successfully than by required training *(Proportion of inevitable training: low).* Even when a particular event occasionally increases the training activity, the overall tendency is to minimise training activities, even when no explicit strategy shapes that trend. (Momentum: towards a minimum). Organisational contradictions of various kinds contribute to this state of insufficient training, despite all commitment expressed by the management.

Organisational case study 3: XY Media Austria (20–49 employees)

The firm writes programs for video games consoles. Founded by two young graduates of a technical university in 2001, the company has survived rough times and now is rapidly growing. Nearly all employees are very young and highly skilled, so not necessarily in a formal way. Specialisation is high; any applicant must be greatly involved in the world of computer games. Innovation and quality are key. Given the size of a typical project, the company has to face high risk in project work and risk management turned out to be a major issue. Attracting and retaining new co-workers is the key issue in personnel management. Because there are virtually no applicants with appropriate skills in the labour market and wage levels are considerably low compared to major companies of the IT sector, the enterprise has less employees then it would like to hire. The management has taken advantage of a public cofunding scheme to select and train potential new employees. The development of a structured approach to training is assessed as an important future goal; however, management capacities are not sufficient to address this field now. Moreover, for the highly specialised market segment, little training opportunities are available. Existing programmes are found insufficient (the managers teach themselves many programmes). International fairs and congresses are identified as the single most important yet expansive opportunities for learning. Moreover, the co-operation with experts in various fields (for example, in film dramaturgy) are found most valuable. The gap in management competencies – including project management – is heavily felt. The management is willing to invest occasionally to overcome this bottleneck and to enlarge the basis for further development. The company covers a significant part of the MBA education (fees about 30,000 Euros) for a newly installed assistant of the management, who should further develop the personnel management of the company.

Source: Own summary based on Hefler & Bacher 2008c

(5) The Experimenting Training Culture

Enterprises with an *experimenting training culture* generally demonstrate fairly high to high commitment for training and human resource development topics. This commitment is normally already codified in some way and communicated within the organisation. (*Level of commitment: medium to high*). Training is already clearly understood as investment. The overall training activity is substantial to high (*Level of overall training activity: medium to high*). Compared to other types of training cultures, training activities are already much more extended than in all enterprises with a reactive training culture, but much lower than in enterprises with a further developed expansive training culture. Typically, the development of this type of training culture started because of high incidences of inevitable training; however, the enterprise has developed increasingly genuine practices to use training independently of mere requirements. Therefore, the proportion of inevitable training of all training activities is considerably low (*Proportion of inevitable training: low*). Contrary to all reactive training cultures, enterprises with an experimenting training culture use their training potential in a substantive way (*Use of training potential: medium*). New ways of using training are often developed on a project basis, focussing on a particular problem or a particular group of employees. Mainly based on this kind of project, the average use of training potential shows some peaks, while remaining considerably high throughout the years (*Constancy of use of training potential: medium with spontaneous peaks*). Many employees share training experiences of various kinds (*Distributed experience – proportion of active participants: medium*); however, training activities still focus on selected groups of employees. The enterprise also has successful experience with many ways to use training (*Range of experience: medium*), although this remains a major field for improvement. The capacity to independently develop training projects for various kinds of goals limit the dependency on external drivers: (*Dependency of volume of external drivers: low*). Even when training projects sometimes fail, the organisation strongly believes in the potential of training. Therefore, the annual testing of additional training activities leads – setting aside some up and downs – to constantly increasing overall training activity within the limits of the available training potential (*Momentum: towards full potential*).

Organisational case study 4: XY Training Belgium (10–19 employees)

The firm organises outdoor training supporting team-building processes in organisations. Founded in 1977, the for-profit organisation is well connected in its field nationally and internationally. Most employees have a university education and share different backgrounds (for example, sociology, social work, psychology, physical education). To meet high standards, its core staff requires training. For providing a foundation, all new entrants receive about 50 days of fulltime training, covering a wide range of the specific field of training offered by the company within their first year(s) in the company. As a rule, all employees participate in at least one further education activity within three years.

The companies' experts co-operate with a local university in establishing a postgraduate programme of adventure education. Employees participate in selected modules of this course, while teaching in others. The company covers all costs of further training, even for more expensive programmes (for example, the formal course chosen by the employee participants involves fees of 7,650 Euros). Training time is regularly within working time. Providing opportunity for a wide range of professional training and education is seen as a crucial part of retention strategy and as an incentive to the employees. There is no formal training plan. Being well connected to relevant institutions in the field, it is possible to identify new opportunities for training. Focussing mainly on the individual employee's learning needs, however, the company fails to address more organisationally related training topics. Given the low staff-turnover, training engagement may slow down in the future, when new training opportunities become scarce for experienced experts.

Source: Own summery based on Vermeersch & De Rick 2008b

(6) Evolving Training Culture

Enterprises with an *evolving training culture* share most characteristics of the experimenting subtype. However, the training culture has already developed more stable structures. Commitment for training is clearly high and definitely codified and communicated in the organisation (*Level of commitment: high*). Training is clearly seen as a way to invest for various purposes. While the absolute level of training activity is between medium and high, the proportion of training-potential used is already high and the use remains high over the years (*Proportion of training potential used/ constancy of use: high*). Any inevitable training activity marks only a small proportion of all training activities (*Proportion of inevitable training activity: low*). Consequently, the impact of external drivers on training volume is considerably low. (*Dependency of volume of external drivers: low*). Companies with evolving training culture have already collected a broad range of experiences on different ways to use training and they simultaneously apply several of these approaches (*Range of experience: medium to high*). Normally, there are already highly structured arrangements available (for example, programs for high potentials or technicians; yearly internal training events). Many employees have had training for various purposes. (*Distributed experience: medium to high*). However, developing strategies that are more inclusive for employees with considerable lower training activities remains a concern. A better use of the existing training potential becomes possible only by increasing the inclusiveness of the training activity. By including more employees and further exploring the range of opportunities to use training, the enterprise makes further steps towards a full use of its training potential (*Momentum: towards full potential*).

Organisational case study 5: Omega Precision Engineering (England, 50–99 employees)

The firm demonstrates high commitment to both nonformal training as well as training leading to qualifications. The enterprise positively assessed the process of certifying its HRD with the Investors in People standard and industry-specific standards. ('There's no value in having a set of badges, it's about the process that, the improvements that you get from the process.')

Training is understood as an investment. Support for training includes payments of fees, time off for following the courses, working time accepted to complet education-related tasks. Salaries can be increased after an employees complete educational programmes. Within two years, 35 percent of the workforce has engaged in formal adult education (NVQ programmes and courses, partly leading to qualifications) and 100 percent in other workplace related, in-house learning activities. Training activity remains high over the years and is not tied to particular events. 'Education is seen as an integrated part of the fulfilment of employees.' However, the firm had no particular figure available on working time spent on learning and training activity. Given high participations rates, it can be assumed that the enterprise uses its training potential in a significant manner, but still could further increases its activity level. However, spending on training is considerably low (compared to sector standards), even when considering that only fees are included (an annual average of approximately 250 Euros per employee). Policies to support informal workplace learning include biannual team sessions, regular team briefings and meetings, job rotation and a mentor scheme. Learning conduciveness of workplaces seems to be high for a significant part of the workplaces, given the strong trend towards technical innovation, high quality-standards and ever-changing production of considerable small series of products (often less than 1000 units). In general, the culture of workplace learning seems clearly expansive. Clearly high level of organisational learning is measured by the cycles of updating business plans (two times a year), importance of innovation, range of fields of products, speed of adapting new production technologies and identification of new business opportunities.

Source: Own summery based on Holford et al. 2008a

(7) The Optimizing Training Culture

Enterprises with an already fully developed, *optimising expansive training culture* show a clearly above-average level of training activity. (*Level of activity: high*). Their relative engagement in training is several times higher than the average of all enterprises. Within this type of training culture, the *training potential* is nearly fully used. Training policy is oriented towards innovating and optimising the training activity, while an expansion of the training activity is possible only in a rather limited way, as most potential training is already used. Management focuses on deciding between alternatives in training and replacing particular activities with more efficient and appropriate ones. Therefore, while the training activities remain on a very high level over the years (*Constancy of use of training potential: constantly high*), the training activities are constantly renewed. Because training is clearly seen as investment, optimising also means to replace less efficient training approaches by ones that are more efficient. Investment in technologies (for example, e-learning, blended learning) often reflects a way to gain space for other training activities by improving efficiency. Inevitable training generally plays a minor role (*Proportion of inevitable training: low*). However, legal training requirements limit the voluntary use of scarce training potential, therefore, much effort is invested in matching organisational goals with external requirements. Most of the workforce shares experiences with various kinds of training and thus have available a common understanding. Supervisors as well as workers could give advice on successfully using particular training and education. They share a common knowledge of what does and does not work. Recommendations for particular training programmes or experts are available (*Distributed experience: high*). The range of opportunities to use training is very broad (*Range of experience: high*). Training policy focuses on innovative training projects, while constantly improving well-established ways to use training (*Momentum: towards full potential*).

Organisational case study 6: A+ Pharma Research and Distribution (100–249 employees)

The organisation is engaged in research and production as well as gross sales for a wide range of products needed by medical laboratories. Founded in the early days of Russia's new capitalism by three university researchers, the enterprise experienced rapid growth in recent years, developing from a local supplier to a principal actor in the Russian market. Currently, 85 percent of the staff is highly qualified, 60 out of 200 employees are engaged in research and development activities. Nearly 120 employees have obtained higher education degrees, (almost one fifth of them have two diplomas of higher education). Relevant fields include medicine, biochemistry and chemical engineering. However, qualifications in management (including project management) and marketing become important for trained physicians or chemists. Therefore, while working for the enterprise, many employees, including the founders, have attended formal adult education in these fields. The company works in a quickly expanding yet instable market, subject to external shocks such as quickly changing regulations and tax requirements. Securing 'western' quality at a locally competitive price level is key for the success, requiring continual innovation (not so much in the field of basic research but in directing and combining processes, finding new ways in balancing advantages and disadvantages of the local market situations.) A HRD manager is in place. All employees have yearly appraisal interviews that include discussing individual training plans. Workplace learning is supported by regular meetings, collaboration in multidisciplinary project teams, regular attendance of seminars and conferences and partial job rotation. Nearly all employees are engaged in in-house training activities. Aside from more regular activities in different fields (for example, information on new products), target programmes on a project basis are used (in the year of the interview, a program for all members of the sales staff). About 10 percent (in 2007) attend external educational programmes; in particular, university-based formal programmes. Even without a formal agreement, the company regularly covers 50–100 percent of tuition fees and grants free-days to attend courses and prepare for examinations. Training costs are about 8–10 percent of the wage costs, each employee participates an average of between 5–6 days in training a year. Long-term co-operations are established with various higher education institutions that also provide nonformal educational offers.

Source: Own summery based on Khokhlova 2008

We expect that type of typology to be highly applicable for a broad number of issues; for example, with companies' responses to public co-funding schemes for training, companies' reaction to specific training (such as in the fields of health and safety or equal opportunity) and more general training obligations (such as in individual rights of employees for company funded training) or the impact of up and downs of the economic cycles on enterprises' training activity. Next, we use our typology for understanding companies' support or non-support for formal adult education of their employees.

5.4 Patterns of support for formal adult education

Despite weaknesses of statistical data available, the evidence indicates that enterprises, irrespective of their size, support formal adult education. However, we lack theories explaining the reasons for this support.

Available approaches include 'post-Beckerian' variants of economics of education. According to Becker's original position, formal adult education provides *general skills* – useful for a broad number of employers – and therefore should instil a skill premium for the individual employee; as the beneficiary of the returns, the participant in formal adult education should cover the training costs, while the enterprise stays neutral. Earlier empirical research explains the presence of employer's engagement in improving general skills by, for example, market imperfections, information asymmetries (between the current and a future employer) or risk aversion (of employees not knowing in advance the working conditions with a new employer). Newer accounts (starting with Bishop 1988) highlight the potentially outstanding value of uniquely combining firm-specific experience and general (formal) education and training for the enterprise. By combining firm-specific experience and formal (general) training, firms may unleash their employee's genuine, situated and thereby firm-bound potentials that are hard to copy; this allows for a market premium high enough to pay wages substantially above market level. However, post-Beckerian approaches explain only why the employer's enterprise potentially may also profit by supporting formal (general) education as the do in for firm-specific training. The most general, functional-rationalistic assumptions on the productivity-improving nature of any education and training remain the sole basis to explain why companies engage in training.

In a comparable fashion, the rational choice, institutionalism theories consider collective ways to overcome problems of coordination among employers. Enterprises are expected not to invest in formal initial or further vocational education and training, when their competitors may choose to save on training costs and free ride through poaching other firms' well-trained employees by paying higher wages (Estevez-Abe et al. 2001). Effective coordination between employers may limit free-riding; however, the benefits of training are taken for granted and enterprises are expected to invest as soon as the threats for benefiting from their investments are removed.

Other explanatory frameworks rarely distinguish between formal adult education and nonformal training (with the important exemption of Scott & Meyer 1994). Summing up, few specific explanations exist for how and why enterprises should support formal adult education.

To explore support for formal adult education on a company level, within a subproject of the 2010 project, case studies on the importance of formal adult education in SMEs were provided by teams from twelve countries (Austria, Belgium's Flanders region, Bulgaria, England, Estonia, Hungary, Ireland, Lithuania, Norway, Russia, Scotland and Slovenia). Our analysis builds on these case studies as well as national reports based on the same material and prepared by the various national teams. Evidence was available for 86 enterprises and 126 participants in formal adult education. Hefler (2010a) provides more information on methods applied.

Typically, theories on the reasons for supporting formal adult education of single or group of employees develop from case-by-case analysis, where company-provided support or non-support is determined according to individual cases. Overview 17 summarises the various ways of supporting participation found in our case studies (for more details, see Hefler 2010a, Section 7.5). However, instead of examining support on a case-by-case basis, I am more interested in developing general explanations of why enterprises support formal adult education. Therefore, we developed a typology of support patterns, highlighting how far support for formal adult education can reach and how systematic support is established on an organisational level.

Overview 17: Ways of supporting participation in formal adult education of employees in small and medium enterprises

Support offered	Patterns to do so
Ways in which the enterprise may support an individual's decision to participate in formal education	
Strengthening motivation	- Consenting to the participation - Acknowledging symbolically individual participation - Declaring explicit support for formal adult education
Easing time constraints	- Providing time flexibility (while work assignment remains unchanged) - Rearrangement of work schedules - Adjusting working time and extension of work (reduction of long hours ...) - Accepting an educational leave - Devoting paid working time for participating in formal adult education - Using and granting work assignments within the educational programme for enterprises' purposes
Supporting competence development	- Using business cases/projects from the employer within the educational programmes - Allowing consultation with company's experts - Assigning activities in relation to the educational activities
Reducing individual financial burdens	- Using enterprise's infrastructure for educational purposes - Covering (a part of the) fees or accompanying costs of educational programmes
Inspiring individual participation by providing advancement options	- Offering increased wages for successful completion - Offering promotion for participation/completion in a programme
Ways in which the enterprise may encourage an individual to enrol for a particular qualification	
Initiating individual participation	- Suggesting that an individual enrol for a particular qualification(in the course of individual career agreements) - Agreeing on participation to support an employee in a new position
Initiating participation of groups of employees/ types of positions	- Initiating a programme for staff on a project basis - long-term co-operation with an education institution - systematic integration of attendance of formal programmes in the strategic personnel development (e.g. by regularly offering participation to specific groups of employees or job holders) - organising formal programmes on a permanent basis

Source: Hefler 2010a, Chapter 7.5

We propose five types of organisational patterns of support for formal adult education of employees: (A) Ignorance, (B) Acceptance, (C) Individualised Support, (D) Principle Support and (E) Integrated Support. Types build on a double hierarchy running from *less* to *more* support and from *no* to *substantial* organisational activity to initiate formal adult education. Overview 18 summarises our dimensions used to identify the patterns. As we construct a hierarchy for moving from one type to the next, the behaviour of enterprises are classified according to the seven criteria specified. We discuss the criteria later, when describing the support patterns and provide selected summaries of our case studies.

Overview 18: Typology of patterns in supporting formal adult education in enterprises

	A	B	C	D	E
Types	**Ignorance**	**Acceptance**	**Individualised Support**	**Principle Support**	**Integrated Support**
Level of support	Low	Medium	Medium	High	High
Level of organisational initiative	Low	Low	Medium	Medium	High
Requirements					
[I] Acknowledge verbally the individual interest and accept interference	-	√	√	√	√
[II] Regularly support activities of any kind	-	√	√	√	√
[III] Substantial support at least in particular constellations	-	-	√	√	√
[IV] Co-initiate at least in particular situations	-	-	√	√	√
[V] Generally adjust organisation needs and participation requirements	-	-	-	√	√
[VI] Generally offer at least financial support or working time	-	-	-	√	√
[VII] At least one project initiative to increase formal adult education for a group of employees	-	-	-		√

Source: Hefler 2010a, Chapter 7.6 (with adaptations)

Type A Ignorance

As the base line, we use the pattern 'Ignorance'. Here, the enterprise takes no initiatives to promote participation in formal adult education. The enterprise shows little support for formal adult education, which plays no role in the enterprise's wider training or HRD policy. If any support exists, it is cursory and without any guarantee for prolongation. Participation in formal adult education takes place without acknowledgement from the employer.

Type B Acceptance (medium level support, low level of organisational initiative)

Enterprises are classified among the type 'Acceptance', when they meet at least two basic criteria and none of the other five criteria stated. First, they [I] *verbally acknowledge the individual interest in formal adult education and accept interference of organisational and individual spheres.* We define a minimal level of support as personnel management explicitly accepting formal adult education as a topic. This implies accepting some restriction on an employee's capacities during the participation. When formal adult education is approved in principle, employees could communicate on their participation and look for arrangements and, for example, even ask for financial support where necessary. Participation could also become visible to other workers. Second, as an additional requirement, some [II] *supportive activities of any kind* of the 'menu' presented in Overview 17 has to be in place, documented for a number of individual cases. To sum up, the enterprise takes no initiatives to promote participation in formal adult education, however, in individual cases, the enterprises offers some forms of support, mainly with regard to work schedules and the permission to use actual work activities also for educational purposes.

Organisational case study 7: XY Metals Norway (20–49 employees)

The company's strategy built on artisanship and experience to provide reliable quality in a low-tech production regime. The enterprise has an apprenticeship scheme and provides internal courses for staff to develop the specific necessary skills. Their training meets required standards of the applied quality management system. Moreover, the enterprise follows a peer-learning approach, where experienced employees personally pass their knowledge and skills to less experienced workers. In principle, the company welcomes any learning activity, including participation in formal adult education, but does not initiate participation. There is no general rule concerning formal adult education. The company provides its workers with informational material on free-of-charge formal education offered to union members. When employees participate in formal training, they individually negotiate a schedule and some time off for educational reasons.

Source: Own summary based on Ure & Bjørg 2008

Type C Individualised Support (medium level support, medium level of organisational initiative)

Enterprises which meet already stated criteria, and provide support on an individual basis and at least occasionally co-initiate participation in formal adult education, fit the 'Individualised Support' pattern. They provide [III] *substantial support at least in particular constellations.* As a threshold for the 'substantial' category, we use the following criteria: pay more than 50 percent of the participation fees; accept participation during working hours of at least 30 percent; support the work on a thesis or other educational project using examples or resources of the company or offer some clear reward for completion, for example, a promotion or wage increase. Moreover, the enterprise [IV] *co-initiates, at least in particular situations,* the participation. Here, enterprises explicitly accept that formal adult education has a role within the participating individual's organisational career path, for example, preparing for or as a supportive measure after a promotion. Formal adult education is thereby accepted as a potential part of the organisations' human resource development. Enterprises do not necessarily directly initiate participation, but support employees in adjusting personal aims to fit the organisational aims. Bringing the criteria together, the enterprise supports individual participants in formal adult education, but does not set up projects; support is mainly agreed to with individual employees, can be substantial, and includes financial assistance and/or dedication of some working time to the programme.

Organisational case study 8: Copper Products Incorporated (England, 50–99 employees)

The firm offers individualised support for formal education. The company does not distinguish between formal and nonformal adult education, but compares any form of taught activity to forms of informal workplace learning and on-the-job training. However, the enterprise values the National Vocational Qualification (NVQ) and supports employees willing to take courses leading to an NVQ. The management positively regards NVQ courses for both the individual employees and the enterprises. The enterprise fully pays obligatory courses of great interest to the enterprise. Moreover, the enterprise co-operates with a non-profit provider offering courses leading to NVQ. The enterprise regularly covers tuition fees; however, only exceptionally grants work-release time. Time off the job for educational purposes is regarded as a main challenge to the organisation and therefore seldom arranged. Support for formal education is embedded in a supportive HRD culture that adheres to the 'invest in people' principle.

Source: Own summary based on Holford et al. 2008b

Type D Principle Support (high level support, medium level of organisational initiative)

Enterprise may explicitly provide support for formal adult education, not on a case-by-case basis but as a rule. We identify 'Principle Support' when enterprises in addition to the already stated criteria arrange general *adjustments of organisation needs and participation requirements.* Management clearly states that the enterprise would adjust individual work schedules and activities for the duration of participation in formal adult education. This adjustment is to be granted irrelevant of the employer's interest in the individual educational programme. Moreover, [VI] a*t least financial support or working time is offered on a general basis* for supporting formal adult education. Enterprises must have a policy of contributing at least 50 percent of the fees for each participation case in formal adult education, or accepting at least 30 percent of course work (up to 120 hours a year) to be within paid working time. To sum up, the enterprise offers support for formal adult education in several ways and its general policy includes financial support and/or devotion of some working time to the programme – at least sometimes, the enterprise initiates formal adult education.

Organisational case study 9: XY Chemicals Slovenia (100–249 employees)

The company is strongly expanding its workforce based on a globally leading position in a niche market. The HRD strategy focuses on improving the workforce's skills, in particular in the area of technical education. Due to shortages on the local labour market, promoting participation in formal adult education in technical fields is important within personnel development strategy. Employees, who hold a position or are preparing for a certain position, where a particular qualification seems to be favourable, are openly invited by the enterprise to take up formal adult education. A formal education contract is fixed for participation in formal education in line with the organisational requirements. On the basis of an individual study contract, the firm supports the student financially by paying the tuition fee and some compensation for transportation costs, guarantees time off needed to attend lectures, seminars and exercises when those are delivered during working time and the time for preparation for exams. When education is in line with the HR plan of the firm the workers get promoted after the completed education to more demanding work or their existing work is broadened by additional or more complex tasks. Support for formal adult education is restricted to programmes also meeting the company's needs.

Source: Own summary based on Mirčeva 2008

Type E Integrated Support (high level support, high level of organisational initiative)

When enterprises not only principally support (Criteria I–VI), but initiate participation in formal adult education as part of their HRD policy (VII) *At least one initiative on project basis to increase formal adult education for a group of employees),* we categorise them under the type 'Integrated Support'. Management invites employees to participate in a formal educational programme, either as a group (for example, in a customised programme by an education provider) or based on a strategic decision, for any employee eligible for or promoted to particular career trajectories (for example, any skilled worker to be promoted to a supervisory position). In short, the enterprise offers support for formal adult education in several ways, some of them on a regular basis, including financial support and the devotion of working time. Programmes leading to formal adult education are established for one or more groups of employees.

Organisational case study 10: XY Chemicals Austria (50–99 employees)

The company faces strong competition for skilled workers in chemical industries in the regional labour market. The company invests substantially in training and systematically provides training on all staff levels. One major approach is to hire unskilled workers trained in another trade (for example, carpenters) and to offer them extended training on and off the job, before they start to work as helpers within the shift-work teams. To become a full member of the organisation and to benefit from the substantially higher wages for skilled chemical workers, unskilled workers are openly invited to prepare for a particular type of apprenticeship examination (Außerordentliche Lehrabschlussprüfung) available only for adult learners and that provides a formal qualification on ISCED 3b level.

To help workers prepare for this examination, a former trainer provides one lesson per week over an 18-month programme at the work site. The company covers all costs of the courses, which take place mainly during paid working time; the firm also arranges the participants' work schedule to accommodate the course work. After passing the examination, participants become 'skilled chemical workers' and enjoy a statutory pay-raise. Furthermore, the company supports the preparation for the master examination (Meisterprüfung) in chemical work. The examination is classified at ISCED 5b level. The company supports this step on an individual basis, paying the high course fees. Although there is no specific policy, the company generally offers a promotion to white-collar positions, including a considerable pay rise, after the completion of the programme. Available next steps in careers within chemical industries, either attending a higher secondary education evening school (ISCED 4b Level) or a university for applied science (ISCED 5b), both of which would take three to four years of study, would be also supported by the company. For white-collar employees, programmes in continuing higher education (including MBAs) are supported based on individual negotiations (two cases are reported).

Source: Own summary based on Hefler & Bacher 2008a

The cases selected illustrate a wide range of possible forms of support for participation in formal adult education. By defining criteria, it became possible to arrange these forms into patterns of support and to classify these patterns. At least among our non-representative sample of small and medium enterprises, we identify a considerable number of small and medium enterprises that have a policy towards formal adult education that clearly goes beyond occasional contingent support of single participants.

5.5 Outlook: Assessing the interdependence of support patterns for formal adult education and training cultures

So far, we have seen that formal adult education marks a considerable, although underestimated, topic within training and HRD policies throughout the countries studied. As a life event, participation occurs as frequently as parental leave; companies must consider carefully how to react and whether to support individuals participating in formal adult education. During their working life, a fifth or more of all employees may participate, and even more among particular groups. Between one third and two thirds of all participation cases are clearly related to organisational training and HRD policies, as they are (partly) paid by the employer or take place (partly) within paid working time. Enterprises do not only support formal adult education on a case-to-case basis, but develop overall patterns or policies towards training, which we have classified in five types. Next, we have argued for the necessity to grasp enterprises' more general 'cultures' in supporting training and development, and have referred to a dichotomy of reactive versus expansive training cultures. Thus, while enterprises undoubtedly support formal adult education, it is unclear to what extent this support results from developed training cultures or from other factors. For an initial approximate answer to this question, we compare the support patterns for formal adult education with the types of training cultures of our available case studies.

With regard to our six examples, we find limited support for formal adult education with reactive training cultures in Case Study 1 and 5 ('Acceptance'/'Streamlining'), some support for formal adult education within a reactive training culture in Case Study 2 ('Individual support'/'Orientating') and strong support for formal adult education paired with expansive training cultures in Case Study 6 ('Support in Principle'/'Optimising') and Case Study 5 ('Integrated Support'/'Experimenting'). Unsurprisingly, companies with expansive training cultures are also more likely to adopt more extended support patterns for formal adult education. More than half of all enterprises in our sample are classified as having an *expansive training* culture and also have a policy of systematic support for formal adult education. Slightly less than half of enterprises with *reactive training* cultures provide little support for formal adult education of their employees. However, we are more interested in the more unexpected combinations of training culture and support for formal adult education as in Case Study 3 ('Streamlining'/'Support in Principle'), where an organisation is combining a restrictive training culture with a strong support for formal adult education.

Overview 19: Cross tabulation of Training Cultures and Support Patterns in case study firms

	'Ignorance' 'Acceptance'	'Individual Support'	'Principle Support' 'Integrated Support'
Reactive Training Cultures	44 %	30 %	26 %
Expansive Training Cultures	13 %	33 %	54 %

Source: LLL2010/SP4 Data N=74

Among SMEs with reactive training cultures, we find many that openly support formal adult education. We have learnt that in most countries, individual employees of small enterprises are as likely to engage in formal education as employees in larger ones. Thus, the issue could not be ignored by the organisations. Extended, multi-year, formal adult education programmes have the potential to systematically support the development of individual capacities and thus help to overcome the shortcoming of a firm's rudimentary human resource development policies. Individuals' readiness to contribute substantially to the costs of education may help overcome restriction established by a reactive training culture. Moreover, particular conditions in the organisations' environment – as in Case Study Example 3 the combination out of a lack of formally qualified employees in local labour markets combined with strong regulative enforcement for the use of properly qualified personnel – can introduce support for formal adult education as an explicit strategy. To sum up, there is evidence that formal adult education could substantially add to the personnel development policies of SMEs: small enterprises may start with supporting formal adult education of their employees as a first step to developing more supportive cultures for human resource development. When considering existing theories that see formal adult education mainly as a topic of large corporations (for example, 'corporate universities'), this comes as a surprise. More research is needed to explore, confirm or challenge this result. In particular, we have to learn more about the types of formal adult-educational programmes and their institutional embeddedness within careers: we come back to this point later.

Contrary to our expectations, we also find a considerably high proportion of small and medium enterprises that expansively support nonformal training, but provide disappointingly little support for formal adult education and do not go beyond individualised support. A high proportion of working students and legal frameworks (for example, tax regulations in Estonia or Bulgaria) reduce the incentive for the employer to pay, for example, for tuition fees in formal adult education (because the beneficiary must pay income taxes on the tuition benefits). We have some indication that enterprises are less inclined to support formal adult education where 'education' – leading to individually earned 'credentials' of considerably lower vocational specificity – is more clearly distinguished from vocationally oriented and more organisationally specific nonformal 'training'.

However, the relative dependence or independence of policies for formal adult education within enterprises' general training cultures seem to vary with countries' dominating qualification and skill formation systems (see Streeck 2011, Hefler 2010a, Chapter 7): In countries, where vocational qualifications are considerably narrowly defined and where credit-based provision of vocational qualifications is well developed – as in England, Scotland or Ireland – the differences between 'formal' and 'nonformal' adult education (with the exception of higher education) are considerably weak and so are the differences between organisations' policies for formal and nonformal adult education. In countries, where vocational qualifications are frequently bound to comparatively broad and legally defined occupational profiles, typically available only by extended and centrally controlled vocational educational programmes – as in Austria, Slovenia or Norway – the differences between 'formal' and 'nonformal' education tend to be clearer and more significant for enterprises. Consequently, more independence between policies for formal and nonformal adult education is in place. Anyway, more research is needed for the impact of skill formation systems on the interdependence of SME's support for formal and nonformal training as we are going to discuss in our outlook.

Chapter 6: Opportunity structures for formal adult education – Towards a framework for comparative research

6.1 Introduction

Cross-country comparative research has made clear, that it is misleading to describe either the 'education system' or the 'employment system' in isolation. Without analysing the link between education and (gainful) work, the former could not be understood. In a similar vein, the 'employment system' owes much of its characteristics to the ways education is organised within a society. Simple models of 'demand' (economy) and 'supply' (education) do not work as considerably autonomous changes in the education system may successfully alter the organisation of work. Finally, 'instruction' (being taught) and 'learning' are by no means restricted to the 'education system': the world of work is not a simple consumer of education, but a site of instruction and learning as well, which potentially even outstrip the education system when it comes to vocational learning and the development of craftsmanship and professional expertise. Potentially, as historic exploration could easily demonstrate, the world of work could do without any 'education'. For long historical periods, most learning required in the workplace, certainly, could be made available within the world of work itself, making any education an intruder of ambivalent status.

As the need for a joint analysis of education and work has become widely accepted, various proposals for how to achieve an integrative perspective have been made. Among various proposals as 'human capital development systems' (Brinton 2005) or 'qualification systems' (OECD 2007), the concept of 'skill formation systems' seems today the most broadly used label for comparative research on the education-work-link. However, the concept of 'skill formation system' is poorly defined and various understandings of the concept are in use: a detailed account of the history of the concept is missing. For the purpose of my analysis, at least two lines of reasoning have to be considered.

Firstly, in the early 1980s, scholars have developed the concept of skill formation systems for comparing the position of education, continuing training and informal learning in Japanese and American manufacturing, focusing on the functioning of internal labour markets as a core area of skill formation. While the US system was taken as the 'normal case' of segmented internal labour markets, the Japanese system was analysed in more detail. Large Japanese enterprises provide not only 'life-time employment', but craft a space for extended vocational education, the development of professional experience and 'organisational learning' as the basis for incremental innovation. For the individual, the enterprise becomes the focal, *identity* providing space – the ba (Brinton 2011, Nonaka & Toyama 2007) – defining social existence. Moreover, the organisations become the backbone for vocational education and the creation of skill, unmatched in importance by the initial education system, allowing for a Japanese way of production, which has become a 'world standard', competing with Fordist production regimes. With Japanese manufacturing, withstanding a division between 'usual' and 'unusual' activities (Koike & Inoki 1990, 7f), workplace learning as an innovative group activity becomes a major source of skill formation. The strength of skill formation within the company system determines the features of the initial education system, which withdraws from vocational preparation to provide more general education, yet in highly competitive settings with a strict hierarchy of educational pathways and prestige of educational providers. Schools are defined by their power to provide access – based on stable co-operations and institutionalised mutual commitments, not by their curricula specificy – to the most prestigious employers: The link between the content of education, entrance level positions and future careers are weak. Otherwise, the link between the prestige of schools and universities, entrance positions and future careers is strong. While in one part of the literature, the Japanese skill formation system was analysed as a particular source of competitive advantage, a model of the power of (informal) workplace learning and unmatched basis for knowledge creation and innovation (Nonaka & Takeuchi 1995), other contributions have dealt with the societal consequences of the arrangements, also found in other societies in East-Asia. Effects include the still strong exclusion of women of more prestigious work (yet, not of education) (Brinton 2011), or the competitiveness of education systems ('examination hell'), providing one way ahead only, yet, dooming not selected adolescents to a life without any prospect for advancement. Consequently, the particular 'skill formation system' becomes identified as constitute for the society as a whole, shaping any other area of social life and being reshaped by any fundamental change in other societal fields as well.

Secondly, a differently pronounced understanding of 'skill formation systems' has been introduced since late 1980s by a group of British scholars in political economy, including David Ashton, Francis Green, Andy Green, Hugh Lauder, Philip Brown and Colin Crouch (Ashton & Green 1996, Crouch et al. 1998, Sung et al. 2000, Brown et al. 2001, Crouch 2002, Finegold 2006, Crouch 2006). Skill formation – contrary to general education – is identified basically as field left to employers and workers, yet, not taken as atomistic actors, but as collective ones, namely business-interest organisations and trade unions, competing for power and control over the organisation and remuneration of work. How work is organised and what types of skills are required, is vital for the interest of both parties of the employment contract. Employers and trade unions could seek advantage for their members by pressing for particular arrangements both, for initial vocational education and institutionalised patterns of organising work and using skills. Skill formation and the certification of skills become thereby a focal point in the system of industrial relations. By comparing education and training systems in leading industrial societies (in an early phase, Great Britain with France and Germany, later with the US, Japan and the 'Tiger states' in East-Asia), they took a particular interest in the role of the state in the provision of vocational skills. The state – influenced by organised interest groups of employers and employees – could intervene in the skill formation process and constitute by legal means particular institutional settings, which shape the future prospects of the labour market parties and the individual opportunity structures of individuals as well. The state could – as for example, in France – even expand its authority from general to vocational education and running strongly regulated vocational education systems, following the pattern of compulsory and secondary academic education. Regulation becomes important for both initial vocational education, the certification of skills and the rights and limits for the exploitation of occupational and professional skills. Established ways of creating and using skills, however, form mutually re-enforcing institutional packages, expected to lead to two ideal types, namely low-skills versus high-skills equilibriums.

When initial vocational education is weakly institutionalised and skilled workers make strong claims based on their rare skills, employers may opt for a type of work organisation of the 'Fordist' type, with high numbers of jobs with little skill demand and low levels of discretion, assisted by and overseen by a small group of skilled or professionally educated workers, technicians and managers. More advanced position are available only to more highly – typically university – educated people, while most workers remain limited to poor jobs, providing more restricted opportunities for learning and progress. Consequently, individuals have an incentive to go for general higher education, yet, little motivation to invest in their vocational skills, which make not much of a difference. Typical occupational skills are scarce because of poor individual incentives; therefore, employers risk seeing their employees being poached when they initiate vocational training. This constellation is labelled 'low-skills route' (Ashton & Green 1996, 117–136) or 'low-skills equilibrium' (Finegold & Soskice 1988) to stress its self-enforcing qualities: the ignorance of the state leads to a stable pattern hard to break out for either employers or employees and resistant to simple 'supply side' interventions by lifelong learning policies; for example, by subsidising company training. Great Britain (prior to the 1990s) has been described as a model for the low-skill route.

When the state strongly intervenes in initial vocational education – no matter if more directly or by more loose framework regulations for empowering the social partners – and reserves access to particular occupations to holders of vocational certificates, then all employers must reflect agreed-on qualifications bundles or *Berufe* (occupations) in the ways to organise work. Work processes could not be deliberately divided; however, skilled workers have to become empowered to use their skills to a maximum. Consequently, work is organised differently, with less managerial oversight and technical support, and more learning opportunities, discretion and responsibility on the side of the skilled workers, which make up most of the workforce, accompanied by a comparatively small group of unskilled helpers and a group of employees with higher (mainly technical) education. Vocational training pays off, so that more individuals opt for vocational education instead of no training or prolonged academic or higher education. Higher secondary and particularly tertiary education remain a requirement for only a small fraction of high-level positions, which fits well with more rigid access routes for higher education and higher rates of drop outs of university studies. High proportions of participants in vocational education (up to higher secondary levels) are therefore combined with comparatively low attendance rates in tertiary education. As individuals are motivated to invest in vocational training and all employers are bound to make use of defined qualifications, vocational skills abound. Employers do not have to fear poaching nor being 'held up' by their skilled workers, who could not use their power of their hard-to-replace qualifications for unfair wage claims. The resulting 'high-skills-equilibrium' was modelled according to the 'German Skills Machine' (Culpepper & Finegold 1999) prior to the 1990s.

Skill-formation systems are typically studied either within a rational choice institutionalism framework (Estevez-Abe et al. 2001) or within the framework of historical institutionalism (Thelen 2004, Mahoney & Thelen 2009). Both streams of study require the inclusion of more characteristics of societies and their 'institutional packages' (Mills et al. 2008), as their systems of industrial relations or welfare states (Ebbinghaus & Kittel 2006). Consequently, skill formation systems become frequently studied within the 'Varieties of Capitalism' framework (Soskice & Hall 2001), which shares many lines of argument with the British school of thought on skill formation systems. Various studies focus on the complementarities between skill formation systems and other institutional settings, for examples, the arrangements for collective wage bargaining (Busemeyer & Iversen 2012). Typologies on 'training and education systems' or skill formation systems aim at classifying countries according to their systems, taking – as Ellu Saar and Odd-Bjorn Ure show in their overview on recent typologies (Saar & Ure 2012, forthcoming) – either the education system, the employment system or the overall institutional setting of welfare states or market regulations as their starting point.

In this chapter, I start to explore the impact of skill formation systems on provision of, incentives for and barriers to formal adult education. I am going to explore the *opportunity structures* for formal adult education and the particular role of the organisations in their creation and maintenance. By *opportunity structure* – in accordance with the widely spread use of the term since its introduction in the early 1960s (Bruce & Yearley 2006, 221) – I mean the options of individual choice, determined by structural and institutional properties of the societies, open for an individual on a particular social place within this society. Individuals may – based on personal abilities or chance – transcend their prearranged and statistically likely future; however, opportunity structures shape the options typically available for a member of a society of a particular social class, biological age, gender, educational attainment, occupational career pathway and seniority, race, migration history and the like. While structures and institutions provide and restrict available opportunities, individual agency and skills are required to take advantage of the opportunities available. Heirs not willing to living up to their golden future will lose their place on the sunny side of life, as Bourdieu so skilfully showed when reinterpreting the faith of Flaubert's hero in *L'education sentimentale* (Bourdieu 1995). Any mere option has to be actively made part of the individual *life structure*. Consequently, social and institutional structures and individual choice are studied in their interrelations, not as opposing concepts.

The provision of formal adult education has been globally diffused; however, there are countries, where formal adult education is practically unavailable, countries, where – even when controlling for statistical difficulties – provision of formal adult education is abundant and countries, where – for various reason and compositional effects – medium levels of provision could be observed. As my basis for achieving an informed guess, I take UOE data or the best estimates available (for Japan and the U.S). For embedding European data, I widen the scope of my analysis to, by world standards, two extreme cases. I take the United States as the extreme case for high levels of formal adult education and Japan as an extreme case for low levels of formal provision. Four European countries complete the picture: While Scotland – or Great Britain more generally – belong to the countries with high participation, Austria and Germany represent countries with moderate, on-average participation in formal adult education. Finally, I take France as a country with a low participation rate comparable to Japan (see Diagram 10).

Diagram 10: Participation rates (estimates) for participation in formal adult education 2007 according to the UOE concept (age breakdowns 25–64)

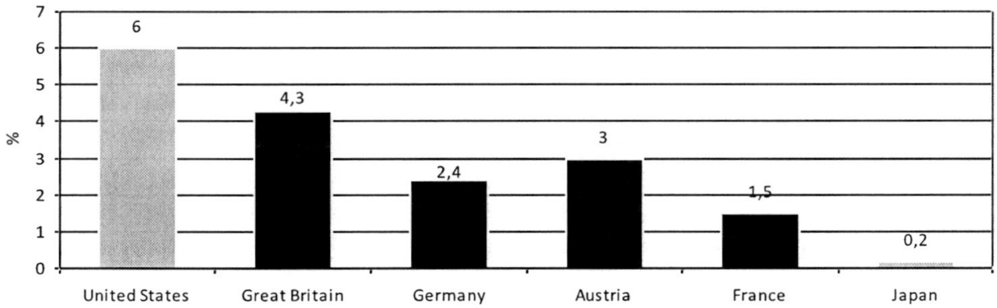

Source: UOE, own calculations, Brinton 2011 for Japan, for the US own estimates for 2004/2005 based on National Centre for Education Statistics 2006

Even when carefully considering difficulties of measurement, countries will likely differ in their opportunities structures for formal adult education. Some countries have more offers of formal adult education and programmes attract more participants. Other countries have fewer programmes available and with little attraction to adults or their employers.

The chapter is structured as follows. In Section 6.2 I turn to the now classic framework of 'societal analysis' (Maurice et al., 1986), which has informed – as a forerunner – much of the literature on skill formation systems. The framework allows for an understanding of the different role of formal adult education in Germany and France up to the early 1980s. In Section 6.3, I explore recent (2008) case-study findings for Austria and Scotland to see if the reconstructed framework is useful for other countries and today's situation. In the conclusion (Section 6.4), I combine the developed arguments with my reasoning on the seven organisational fields of formal adult education and point towards a future framework for comparative research, referring to the world extremes, U.S. and Japan, and to the four European countries analysed in the previous sections.

6.2 Formal adult education within institutionalised career patterns: 'Organisational Space' versus 'Skill Space' dominance

The Social Foundations of Industrial Power – A comparison of France and Germany (Maurice *et al.* 1986) has become a landmark study of the sociology of education (Brinton 2005, 579). Although the empirical analysis was done in the 1970s, the identified relationships and concepts remain highly relevant. The distinction drawn between 'organisational space' and 'occupational space' (or skill space) is among the fundamentals for comparative research on work and education (Shavit & Müller 2000). Their overall approach of using 'institutional packages' to explain the relationship between education, work organisation, industrial relations and social stratification is mirrored by today's dominating schools of comparative research, including the *varieties of capitalism* approach (Soskice & Hall 2001), the *business system* approach (Whitely 2007) or the new political economy of *skill formation systems* (Crouch *et al.* 1998).

The initial question of Maurice *et al.* was: Why does France have much higher wage differentials than Germany? They show that French firms in manufacturing employ considerably more white-collar personnel with management authority than German firms. While France has comparably low wage differences between unskilled and skilled personnel, it has much higher wage differences between non-management and management employees. How could one explain these differences that lead to considerable differences in social stratification?

Obviously, the empirical basis of the *Social Foundations of Industrial Power* is both dated and limited in scope. The book is based on organisational case studies completed in the middle of the 1970s, and the study was restricted to medium and large enterprises in the metal and chemical industry. Vocational education has changed in both countries significantly, so the findings by Maurice *et al.* do not account for today's situation (see Powell *et al.* 2009). Of course, their findings do not represent 'national cultures' or country systems as a whole.[26]

Yet, the way the authors conduct their research and construct their arguments remain highly illuminative. To answer their research question, the research team conducted case studies in Germany and France in carefully paired companies, which were highly similar in size, sector, products, technologies used and overall work organisation (for example, production by unit, batch or continuing process). Rejecting deterministic frameworks, the authors highlight the considerable leeway of organisations to decide how to organise work and how to reward workers. While the firms' behaviour is not determined by, for example, technology or market structures, the societal environment clearly influences firms; thus, German and French firms have distinct features. The authors seek an alternative to the most common 'system-environment' scheme and explore the firms' strategic reaction to various factors in their environment.

They model, within the organisation, the social relations among workers, employees and management in various 'fields', 'domains' or 'spaces'. The relations between unskilled workers and skilled workers found within the enterprise coexists with the relation between the two groups within the 'educational space' (for example, trained in similar or different educational tracks), the 'skill space' (for example, clearly separated by formal qualifications or not), the 'space of class relations' (for example, high/low differences in average wages) and the 'space of industrial relations' (represented by united trade unions or by vocationally specific, differentiated unions).[27] Clearly, various spaces shape each other, while preserving, at the same time, considerable relative autonomy.

Any firm enjoys considerable autonomy to organise work and thereby create particular social relations among various groups of co-workers. However, the freedom to organise is limited, because the world inside the organisation simultaneously belongs to various social spaces outside the company. Finally, organisational behaviour itself becomes a major influence for the various spaces (for example, educational space, space of industrial relations) requiring the conceptualisation of and

---

26 They do not reflect gender segmentation nor other lines of discrimination (O'Reily 2000), although gender or migration background matter. Germany had larger wage differences, for example, among women than France; dual apprenticeship implies frequent dead ends in sectors with a high proportion of female employees (O'Reilly 2000; Krüger 1999). Societal analysis fails to reflect the employer's active role in workplace discrimination, which carefully studying forms the main achievement of contemporary approaches in organisational-stratification research (Baron & Bierbly 1980; Baron 1984; for a recent review of literature see Stainback *et al.* 2010).

27 The number of 'spaces' studied was explicitly not intended to be exhaustive (Maurice & Sorge 2000, 3); for example, Marc Maurice later introduced the 'innovation space' (Maurice 1995) or other authors analyse the 'space of gender relations' (O'Reilly 2000) or the 'family space' (Maurission-Barrère 2000).

the description of how organisations become *enabled and restricted* by various spaces and how they enable and restrict these spaces themselves. For example, social stratification shapes organisational behaviour that, at the same time, generates inequality or discrimination.

Organisational space (the behaviour of comparable employer organisations) and *skill space* (the particular interplay of educational provision and the learning opportunities provided at work) create and limit an organisation's capacity to use and produce skills, organise and reward work, and provide access to various career paths within the firm. Clearly, both spaces coexist in any society, but given their multiple properties, either space can dominate the organisation of work. Maurice *et al.* (1986) introduce this fundamental assertion in the following:

> *Theoretically a firm can organize its work system in one of two ways: it can define jobs according to its own criteria and require workers to adapt or train them to fit the job definition, or it can take account of the existing qualifications of the work force and design jobs around the capabilities of the workers. In the first case, job demands determine the workers profile. In the second case, the worker's profile exerts an influence on the job definition.* (p. 67)

When the organisational space is dominant,

> *definition of the job by the firm using its own criteria, is more likely to occur [...] As a result the firm finds it possible to set work organisation criteria of its own in such a way that there is a sharp distinction between nonsupervisory positions, which require only a short period of on-the-job training, and positions involving design and organisational responsibility. This type of job definition tends to devalue the former kind of job relative to the latter.* (p. 67)

When the *skill space* is dominant,

> *firms will tend to organize production around the norms of the training system. In this case the work system will place greater emphasis on the relative autonomy of the workers and reward the productivity associated with their qualifications rather than their adaptation to the organisation. (p. 68)*

It is important to note, that the authors understand their concepts of *spaces* (in French, *espace*) as an alternative to *markets*. The analysis of the dominance of either organisational space or skill space is developed as a critical exploration of the theories of segmented labour markets, in particular of Michael Piore's contributions (Maurice *et al.* 1986, 210–212). Later, however, in important contributions to the field (Eyraud *et al.* 1990; Shavit & Müller 1998; Mardsen 1999; Müller & Gangl 2003), organisational space is taken to mean 'internal labour markets' (ILM) and skill space to mean 'occupational labour markets' (OLM), which implies losing much of the critical potential of Maurice *et al.*'s analysis. The societal relations within specific 'spaces' do not follow general laws and could not be explained by aggregated rational behaviour of individual workers or their employer organisations. Both 'organisational' and 'skill' spaces are forms of institutionalised processes, specific to one society and not the 'economic rational' answer to given problems of control and exchange.[28]

The dominance of either skill space or organisational space is crucial for any workplace learning, informal[29] and nonformal training, or formal adult education. Maurice *et al.* do not particularly analyse formal adult education beyond their interest in the 'span of qualification' (p. 56), that means, the career pathways available after earning a particular qualification. Thus, what I am presenting in the following is our interpretation of what might be concluded for formal adult education from their more general arguments. I review steps within organisational careers – the career pathways typically made available by an organisation for their long-term employees, (see Overview 20) and their link to formal adult education. I start with organisational careers under the dominance of skill space.

---

28 For an excellent account on social control of skill in industrialised countries, see Streeck (2011). Maurice *et al.* are more explicit in describing the features of the German-style skill space than in describing a skill space in the absence of a strong vocational education system, as in France during the 1970s, or for the features of the organisational space in Germany. However, an organisational space clearly exerts an influence on work organisation and is shaped itself, for example, by the educational space or the space of industrial relations. We think that the concept of organisational fields (Wooten & Hoffman 2008) provides here a promising tool for clarification. Organisational institutionalism makes the case for the emergence of highly institutionalised patterns regulating work organisation and employment even in the absence of formal regulation by law – coined as the paradox of the weak state (Dobbin & Sutton 1998).

29 The dominance of either skill space or organisational space is also highly important for informal workplace learning. Maurice *et al.* describe how, in Germany, complex and demanding work is assigned to work teams. Teams typically have workers with different levels of experience. As a team, shop-floor workers are responsible for tackling both the regular and the extraordinary requirements of the production process. Maintenance departments play a much more selective role than, for example, in France. All team members participate in a steady learning process. Moreover, pay schemes back up informal workplace learning, as individuals are paid based on their qualification level *and* on the level of team performance. Under dominance of *organisational space* in France, methods of wage determinations require narrowly defined individual workplaces, which discourage workplace learning. Shop-floor workers are typically not expected to deal with extraordinary situations, nor receive any bonus for successfully addressing problems. On the contrary, any demand for extended competence of shop-floor workers would imply a pay-raise and thereby a change in the overall pay structure. To avoid this type of claim, organisations restrict job discretion. Therefore, considering the dominance of either skill space or organisational space helps to explain the 'double nature' of skill as an attribute of either workers or workplaces (Attewell, 1990), the national differences in levels of workplace discretion (Dobbin & Boychuk 1999) or differences in the institutional basis for implementing *High Performance Work Systems* (Appelbaum *et al.*, 2000).

Overview 20: Steps in organisational careers discussed in Maurice et al. (1986) for Germany (skill space dominates) and France (organisational space dominates) non-/related to formal adult education

		Dominated by Skill Space	Dominated by Organisational Space
(a)	Access to the organisation	Differentiated for specific occupations; dual apprenticeship system; separate for core segment/secondary segment	Low level of occupational diversification; competitive, based on credentials in general education
(b)	Access to the core segment of the internal labour market	Typically, not foreseen within organisational careers ('strict segmentation') (individual 'second-chance education') – however, co-optation strategies in case of skill shortages	After extended probation; on-the-job/off-the-job training plus 'job ladders' from most elementary to more complex and responsible jobs
(c)	Skill adaptation when moving between related jobs/when jobs are adapted – Ongoing career development	Little career mobility outside significant career steps; increased abilities and demonstrated motivation (*Leistungsbereitschaft*) lead to higher premiums on individual/team level	On-the-job training and short-term (non-formal) off-the-job training; Frequent change between workplaces, moving to jobs ranging higher in job classifications/paying higher wages, following established job ladders
(d)	Access to medium-level management jobs; Mobility between blue-collar/ white-collar employees	Completion of a formal training programme (*Aufstiegsweiterbildung*) is required	After being chosen, based on seniority and job appraisal, extended phases on company sponsored off-the-job preparation (6–9 months, full-time) in corporate (nonformal) training programmes
(e)	Access to engineering jobs/upper-level management jobs	For medium-qualified, non-graduate employees; upper secondary technical schools or applied higher technical education must be completed	Reserved for hired graduates after an extended probation and socialisation period

Source: Own description based on Maurice et al. (1986)

When skillspace dominates organisational career patterns: German manufacturing in the mid-1970s

Within the 'skills domain', job openings are specified according to vocational profiles: only holders of the specific occupations can apply and higher levels of general education cannot make up for a lack of vocational training. The 'dual apprenticeship system' forms a particular route into the organisation, as enterprises fill vacancies with their former apprentices or equally qualified candidates. The internal labour market's core segment has skilled blue-collar jobs. Vocational education forms an entry path into the organisation and into its higher ranks, at least for the most prestigious, technical vocations. Young individuals with working-class backgrounds choose the apprenticeship system because of skilled workers' strong occupational and class identity and career opportunities for holders of vocational degrees. At the time of the study, completion of training was not required to get a job in German manufacturing, but the primary segment of the internal labour market can only be accessed with a vocational qualification.

Binding social-partner agreements have reserved skilled work for skilled permanent employees. Unskilled work, however, is mainly organised with the internal labour market's secondary segment, where jobholders do not have the appropriate vocational training. For workers without the proper vocational education, this arrangement implies a barrier within the internal labour market: without proper qualification, they are not supposed to become part of the core workforce. If enterprises can attract appropriately skilled workers or retain former apprentices, there is little need to provide formal vocational training for employees. Only when attracting skilled labour becomes difficult, then enterprises offer to 'unskilled' employees the training that leads to a formal qualification. Individuals, however, have a strong incentive to gain vocational certificates, so that they become eligible for the core segment of the internal labour market.

Formal adult education becomes important when we consider upward mobility within careers. The change from skilled blue-collar jobs to white-collar technical or supervisory jobs generally involves extended formal adult education, which individuals have to master successfully, before being promoted. Maurice *et al.* describe in detail two types of formal programmes covered by the concept of *Aufstiegsweiterbildung*[30] (advanced further training): programmes that prepare for the *Meisterprüfung* and work-related, part-time programmes in engineering that lead to a higher secondary technical education. *Aufstiegsweiterbildung* forms a core element for employees in firms dominated by skill spaces: the organisations hardly have other choices than using these existing educational opportunities to generate medium-level managers and technical workers. Consequently, organisations encourage particular employees to seek further vocational education and the firms may support the costs of the formal education.

Aufstiegsweiterbildung also provides access to upper-management positions and positions requiring high levels of expertise. *Fachhochschulen* (Universities of Applied Sciences) arrange part-time studies in higher vocational education to enable further advancement. In the 1970s, only a small number of positions were reserved for university graduates with research-based degrees – in particular natural and/or technical sciences. Given a strong preference for technical education, university-educated technicians or scientists are also likely to be appointed to higher management jobs. While university-based degrees are one promising starting point for higher-level employment in manufacturing, they are not the only access routes to advanced positions. In general, because career alternatives are available within the organisation, university education for adults is not encouraged.

30 The distinction between *Anpassungsweiterbildung* and *Aufstiegsweiterbildung* can hardly be translated into English. The IAB Glossary distinguishes between 'refresher training, refresher course(s), updating course(s)' and 'advanced (further) training', explaining the latter as follows: 'workers wishing to obtain promotion may well decide to undertake advanced training; a clear distinction must be made between refresher training and advanced training for workers seeking promotion.' (Werner *et al.* 2004, 716).

When organisational space dominates organisational careers: French manufacturing firms in the mid-1970s

When organisational space is predominant, a decisive factor is education of credentials – particularly, the level achieved and the symbolic value of the awarding organisation. Organisations may require a minimum qualifications level, yet, the hierarchy of educational credentials is more important than the potential match between a job and an applicant's profile. Given the low status of vocational qualifications, any higher general education is more important than any vocational qualification. Applicants are selected for career pathways in ever-changing positions within the organisation, not for a particular job profile. Typically, any hiring decision is temporary and based on a formal or informal probation: employees start in the temporary segment of the internal labour market, although their credentials affect their chances to enter the core segment as well as the length of time needed for this change. Job advertisements are loosely structured according to the level of general education and less by vocational specificity. Therefore, individuals place top priority on struggling ahead within the general education system – at least until the final examination within higher secondary education – and avoiding marginalisation within vocational-oriented programmes.

In the mid-1970s, France's educational system had little to offer those who could not deal with the burdens of extended schooling, who were sceptical about their abilities or who faced negative assessment of their performance within the school system. Thus, relying on an organisational career became the logical alternative after dropping out of the general education system. Dropping out of a competitive general education system is understood broadly as terminal: 'second chance education' is available only for individuals who recently dropped out of school, not as an alternative standard route available at any time during the career. Highly competitive entrance examinations for the more prestigious schools make it difficult for the 'drop-outs' to compete with the brightest of younger cohorts.

Within organisational-space dominated firms, virtually anybody, regardless of his or her qualification, starts within the 'secondary segment' of the internal labour market. However, depending on the general and vocational qualification, 'membership' was either granted after a comparable short probation, or – particularly for those with lower formal qualifications – after an extended period of service. A vocational qualification is no requirement for receiving 'full membership' and permanent-worker status. Hence, formal adult education does not play a role in transcending job hierarchies.

Maurice *et al.* emphasise that, in the 1970s in France, to motivate employees and inspire commitment and loyalty among blue-collar workers, the employers' key strategy was to move employees up a job ladder that promised higher responsibility, more demanding skills and higher pay for each consecutive step. Moreover, the social-partner negotiations determined salaries based on very detailed job classifications that made it impossible to reward individual achievement. Therefore, performance is mainly rewarded by progression on a job ladder.

For more demanding jobs and, in particular, medium-level management, organisations chose employers primarily based on individual appraisals; the firms then provided an extensive nonformal, off-the-job training that lasts from several weeks to several months. The training programmes improved the chosen workers' skills and marked and legitimised the transition from non-managerial to managerial jobs. Thereby, corporate training programmes became a *rite de passage* from one job category to another.[31]

Access to upper-level management jobs and any job requiring higher levels of expertise are reserved for graduates of the higher education system. Higher-level jobs have particular organisational career trajectories that often include work in lower-level positions. Consequently, for non-graduates, organisational careers do not lead to any high-ranked positions. This structure implies a strong incentive for higher education within initial education. Overview 21 summarises the findings about the link between particular types of formal adult education and organisational careers in the two countries.

Overview 21: Formal adult education within organisational careers

	Skill space dominated	**Organisational space dominated**
General		
Differentiation on firm level between 'formal' and 'nonformal' adult education	Clear-cut and decisive	Blurred and not decisive
Present 'reference models' for 'formal adult education'	Apprenticeship programmes (for adults); Programmes preparing for *Meisterprüfung*; Part time evening higher secondary technical education or higher education at universities for applied sciences	Long corporate programmes (formal programmes in continuing higher education may replace nonformal programmes)
Timing within organisational careers	Promotion *after* the completion of the programme	Promotion (decision) *before* the programme
Importance of higher education	Low(er) (alternative routes based on formal adult education)	High(er) (graduation forms a new starting point for career progress)
Formal adult education within specific career steps		
Access to the permanent workforce for unskilled (not field specific skilled) workers	Formal vocational training required (little chance for access for employees labelled as unskilled)	Not required (experience and nonformal training sufficient)
Upwards mobility	*Aufstiegsweiterbildung* (craft master; higher secondary technical education) required	Not required (experience and nonformal training sufficient)
Access to higher-level jobs	Higher vocational education (universities of applied science)	Impossible with organisational careers (alternatively, new start after completion of higher education)

Source: Own description

31 Here, Maurice *et al.* provide an analysis of the function of corporate-training programmes that resonates perfectly with analysis by organisational institutionalism for training programmes in American organisations (Scott & Meyer 1994).

6.3 Assessing the model – Formal adult education in small and medium enterprises in Austria and Scotland

In the following section, I explore the argument about formal adult education in organisational or skill-space dominated countries in relation to Austria and Scotland. Because Maurice *et al.* (1986) focus only on a narrow spectrum of sectors and types of work, wanted to explore examples beyond skilled males in manufacturing. Nevertheless, enterprises selected and participants included do not represent all enterprises or participants in formal adult education in one country or overall. My conceptual arguments result from analysing all case studies and countries involved, but because of limited space, share only a few illustrative cases from Austria and Scotland.

Austria – bridging power of a strong skill space

Beside Germany, Austria is frequently cited as an example of a country in which the skill space is dominant. Despite differences in detail, Austria and Germany share traditions of in welfare policies, industrial relations and education and training systems: A strong and highly prestigious vocational education system with more than two thirds of a youth cohort choosing either the apprenticeship system or school-based vocational education. In both countries, the tertiary education sector is traditionally small (with a low number of academics), and only recently started to open up. In Austria, higher secondary technical education was traditionally highly appreciated and was supplemented by *Fachhochschulen* only in the 1990s. However, part-time study opportunities are still restricted. Adult education is almost exclusively seen as traditional liberal education without any formal qualifications provided or required. Austria does not have general systems to recognise informal learning. European education policy only recently triggered the development of a national qualification framework. Skill space is particular strong where the apprenticeship system is strong, which is trade and industry.

When visiting XY Chemicals, we encountered an almost ideal-type linkage of formal adult education and organisational careers when skill space is dominant (Hefler & Bacher 2008a). The medium-sized company (50–99 employees) was founded about ten years ago during the dismantling of a much larger corporation. Production facilities are highly capital intensive and work organisation is characterised by continuing-process production[32] in shift work. The company faces strong competition for skilled workers in chemical industries in the regional labour market. On the shop level, all current employees are male.

32 'In continuous-process production, the entire process is mechanised. There is no starting and stopping. [...] Automated machines control the continuous process, and outcomes are highly predictable. Examples would include chemical plants, oil refineries, brewing plants, pharmaceuticals and nuclear power plants.' (Daft et al. 2010, 270). One type besides 'small batch or unit production' and 'large batch or mass production' of work organisation described by Joan Woodward in her seminal study (1965).

The company invests substantially in training and systematically provides training for staff at all levels. One major approach is to hire unskilled workers trained in another trade (for example, carpenters) and to offer them extended training on and off the job, before they start to work as helpers within the shift-work teams. To become a full member of the organisation and to benefit from the substantially higher wages for skilled chemical workers, unskilled workers are openly invited to prepare for a particular type of apprenticeship examination (*Außerordentliche Lehrabschlussprüfung*) available only for adult learners and that provides a vocational formal qualification on higher secondary level, yet without university entrance permission at ISCED 3b level.[33] To help workers prepare for this examination, a former trainer provides on-site, one lesson per week over an 18-month programme. The company covered all costs of the courses, which take place mainly during paid working time; the firm also arrange the participants' work schedule to accommodate the course work. After passing the examination, participants become 'skilled chemical workers', enjoy a statutory pay rise of about 400 Euros a month, and can even become shift leaders in small shifts.

As a next step in the career progression of skilled workers, the company supports the preparation for the master examination (*Meisterprüfung*) in chemical work. The examination is classified at vocational higher education level ISCED 5b level, yet do not include entrance permission for any general university study. The company supports this step on an individual basis, paying the high course fees. Although there is no specific policy, the company generally offers a promotion to white-collar positions, including a considerable pay rise, after the completion of the programme.

One employee (male, between 25–30) made clear in our interview that he understands his current formal adult education as a quite natural step within his career, providing access to more challenging and better-paid, white-collar work. Although he had no further plans at the moment of the interview, he understands there are at least two further steps within formal adult education available for him: either attending a vocational higher secondary education evening school (ISCED 4b Level) or a university for applied science (ISCED 5b), both of which would take three to four years of study. However, this would require a substantial rearrangement of his life during the years of participation.

The case study demonstrates how formal adult education is integrated in organisational careers and firmly bridges the gulf between education and work. Various formal training opportunities are institutionalised and mirrored by the work organisation of the enterprise. The actual work processes are adjusted to learning within formal programmes. Individuals can invest in their further training, because the ad-

33 ISCED stands for International Standard Classification of Education (UNESCO 1997). For a discussion of its use in cross-national research see (Schneider 2008).

ditional certificates typically improve the career path with their present employer or – as an alternative – with other possible employers within the occupational field.

Three of the eight other Austrian case studies also demonstrated the interplay of work and formal adult education under the dominance of the skill space. However, in two cases, the most frequent entrance qualification is no longer the dual apprenticeship (ISCED3b), but higher secondary vocational education (ISCED 4b), and the participants study part-time at a university for applied sciences (Hefler et al. 2008).

Finally, the remaining four case studies highlight that the dominance of skill space is hardly a universal property of the country. For example, XY Plastics Austria (Hefler & Bacher 2008b) uses a highly idiosyncratic production technology, but no vocational training is available for the required skills. Therefore, as Baron & Bielby (1980) described for typical organisational-space dominated enterprises, the company trains and develops its work force, using particular job ladders, where employees proceed from more elementary to more advanced jobs. Workers are granted lifetime employment and above-average wages for shift work in a region where industrial work is scarce. Typically, most workers hold various types of vocational or even higher secondary education, yet are classified as unskilled workers. Important for career progression is the mastering of firm-specific skills and competence, not vocational qualifications. Despite tendencies to generalise patterns through all economic fields, arrangements remain specific to particular economic sectors, better understood as 'organisational fields' (Wooten & Hoffman 2008). Organisational space and skill space dominance can therefore co-exist in one country, an argument also highlighted within organisational institutionalism (Fligstein & Byrkjeflot 1996, 29f.).

Scotland – Dominance of organisational space moderated by professional space

In contrast to other authors (for example, Eyraud *et al.* 1990) who compare Great Britain with France, we assume a dominance of organisational space in Scotland with a clear supremacy of general education above vocational education, low importance of standardised vocational qualifications industry-wide, a restricted 'qualification span' of vocational education, a high proportion of blue-collar workers without vocational education in narrowly defined workplaces and low pressure on enterprises to use broadly defined vocations as the basis for organizing their work. In contrast to Germany, an apprenticeship system was never fully backed by the state (Thelen 2004). Only a comparatively small fraction of skilled blue-collar workers, predominantly in tool making and maintenance departments of manufacturing, use an apprenticeship system. Thus, it has never become the backbone of industrial work as in Germany (Maurice *et al.* 1980). In the 1980s and 1990s, new initiatives attempted to re-strengthen vocational skills, both in the education system and at the workplace; for example, the introduction of a qualifications framework (Franklin 1997) or the implementation of the 'modern apprenticeship' scheme (Fuller & Unwin 2003). However, skill space is clearly more strongly developed than, for example, in France.

The early establishment of modularised and credit-based qualifications led to a broad understanding of formal adult education.

XY Manufacturing, a family owned, medium-sized company (250–499 employees) represents an organisation, typical for organisational-space dominated sectors or countries, yet skill space also influences it (Ahlgren *et al.* 2008a). The firm produces large-scale refrigeration systems, and its work organisation could be described as customised unit production. Most employees (nearly all male) work on the job floor. The enterprise has existed for about four decades and offers long-term employment opportunities, with a considerably high turnover rate.

The company's internal labour market has visible career opportunities, but not formalised as career ladders. Workers could go from elementary to more advanced jobs, and engineers were encouraged to go from apprenticeship to the top-level engineers within the company. The job floor has a considerably low level of required formal qualifications; however, in-house and on-the-job training forms the backbone of the skill-formation strategy. The organisation decides on career advancement based on an appraisal system. The company highly acknowledges formal adult education as an extension of in-house training, yet, not as a structuring principle in its own right. Various formal educational opportunities could be used, if they meet the requirements of organisational career development.

One interviewee, Kevin, in his 20s, joined the company seven years earlier, right after school. Through the company, he achieved most of his vocational qualifications such as a forklift driving licence and a degree in welding (recognised within the Scottish vocational qualification framework). Training on the job and within specialised courses provided particular skills required for his specific career pathway through the company. However, Kevin has never participated in an industry-wide-recognised, standardised and comprehensive vocational training programme. Based on his work experience and his demonstrated abilities and traits, he was recently promoted to a supervisory role, implying a change from technical work to a more managerial role.

To support his new management role and to prepare him to take on more responsibility, the company encouraged him to start a four-year, part-time university degree in engineering management at a local, further-education college. Given Kevin's prior qualification, he was allowed to skip two years of the programme. The employer pays half of the tuition fees. The programme was provided entirely outside the workplace, two evenings a week, three hours per class. Classes are a mixture of lectures to a group of 4–5 students and one-to-one tuition. Homework requires, on the average, one day of each weekend.[34]

34 It is important to emphasise that the chosen programme on the higher-education level shares more of the characteristics of nonformal training programmes (for example, small groups, one-to-one tuition, flexibility) used by companies in internal training programmes rather than traditional university programmes.

The formal programme is clearly in line with the career pathway within XY Manufacturing. Kevin's line manager expects to promote him to supervisor in the near future. Kevin's recognised vocational qualification would, however, also increase his opportunities for employment elsewhere. Kevin has thought about this option if he is not promoted within a couple of years after finishing his programme. Therefore, where organisational space dominates, formal programmes mark no defined requirement within organisational careers (although they might be used for reasons of convenience). Formal programmes are generally recognised in the labour market; however, their value is less firmly institutionalised than in countries where skill space exerts a much stronger influence.

Four of the six Scottish case studies represent a considerably different type of enterprise and point towards a different type of space (Ahlgren *et al.* 2009). They represent 'professional organisations' (Leicht & Fennell 1997), employing predominately university-trained employees such as scientists, certified engineers, lawyers, architects, accountants, project managers, etc. The literature on professional work (Abbott 1988; Freidson 2001) notes that professions are regulated in a way which could be addressed as *professional space.* We review one typical case study in this section and discuss this point in the concluding section in more detail.

XY Oil Exploration is a medium-sized (50–99 employees), knowledge-intensive organisation specialised in searching for oil in fields already shut down (Ahlgren *et al.* 2008b). Daily business is strongly based on projects, because the company identifies and sets up exploration projects together with its subsidiaries and a global network of partners. Employees typically hold a Master's or PhD degree. Training and further development of all employees were strongly supported; for example, the average, annual training budget per employee is about 3000 pounds sterling. Professional polyvalence – the ability to shift between various work places established within one organisation, based on a broad basis of skill and competences (Maurice et al. 1986, 68) – is strongly encouraged. However, the employees orient themselves to the standards and norms set by their professional fields, which may not only imply mandatory continuing education, but also provide a structure for formal training opportunities leading to the next step within a hierarchy of defined professional levels, as we could see in the following case.

Based on his university degree, Pete chose to enter the accounting profession and to acquire an accountancy qualification provided by the Association of Chartered Certified Accountants, one among several professional organisations entitled to recognise professional-accounting education. The course consisted of four modules, preparing for on average of four exams. Including time to resit several examinations, Pete needed three and half years to complete the programme. He had started his programme, when he was employed with his former employer, yet, after six months, he quit and took on a position as a junior accountant with XY Exploration. His current employer agreed to cover the full costs of the programme and 15 days of paid study leave. Moreover, Pete gained the opportunity to work immediately in a highly challenging field of global cross-border accounting within an expert team. After completing the programme, he could get a professionally defined, responsible position within accounting.

It is important to note how organisational space and professional space interact, making the formal qualification both a required step within a professional career and a requirement within organisational career development. However, not all countries organise accounting as a profession; for example, many skill-space dominated countries train accountants in a broad vocational education (for example, on higher secondary level). Further specialised training in particular fields of accounting may often be understood as nonformal and not as formal education. Therefore, professional space as an alternative for skill space has clearly different possibilities in distinct countries.

The societal effects school introduces the concept of 'space' for modelling the interrelatedness of various autonomous areas of the social world – or, in the words of organisational institutionalism, autonomous fields of institutional life – such as general education, vocational education, industrial sectors or industrial relations. Therefore, dominance by either skill space or organisational space does not merely translate features of the education or skill formation system into a new typology, but instead models a totality of societal relations. Consequently, although the dominance of either skill space (for example, in Germany, Austria, Switzerland or Denmark) or organisational space (for example, in France, Scotland, England, the United States or Japan) may point in one direction, the actual differences in, for example, organisational spaces between countries may be of equal or even higher significance for the overall institutional effects of formal adult education. For example, the virtual absence of second-chance education in France seems to be more the result of the state-enforced strong and highly legitimised competition for scarce places in prestigious educational tracks (Hage & Garnier 1992, Resink 2007) than of the dominance of organisational space. Consequently, only using quantitative indicators cannot determine the relative dominance of skill space or organisational space.

Our assessment based on recent case studies in Austria and Scotland has shown that the assertions connected to the dominance of either skill or organisational space provide a useful analytical tool for understanding the role of particular types of formal adult education within organisational careers. By exploring the Austrian cases, we have learned that analysis should focus on more local contexts, because, within one country, either skill or organisational space may be dominant in different fields. Within Scottish cases, we referred to the importance of the professional space as an important source for the institutional charter of formal adult education.

Beyond skill space, the *professional space* provide an alternative institutional basis for securing the occupational relevance of formal adult education. We would follow Neil Fligstein and Haldor Byrkjeflot in their short definition of 'professionalism' as a third logic for controlling work beside 'vocationalism' (=skill space) and 'managerialism' (=organisational space). The authors characterise the institutional framework of professionalism as follows:

> 'Professionalism is a conception of work that references a professional peer group, uses associations to maintain collegiality, and relies on universities for the training of personnel. Careers are centred on professions, not firms or industries, and once in a system of professions an individual, tends to stay for life.' (Fligstein & Byrekjeflot 1996, p. 12).

Professional spaces seem to expand particularly in countries where organisational space is dominating and skill space exerts little influence on work organisation. Fligstein & Byrekjeflot (1996) characterise the employment system of, for example, the United States or Great Britain as a combination of managerialism (for unskilled and skilled work) and professionalism (for highly skilled work). In the absence of other strategies for securing the interest of employees, professionalism – ranging from the traditional liberal professions over, for example, general management or accounting to various para-professions, for example, in counselling or medical services – may become an equally dominating form of work organisation in societies otherwise dominated by 'organisational space' for up to a third of the working population (Scott 2008c, Baker 2011). Within professional space, (continuing) professional education imparts new functions to formal adult education, because it enables insiders to act professionally and ask for proper remuneration while introducing ever-tightening requirements for outsiders to enter the field.

To understand the institutional bridges between formal adult education and the world of work, we must consider how the interplay of organisational space, skill space and professional space has an impact on work. Maurice *et al.* provide a fruitful starting point. For a new comparative framework, organisational institutionalism provides additional insight, in particular with regard to organisational and professional space. Individual, organisational and societal benefits of formal adult education – and more generally, lifelong learning – depends on the institutional bridges available between education and work. Policy discourse is mainly concerned with raising participation numbers. However, steering demand for skills by enterprises, aiming at a 'high skills equilibrium' (Crouch *et al.* 1998), may also fall short, as it leave out questions of social relations, collective identities and autonomy at work. Creating new bridges between adult learning and work requires collective actors – social movements, occupational communities, interest organisations – to work towards their proper interests, confront their organised opponents, negotiate compromises and change how work is organised and how people relate to each other. Therefore, even if we focus merely on labour-market issues or economic performance, lifelong learning is crucially connected to collective emancipation and societal change. These institutional processes connected to formal adult education may be of particular interest to comparative research.

6.4 Towards a comparative framework on opportunity structures for formal adult education

Opportunity structures for education over the life course are frequently discussed by referring to 'drivers' and 'barriers' for participation, reflecting both institutional settings increasing or reducing life course flexibility and personality characteristics conducive or not for participation (for a review see Setftersten & Lovegreen 1998). While all industrialised nations have similar promoting and hampering factors, particular institutional settings cause the factors to have varying impact in different countries. The same perceived barrier for participation – for example, as measured in surveys on individual motives for non-/participation – may lead to different outcomes in different institutional frameworks (Rubenson & Desjardins 2009).

I propose to analyse the *opportunity structure* for formal adult education by considering six dimensions, summarised in Overview 22 and described in the following section that includes examples concerning our countries under study.

(A) Availability and Accessibility

Clearly high levels of participation require high levels of availability. Countries with moderate to high participation rates should show a clearly identifiable set of organisations and programmes devoted to formal adult education. In the United States, a whole sector of the higher education system – the community colleges – has developed into a major provider for formal adult education. In Germany and Austria, a range of evening schools or types of programmes (preparation for craft mastership examination) are in place without interruption since the Second World War. However, despite the status of formal education in Japan and France, they have few comparable programmes. Of similar importance is the accessibility of organisations and programmes for adult 'non-traditional' students, belonging to initial education, notably the higher education sector. The U.S. has more and more adult students entering higher education organisations, making up most undergraduate students. Increasing participation of adult students in higher education – at least, in its less prestigious organisations – has been a long-time, recently strongly enforced policy for British universities. Higher education also plays an important role for formal adult education in German and Austria, even without any explicit support (Markowitsch et al. 2012, forthcoming). In contrast, up to the 1990s, universities in Japan simply denied access to 'off time' entrance (Brinton 2011). Finally, competitive entrance procedures may strongly reduce adult learners' access to more prestigious programmes or organisations, when they cannot compete with traditional-age applicants, who can devote all their time to training for the entrance examination. However, there might be places reserved for adult applicants, for example, among study places in medicine for nurses with a number of years of professional experience. Availability and accessibility, moreover, may change over time, requiring longitudinal data. In Markowitsch at al. (2012 forthcoming), we have outlined for Austria the rise of new programmes and the extension of places within programmes of formal adult education within a period of about 15 years (1996–2011). Therefore, the expansion – or contraction – of educational programmes at hand, forms naturally a starting point for any historic and cross-country analysis.

(B) Rigidity and Selectivity

Opportunities for formal adult education differ in their rigidity and selectivity. Countries have more or less selective programmes that differ in their composition – as they do for the provision of pupils and students in initial education. Many dropouts of the initial system – naturally a target group for formal adult education – might not participate in formal adult education because their experiences with initial education and the current practice within formal adult education lead to low expectations of success. Selectivity reflects both the demanding nature of curricula and the levels of available support structures. Countries such as the U.S. or Scotland with less selective programmes have more participation in formal adult education. Participation is clearly low where rigidity, selectivity and competitiveness of initial education shape a society, as in France or in Japan, based on 'selection by educational failure' (Maurice et al. 1986, 32).

(C) Public support for participation

Countries differ widely in their provision and distribution of public resources for adult education. Many countries provide the most important support through funding programmes and organisations devoted exclusively to formal adult education or of study places for non-traditional students in higher education. Adults can typically participate at no or low tuition fees, clearly below the costs involved in their education. Co-funding schemes for tuition fees may or may not be available. For full-time participation, grants or credit schemes for covering living costs may or may not be in place. In some countries, adults can use grants for higher secondary and tertiary education also available for traditional students; in other countries, an age threshold excludes adults from these schemes. Educational-leave schemes may allow for a break in employment without losing too much income or the right to return to the job. Regulations on tax deductibility for the costs of formal adult education may have a strong impact on the individual costs of participation: regulations range from no deductibility to extended opportunities (such as deducting past costs from taxes for future incomes, see CEDEFOP 2009). Countries differ greatly in their tuition fees for comparable programmes; low-fee programmes clearly have an impact on accessibility. Support for living expenses relates to high participation in formal adult education, as in Norway or Sweden; this reflects high levels of support for students, irrespective of age. However, the U.S. example shows that adults may pay high tuition fees and support themselves during their formal education where paying for individual (higher) education is the societal norm. Individual financial aid is maybe the best-studied driver for participation rates: yet, financial barriers to participation are not decisive and their removal alone does not prompt expansion in formal adult education.

(D) Flexibility of career trajectories

Participation in formal adult education requires typically flexibility of work assignments during participation and also the opportunity to change between career trajectories later in life. Enterprises allow for more or less flexibility in individual careers, such as taking a career break, changing between workplaces within an organisation or changing between organisations. Changing careers successfully is more or less likely and comes at a price for breaking with the institutional expectations. Employment systems could be highly rigid and controlled by management and/or trade unions; they allow for little flexibility so that individual preferences do not subvert carefully crafted vacancy chains (White 1970, Chase 1991). Unionised 'closed shops' firms in Great Britain and internal labour markets in bureaucracies or large manufacturing enterprises in the United States of the 1950s and 1960s or Japanese manufacturing firms up to the late 1980s have been described as being close to the ideal of 'total control' over career entry and career progress. Institutionalised agreements between employers may block any exit strategy within one industry, when employers do not hire any former employee of competitors (Streeck 2011).

Private 'failure' to meet predefined expectations due to pregnancy, family obligations or health problems may lead to relegation to dead-end positions, to dismissal of or even exclusion of a whole sector. Without a rigorous enforcement of equal-opportunity principles (Dobbin 2009), negative sanctions for 'deviation' often outlive formal policies (for example, 'marriage bans'), which have been legally prohibited. Strong preferences in recruiting, such as for graduates of a particular university at the typical graduation age, shut down opportunities for any type of 'non-traditional' student in less dominating organisations (for Japan, Brinton 2011; for U.S. top consulting firms, Rivera 2011). The changes in union power, internal labour markets and human-resource management and development practices resulted in strictly defined career ladders giving way to more adaptable trajectory systems that emphasise individual capacities and motivation to contribute and develop rather than filling pre-structured schemes. However, new flexibility comes at a price; it reduces job security and the occurrence of lifelong employment patterns within one organisation. Organisational behaviour allows for more life-course flexibility and also follows the deeply ingrained values of individual opportunity and well-being that gained ground in the prosperous periods from the 1960s onwards. However, remarkable differences still exist between countries and sectors, developments even include trends for more career rigidity. Evidence indicates that overall flexibility of career patterns is larger in the United States and in Great Britain, more restricted (in particular, mid-career onwards) in countries such as Germany or Austria and comparably low in France. Japan is the extreme case of low career flexibility within the more privileged segment of the labour market.

(E) Recognition/Institutionalisation of formal adult education within career patterns

As we have seen, countries clearly differ in the extent to which various career patterns require formal adult education. Obviously, formal adult education plays an important role in professions in all countries. However, formal adult education could become institutionalised within established organisational career patterns (such as ritually following promotion to upper management with an offer to participate in continuing higher education) and, even more likely, within occupational career patterns. For the latter, the craft master examination provides the most significant example. When formal adult education is established within a career pattern, than an individual following a particular career sequence will also choose an expected type of formal adult education. For example, in the USA, formal adult education became widely institutionalised in an ever-expanding number of professional and para-professional fields that require licensing (Baker 2011). In Germany or Austria, formal adult education is clearly established within occupational careers. In Japan, by contrast, highly developed sequences of on-the-job and off-the-job training within internal labour markets of large employers are not organised as formal adult education at all.

(F) Fundamental changes over time in educational provision (intra-/intergenerational change)

Formal adult education is clearly a way for making up for an opportunity missed at the typical age for participation and also for reacting to dramatically shifting qualification structures. The dynamic of educational expansion and fundamental shifts in educational policies and/or government systems may substantially change the accessibility of higher secondary or tertiary education. From 1950 to 2010, older cohorts may have had much less educational opportunities then younger cohorts. Formal adult education may provide a way to overcome the disadvantage of belonging to a particular cohort or 'generation'. To understand differences in country patterns in participation in formal adult education, it is important to consider substantial shifts in availability of educational opportunities. The 'GI Bill' in the USA that allowed (non-black) veterans access to higher education is an important historical example for a structure changing power and resulting in a generational effect in participation in formal adult education (Bound & Turner 2002). Restrictive regulation and the consequent contraction of higher education in the early 1970s in at that time communist countries (Reisz & Stock 2006) – paired with the strong competition on domestic labour markets – form a background for expanding participation in higher education of adults in these societies. Consequently, adults frequently take advantage of educational opportunities unknown when they had been in the 'typical' age of participation.

Overview 22: Dimensions shaping the opportunity structure for formal adult education

	Guiding questions and examples for sub-dimensions
A. Availability and Accessibility	How many programmes are available? How accessible are programmes? - establishment of particular programmes/organisations for adults - open/restrictive policies of organisations in initial education - formal requirements for entrance - selectivity/competition for entrance of favourable programmes/organisations
B. Rigidity and Selectivity	How high/low is the likeliness of success and failure? What is the range of performance acceptable? - retention and success rates of programmes in formal adult education - selectivity and rate of drop-outs in initial education
C. Public support for participation	How many resources are provided for organisations catering for adults? How many resources are provided to adults for co-financing tuition fees, living costs and social-security payments? - Extension of free/low fee programmes - Availability of grant, co-financing and credit schemes - Educational leave schemes
D. Flexibility of career trajectories	How easily can an adult take a break or make a change of his/her occupational career? How many points of entry into organisational career pattern are foreseen? - in/flexibility of institutionalised hiring routines (nature of internal labour markets) - preference orders for desirable/undesirable career patterns - openness/closeness of vacancy chains
E. Recognition/Institutionalisation with career patterns	How are formal qualifications used within career patterns? Are there particular qualifications available by formal adult education only? Are particular programmes firmly institutionalised within established career patterns?
F. Change in educational provision (intra-/intergenerational change)	Has accessibility of advanced education changed within a generations' (economically active) lifetime? Has accessibility changed within consecutive cohorts/generations? - presence/absence of fundamental changes in political systems or the orientation of the education system - timing of phases of growth or decline in specific economic or societal sectors

Source: Own description

The selected dimensions contribute to the societal opportunity structure for formal adult education. Even the first short review has made clear that high participation in the U.S. as well as low participation in Japan correspond with features that expand or limit the opportunity structure for formal adult education. Let us conclude with summaries for the 'extreme cases' of the USA and Japan.

The United States has clearly and extensively defined its formal – degree-awarding or credentialed – adult education; the number of adults returning to certified programmes with high workloads seems to be the highest in the world. With abundant programmes available for adults, the highly inclusive education system with its 'contest' oriented, meritocratic philosophy (Turner 1960), invites anybody to stay as long as possible in their individually desired programme. The firmly institutionalised life-course repertoire includes returning to education during adult life (Hostetler et al. 2007). The substantial public support funds the public system of two-year community colleagues and four-year colleges. The private contributions required are typically much higher than in most European countries, yet reflect societal norms of paying individually for education beyond high school. The flexibility of career trajectories is high, even in the core primary segment of the labour market. The declining importance of organisational career patterns in internal labour market have been balanced by a strong increase of 'licensed' employees, belonging to various traditional, new or para-professions. The institutionalisation of formal adult education follows two main routes. On the one hand, a societal enforcement of the value of educational credentials urges employers to take any credential seriously. However, the large differences in prestige of credentials on the same educational level, awarded by different educational organisations, subvert the basis for a strong programme-employment link, at least for degrees of 'less-selective' providers (Baker 2011). On the other hand, the strong trend toward professionalisation and licensing clearly increased the institutionalised use of formal programmes for access and progress in professional careers. Intergenerational expansion in access to higher education is still large, in particular for formerly discriminated against minority groups (Attewell & Lavin 2007). High participation in formal adult education, consequently, results from the highly supportive conditions related to any of the six dimensions outlined.

In Japan, the interlocked institutional environments leave little space for formal adult education. Adult education is clearly restricted to the sphere of leisure and individual improvement; yet mostly excludes both formal and vocational education. Formal adult education (with a 'charter') is not used as a concept, although an extended system of examinations allows for acquiring (narrowly defined) qualifications on defined levels of competence such as in a particular foreign language: however, courses are clearly divided between those preparing for the examinations and the 'formal' programmes that award valued educational credentials. Based on near-to universal, higher-secondary education, Japan already reached universal higher education in 1993; more than 70 percent of a cohort participated in two-year or four-year higher education programmes. Yet universal inclusion is combined with a steep stratification of schools and universities according to prestige; schools are ranked based on their institutionalised linkage, either to prestigious educational organisations or to prestigious major employers that offer lifetime employment, extensive further training and extended career opportunities. Educational processes focus on preparing for highly competitive entrance examinations for the more promising high schools and universities: non-traditional adult students have virtually no chance for winning a place in prestigious institution (Fuwa 2001, 133). Employers use schools and universities as 'selection machines' and trust the recommendations of head teachers and professors with regard to applicants: educational organisations directly negotiate the placement of their graduates with the core segment of the labour market, that is the entrance position in a large corporation. Beyond the procedures for direct placement, educational credentials have clearly restricted value; moreover, they represent mainly a position within a league table, ranking students according to their alleged abilities and, consequently, their 'trainability'. They represent less a set of knowledge, skills or competences valued in its own right: formal adult education hardly allows for a 'second chance' in the difficult competition within a cohort. Vocational education and further training for the various positions within lifetime careers with one organisation are provided by combining workplace learning, on-the-job training and extended off-the-job training provided by employer-run, educational organisations. Large employers in manufacturing, yet, also in public service as health or education run their particular professional education systems (known as *Kigyounai kyouki*, see Fuwa 2001, 128). 'Formal' qualifications earned in continuing education play virtually no role. Consequently, formal adult education cannot claim much of a social charter. Career pathways within the large co-operation are strongly age-graded, allowing for little variants for first entrance. Yet, age-graded, career pathways represent only an example for still highly normative, life-course patterns with a "right" age for anything: education, career entrance, marriage and a first child. Only very recently, the strictness of norms ruling the life course – and gender relations – have begun to erode, reflecting a major crisis in the social reproduction of the Japanese society (Brinton 2011). The highly competitive pathways in adolescence divide the society in 'successful' and 'failing' individuals, recommending the latter to accept their faith – the social withdrawal of quite a large proportion of the Japanese youth is a reaction to a future without opportunities (Furlong 2008).

All six dimensions shaping the opportunity structures for formal adult education are interacting and constraining each other. To study the institutionalisation of formal adult education within career patterns ('social charter'), we need therefore to study local, organisational field-specific settings in their relative, limited autonomy to the backdrop of more general institutional structures dominating in one country.

Finally, while reflecting the importance of *country-level* structures, the local levels – with considerable independence – are determining the opportunity structures, the institutional processes creating both formal programmes, their charter, their use within organisation and consequently their potential roles within individual life courses. To understand formal adult education within one country – and consequently for cross-country comparison – we must return to the organisational fields creating formal adult education as addressed by the typology of formal adult education in Section 3.6. These organisational fields – the companies of an organisational populations and the organisations completing the organisational set – make up the particular charter of formal education.

Institutional drivers for formal adult education do not only evolve within individual societies, but also from evolving patterns of world culture that drive transnational institutional processes by directly affecting relevant organisational fields. When studying the persistence of national patterns of institutionalising the education-employment link, we must not ignore the effects coming from world cultural process (Wiseman & Baker 2006 for a review). Opportunity structures for formal adult education are obviously different and are likely to remain so across countries. However, all over the world, the belief in education as the defining criteria for adulthood, personal agency and legitimate access to social position is continually gaining ground; with this belief comes the increasing power of global policy prescriptions for governing education and lifelong learning. National systems could be expected to comply with international prescriptions on a symbolic level in a first step, for example, by awarding formal status for nonformal educational activities or by moving the line between post-secondary and higher education. Yet, any institutional change – however symbolic in nature and decoupled from a more powerful core – seems likely to produce long-run consequences: In the middle of a worldwide revolution of the cognitive models that societies apply to their education systems, we should expect formal adult education to be a highly dynamic field for the next few years. Roughly a century after the appearance of its early institutional forms and four decades after its invention as a category for statistical use, the very meaning of formal adult education is on its way to a transformation that we know little about yet. Crafting comprehensive comparative frameworks, while concomitantly observing world-level institutional processes (Chabbott 2003, Jakobi 2009, Wiseman 2010), seems the only way to observe, explain, understand, assess and finally consciously govern this ongoing change process.

Chapter 7: Conclusions and outlook

EURYDICE's report (2011) *Adults in Formal Education – Policies and Practices in Europe* marks a recent peak in a renewed interest, observable since about 2005, in formal adult education on a European policy level. Already in 2007, the Action Plan on Adult Learning *It is always a good time to learn* (European Commission 2007), proclaims as a key goal: 'to increase the opportunities for adults to achieve a qualification at least one level higher than before (to go 'one step up')' (EURYDICE 2011, 3). While I was writing this book, many European countries have acted in line with these goals (University of Florence et al. 2010). The goal obviously refers to the European Union's definition of formal adult education: "*education provided in the system of schools, colleges, universities and other formal educational institutions that normally constitutes a continuous 'ladder' of full-time education*" (EUROSTAT 2006, 13) and labels as 'adult' anybody 25 years or older or anybody who has once left school. The vagueness of the definition, which covers highly different types of educational programmes and courses in various member states, implies no obstacle for setting the agenda. On the contrary, as in other fields and as the basis for the 'open method of coordination' (Broek et al. 2010), the vagueness of concepts and indicators allow common policies to be more easily created. It allows for compromises, even when differing in key issues, as everyone finds sufficient leeway for achieving a solution in line with the own preferences. Countries only agree to the common cause as they are allowed to continue in line with their particular understanding of what counts as formal adult education and how it should be promoted; this secures progress towards common goals without requiring – at least in the short run – any fundamental change. Consequently, all countries may promote formal adult education, yet, actually, offer types of instruction representing different local understandings and institutional frameworks. Any statistical representation of 'progress made' will suffer from the paradox of 'comparing the non-comparable' (Maurice 2000); yet this does not hinder the political process.

However, some people argue for dismissing the allegedly incurably blurred 'formal/nonformal' distinction with respect to both 'adult learning' (Colley et al. 2003) and 'taught courses' (Hoppers 2006). Authors of EURYDICE 2011 are somewhat resigned to the fact that differences in understanding of formal adult education are too large to know anything for sure. Moreover, the very idea of 'formal programmes' strictly defined by the state, authoritative providers and standardised curricula seems at odds with much of current educational thought and policies. Today's approaches focus more on learner-centred flexibility and less on provider-governed standardisation, towards more emphasis on output standards and less on curricula input as well as towards more enforcement of modularisation and accreditation of prior learning and less mandatory attendance of entire study programmes.

I strongly argue for sticking to a revised conception of formal adult education that points to highly important aspects at the heart of any understanding of lifelong learning. Certainly, if we dismiss the formal/nonformal distinction for types of education, we would urgently need to recreate an analytical category that could catch the differences between 'any' course and educational programmes with a particular mission. I have proposed to understand and define formal adult education as a social institution. As an institution, formal adult education allows for *taking steps* in adulthood within the social space, by *providing eligibility* for *movements up* or *entering in established career ladders* that *use formal educational qualifications* as defining criteria.

I have proposed in Chapter 3 to reactivate John W. Meyers (1970) concept of the 'social charter' of educational programmes for marking exactly their institutional power to support access to particular social trajectories. Any 'programme' is expected – by parents and students, by future employers and co-workers, by various other institutional players from labour courts to business-interest organisations and trade unions – to typically prepare for sets of 'occupational careers'. Not demonstrated ability, but a shared expectation on what a programme actually prepares for (and graduates are authorised to do) becomes the basis for individual eligibility to enter careers and ascend the available career ladders. These expectations are deeply grounded within societies; they rest on regulative, normative and cognitive structures. One may privately doubt a programme's 'social charter', but this matters little for its societal consequences (Meyer 1977). In brief, I would therefore define 'formal adult education' as adult education with a 'social charter'. To test the 'formal quality', we could ask for the set of careers that the programmes make eligible.

I have shown that formal adult education partakes in the institutional patterns established by the initial education systems. As for initial education, the social charter of educational opportunities in formal adult education results from the particular *institutionalised* use of credentials in career patterns. (The use of qualification results from a complex historical process that reflects both outcomes of social struggles between social classes and more fundamental changes in the process of modernisation.) However, we have seen three reasons that formal adult education is not a simple apex to initial education.

- On the *individual level*, participation of adults is at odds with various elements of the 'moral order' of schools (see Chapter 4). Returning to education has to be integrated into an adult *life structure*, typically determined by gainful work and family obligations. The necessary changes in life structure will turn formal adult education into a personally significant life event; something not usually expected for participating in any nonformal course. Furthermore, adults have already taken a place within society; formal adult education could not simply 'place' them, as initial education typically can. A tension exists between a programme's social charter, the learner's acquired identity and those in the relevant social environments, who have to adopt to a learner's new ambitions and social status institutionally granted by a programme.

- On the level of the *employing organisation*, I demonstrated in Chapter 6 that a balance is required between an institutionalised use of qualification available by formal adult education and a flexibility of career patterns. Otherwise, there is little place for the formal programmes' 'social charter' beyond the fact that participants might have improved their knowledge and skills as expected for any form of instruction. Moreover, as explored in Chapter 5, employers have to deal with their employees' desire to return to education, which is no rare event at all and even more likely to occur for particular age groups (25–40) and occupational groups. However, firms could also profit from combining work with formal education instead of the 'learn first, work later' scheme common for initial education.

- On the level of the *educational providers*, outlined in Section 3.6, various types of formal adult education and their organisational fields typically expand the scope of educational opportunities available within the initial education system. Therefore, the analytical tools developed for 'schooling' are not sufficient for analysing formal adult education. Some types of formal adult education as 'second-chance education' (II) and 'higher education for non-traditional students' (III) are strongly merged with initial education. While other types such as (I) 'Basic skills and remedy programmes, (V) 'Customised vocational/professional programmes for organisations' (VI) 'Continuing professional education' have clearly a more distinct institutional logic and identity: they achieve their 'social charter' in more specific – up to now, under-researched – ways and not by copying institutionalised patterns of initial education.

I have argued that we cannot understand formal adult education in isolation, we have to address it as a total social fact (Berger & Luckmann 1967, 187). We need to craft multilevel frameworks that include the micro level – the individual learners and their life structures; the meso level – educational providers and employing organisations and associated organisational fields; and the macro level – the interaction between various 'societal fields' as well as the exchange between country level and world-cultural developments. My book provides an outline for such a multilevel framework; to further develop the framework, we need studies with more details that focus on single levels and sub-sections.

Social institutions are said to provide collective answers to previously unsolved societal problems: If formal adult education is a social institution, then what problems does it resolve? In this book, I have developed proposals that point in two related directions, which reflect the ambivalent status of education as the most important criteria for social stratification in modern societies. First, formal adult education helps to overcome some limitations of the youth-centred, mandatory educational system; however, it also exacerbates some of its problematic consequences. Second, formal adult education expands the institutional basis for forging compromises in industrial conflict, potentially adding to a 'beneficial constraint' on the side of employers requiring them to value qualification (Streeck 1997).

First, formal adult education helps to solve some problems created by the rise of the education system. I have shown (Section 2.1) that the opposition between 'formal education' and 'adult education' historically arose late in the 19th century with the systematisation of education and the strong enforcement of the link between 'credentials' and privileged 'careers'. When social advancement became possible with the help of formal education, the new possibilities for young people limited the opportunities for anyone past the 'correct' time. The prerogatives of the newly enforced 'formal education system' pressed adult education to go for what remains: education for individual enlightenment and pleasure without any promise for career advancement and upward social mobility. Formal adult education, consequently, has to be invented for offering a 'second chance' for adults to receive from education what education has become able to do: provide eligibility for taking steps on institutionalised ladders of social and career mobility.

The reopening of access to formal education for adults and the creating of particular forms of formal adult education starting in the early 20th century mark the rise of a new type of social institution. Formal adult education refers to this type of new social institution, caught quite uncomfortably between two stools, initial education here, and adult education there. Formal adult education, moreover, remains ambivalent, as it sanctifies and extends the stratification power of the education system: All non-participating adults have to accept their ineligibility for social progress granted to successful participants. Individual social mobility – as highlighted by literature on 'second chance education' of the 1970s (for example, Albrecht-Heide 1974) – comes at the price of legitimating the education system despite its failure to provide equal opportunities to all and to allow for individual and collective emancipation. Class, race and gender-bound social disadvantages, the 'long arm of the family', having subverted equal opportunity in initial education, are found at work again in 'formal adult education', which seems to complete the work of social exclusion of the school system instead of effectively correcting it (Elman & O'Rand 2004, 2007, Hillmert & Jacob 2008, Jacob & Weiss 2011). Paradoxically, an institution, which can effectively help adults with a background of low social status to acquire higher levels of education later in life, is used more often by descendents of well-off families, who have missed a first chance that they thought of as quite naturally theirs. Therefore, while partly a remedy to the social bias and the youth-centred nature of the all-powerful, initial-education system, formal adult education aggravates social injustice instilled by the system. The tension between 'access for all' and reliance on selection and 'social closure' remains central for formal adult education.

As a social institution of its own, different from 'initial education' as well as from 'adult education', formal adult education, consequentially answers problems created by the institutionalisation of youth-centred formal education as the dominating criteria for social placement and progression. It aims at making up for some of the flexibility lost in the institutionalisation of education. It gives back to adults the opportunities lost by the enforcement of formal qualifications. Consequently, formal adult education is instruction for adults that emulates the institutional logics of education as a key social institution and not – as nonformal education has been proclaimed to be – their more appropriate alternative.

Second, formal adult education responds to the societal problem that individuals have no guarantee that their abilities, skills and competences are honoured when working; their skills might become exploited without any compensation. Formal adult education, therefore, contributes to a larger mechanism that uses educational qualifications as a tool for moderating the asymmetry of power within the employment relationship; it constrains the employer's choices in organising work and provides compensation for skills and competences that employees brought into the work process. It adds to qualifications and their institutionalised use for *collectively* securing fair compensation for skills and competencies and individual efforts to develop them.

The 'taken for granted' stratification power of education builds on the institutionalisation of qualifications as a means to control work and wage structures within the industrial conflict. Beyond 'human capital' processes and its market mechanisms that pays for 'productivity gained' and (temporary) 'scarceness' (Rubinson & Brown 1994), the industrial relations system may guarantee that formal qualifications pay off for the individual. Scholars of industrial relations see formal educational qualifications – and consequently, formal adult education as one means among others of acquiring them – as obviously playing a key role in the conflict between capital and labour. As soon as skilled labour is not scarce – reflecting state-funded expansion of educational provision – employers will not pay any skill premium and will exploit the workers' need to work at any rate. Only collective strategies of the employees and their institutional outcomes – from labour laws to collective wage-setting mechanisms – effectively limit employers in using this power. Interest groups could use formal educational qualifications as a basis for enforcing ways to organise work (allowing for using the qualification) and for guaranteeing higher minimum wages reflecting their efforts to become qualified. Those who have earned a formal qualification, should be neither impeded in applying their skills in the workplace, nor abused in their vocational dignity or paid at a rate as low as for workers without qualification.

Formal adult education, consequently, helps provide the infrastructure for working out temporary compromises in the ongoing conflict between the parties of the employment contract, yet also among various competing business-interests groups. Given the deep legal, normative and cognitive institutionalisation of formal education, which legitimately 'makes a difference', formal adult education could not be understood without reflecting on the role of formal qualifications for collectively controlling work, careers and wage setting. One may learn exactly the same things in a nonformal and a formal programme: however, only the latter is typically linked to the collectively secured rights of employees against their employers.

Consequently, the institutionalisation of formal adult education is not a zero-sum game between participants and non-participants, where the latter lose what the former gain. Formal qualifications are at the heart of many collective strategies for defending the dignity of work and securing stable, lifetime incomes vis-a-vis employers' opposing interests. The societal effects of the interplay between initial education, (formal) adult education and career trajectories – as demonstrated by comparing Germany to France – could hardly be overestimated, as they potentially produce different types of income and welfare distributions or even different societies. The logics of educational expansions – as Meyer 1977 argued forcefully – is not limited to games of status competition between graduates 'queuing for jobs'. It could contribute to an institutional infrastructure that could clearly limit employers' disposal over the 'work force', yet, as a 'beneficial constraint' (Streeck 1997), generate space for individual, organisational and societal development.

'Formal' adult education forces us to take seriously the institutional regulations and the societal conflicts about employment relationships – an effort we are typically not inclined to do when reflecting on nonformal education. The somewhat comfortable disciplinary division of labour between 'educationalists' and 'political economist' does not work at all for formal adult education; to understand the meaning and functioning of the institution, we must study both sides of the education/work schism. By analysing the rise of formal adult education as a social institution, we also study changes in what employers are allowed or not allowed to do. Pressuring for higher demands of formal qualification is not only a means for 'status competition' between social class fractions, but a strategy for improving the collective power of employees when meeting their employers. The expansion of the use of formal educational qualifications, fuelled by formal adult education, implies not only *horizontal* 'social closure', where participants have advantages over non-participants, but a *vertical* 'social closure' (Pernicka & Lücking 2012), where groups of employees use educational qualifications to organise and collectively limit employers' omnipotence. While these arguments are expressed in various ways (Fligstein & Byrkjeflot 1996) and are hardly a new insight for the fields of industrial relations and the sociology of labour markets, it is widely absent in the exploration of adult education and lifelong learning. Arguments for 'social closure' as a way for constraining employers' choice and securing individual rights are marginalised in the sociology of education; they have even been forgotten in the study of formal adult education. The radical implications of this view, stated in Meyer 1977 and recently emphasised by Baker 2011, that 'formal adult education' for all may allow for expanding individually guaranteed rights for everyone (while employers might adapt well to the 'constraints' imposed on them) help to counterbalance the image of the 'great training robbery' (Berg & Govelick 1970), where credential inflation (Dore 1976) destroys any basis for individual participants' hopes for profiting from his or her engagement.

To summarise, to study formal adult education as a social institution, we have to deal with its ambivalence, as it allows for:

1. overcoming adults' limited career perspectives and opportunities for change created by institutionalizing youth-centered formal education as the core principle for social selection and stratification;

2. adding to qualifications available for collectively limiting employer's disposal over individual workers' skills and careers and for securing the dignity of (qualified) work that supports more stable career patterns and enforcing fair compensation.

Based on an understanding of formal adult education as a particular social institution, I would like to suggest four ways ahead.

First, to improve our research, we need to achieve a better measurement of formal adult education that is independent of country-specific conventions drawing the line between 'formal' and 'nonformal'. Certainly, any independent measurement of formal adult education is only a transitional, but indispensible stage, for comparative research, because our study should include country-specific perceptions of formal/nonformal. By plotting national data to the backdrop of this new standard, we could learn about the country-specific understanding of 'formal' qualities, something which is hardly achievable at the moment. Diagram 5 in Section 3.7 illustrates my argument for a reclassification. All learning programmes, typified by national conventions into formal and nonformal, should be relabelled according to the questions of whether they include a sufficient workload (using the UOE criteria for half a year of fulltime education) and whether they own a 'social charter' of substantial force. Identifying the social charter implies explaining the institutional mechanisms at work for securing the social charter and the organisational fields involved in 'crafting' the particular charter. Clearly, formal programmes according to national convention may fail the criteria, while programmes defined as nonformal may pass the test and become labelled as formal. By developing a new approach for statistical measurement, following this proposal – for example, to be used within the European Adult Education Survey – we would receive a new basis for cross-country, comparative research and consequently the opportunity for observing the rather heterogeneous components of formal adult education. By clarifying the social charter, we would certainly further develop a typology of formal adult education and collect, consequently, data for the various, rather different types of formal adult education in place.

Secondly, by reflecting on the social charter and how it is achieved at what costs for whom, we would improve our understanding of a challenge at the core of any practical field of adult education: How could the social acceptance of an educational programme and its certificate be socially secured in the relevant fields? It is considerably easy to combine teaching input into an educational programme; it is harder to arrange educational resources in a way that average participants successfully achieve agreed-on leaning outcomes found valuable by the participants and by future employers. It is a particular challenge to arrange for a learning outcome to be valued on an institutional basis. Many well-intended programmes supporting disadvantaged groups in the labour market fail to achieve the 'social charter' guaranteeing their participants better jobs and higher wages. Various newly created programmes in continuing higher education, allegedly responding to the labour market, fail to secure acceptance for their 'credentials', while exploiting their symbolic status and the trust of their (paying) participants. Given the priority of 'formal adult education' within the political agenda for lifelong learning, it is necessary to develop a test for the 'formal' qualities beyond the defining power of public authorities or marketing strategies of resourceful providers. When lifelong learning policy aims to support social (upwards) mobility by promoting formal adult education, one must make sure to choose programmes that deliver what has been promised: providing eligibility for taking steps. When policy aims to promote equal opportunity and social cohesion by access to formal adult education, it is important to observe not only participation as such, but also the access of vulnerable groups to programmes powerful enough to make an institutional difference beyond individual learning.

Thirdly, we need to reflect ongoing changes in the ways that formal education is institutionalised and their possible consequences for formal adult education. Formal schooling continually changes, yet several more recent reform processes may deeply change the ways in which education and formal adult education will actually function. School governance is said to rely less on curricular and inputs and more on standards and outcomes. However, countries differ widely in this respect: the individualised learning pathways allow for change between programmes, modular qualifications, and the accumulation of learning credits not bound to one or even any educational provider. Learning, not instruction, is important; this change breaks ground for accrediting prior (informal) learning. Various new instruments improve the transparency of qualifications; these replace state-governed, more rigid qualification spaces, where credentials have been controlled and rationed like a currency. European and transnational policies unanimously present themselves in accordance with a functional-human-capital understanding of the education-employment link: within a knowledge economy, skills are thought to be naturally valued and qualifications make skills *visible* to prospect employers, paying wages reflecting their exact 'marginal utility' in undisturbed market surroundings. Consequently, this downplays the institutional dimension of the education-work link and the codependencies of the education and skill-formation system, the employment system, the industrial relations, the gender regime and the welfare state. One assumes that there *must* be no difference between a qualification earned in school and a qualification awarded in a credit-based model, as both allegedly only point to an innate ability, certified by an achievement standard. The difficulty lies in distinguishing between ideological claims and actual changes of the institutional foundations of education and consequently formal adult education. Outcome standards and outcome testing independent of individual schools (Kamens & McNeely 2010) instead of curricula governance may or may not alter the institutional logics of schools: in any case, the school someone has attended obviously will imply institutional consequences. Changing rules of the game may alter institutional effects; however, little evidence exists for the loss of relevance for the institutional effects of education – beyond any learning achieved by its participants. Differences between societies – for example, in the meaning of qualification for the labour market – provoke paradoxical consequences, when innovations – such as the implementation of standard-based examinations, accreditation of prior learning or qualification frameworks – imply contradictory change processes and are followed by contradictory (and often no) outcomes. However, as we have seen, some of the institutional innovations – for example, the rise of credit-based qualifications or the creation of qualification frameworks – immediately imprint the national understanding of formal adult education, pointing once more towards the need for a measure independent of any country's conventions.

My final point refers to the dynamic relationship between country-level, societal processes and transnational, world-cultural institutional processes. Formal adult education, following initial education, is also a transnational phenomenon, a multiple-differentiated, social institution diffusing around the globe and an outflow of the globalisation of education policy. Individuals are institutionally constructed as striving for progress and social mobility, accepting education as a basic means to do so (Meyer & Jepperson 2000). Much of the institutional dynamic shaping segments of formal adult education likely results from global institutional processes that shape shared beliefs on the value of education, individual goals and the needs of organisations. Societal level changes in formal adult education may be only loosely attached to local frameworks, yet respond to institutional pressures to comply with world prescriptions. The interdependencies and dialectics between societal differences and global institutional models are at the heart of current debates in cross-country comparative research (Anderson-Levitt 2003, Djelic & Sahlin-Andersson 2006, Morgan et al. 2010). While it is crucial to understand the worldwide expansion of the 'education gospel' (Grubb & Lazerson 2004) and the belief in the sacred power of education to overcome all woes, it is nevertheless important to reconstruct the actual source of education's 'institutional power'. Societies differ widely in the institutions creating the power of education and consequently in their likely faith in any further educational expansion – including formal adult education. So while no revival of a 'de-schooling' discourse is in sight, taking seriously the institutional components of the power of education allows for more fine-grained critical analysis. For education, formal adult education or lifelong learning to fulfil its high expectations requires collective actors fighting for their cause, renewing old or achieving new political compromises, and crafting institutional links between education and work that make education count.

The European Union's 'Action Plan on Adult Learning' – without reflecting too much on the category of formal adult education and its considerable challenges – has promoted adult education as a way 'to go one step up', a tool for 'taking steps'. With this goal, it touched the heart of a promise made by education in modern societies: that we can turn to education for achieving our dreams. This promise in its valid, rational yet also in its and its mythological and ideological components is irrevocably ingrained in the foundation of formal adult education. Research on formal education needs carefully to consider what opportunities are at stake and what illusions have to be disappointed. For this, further improving an institutional view on formal adult education seems to me the most promising way forward.

8 Annex

8.1 The LLL2010 Project

This book builds on research done within the project *'Lifelong Learning 2010: Towards a Lifelong Learning Society in Europe: The Contribution of the Education System'*. The project, coordinated by Ellu Saar (Institute for International and Social Studies, Tallinn University) had been funded within the European Union's Sixth Framework Programme (FP6) by the European Commission. The large-scale project with a total budget of about six million euros lasted from 2005 to 2011 and consisted of five substantial subprojects. Teams from thirteen European countries contributed to the project. Countries and research organisations included Austria (Danube-University Krems), Belgium/Flanders (Catholique University of Louvain), Bulgaria (Institute of Sociology Sofia), Czech Republic (The National Training Fund), England (University of Nottingham), Estonia (Tallinn University), Hungary (Tárki Social Research Institute), Ireland (Dublin City University), Lithuania (Mykolas Romeris University Vilnius), Norway (Institute for Labour and Social Research (Fafo)), Russia (St. Petersburg State University), Scotland (University of Edinburgh), Slovenia (Slovenian Institute for Adult Education (SIAE)). Detailed information on the project, the subprojects, its products and publications, as well as the organisations and researchers involved can be found on the LLL2010 homepage (http://lll2010.tlu.ee) and in the final project report: *Saar, Ellu & Roosalu, Triin (2011) Towards a Lifelong Learning Society in Europe: The Role of Education Systems – Results from multilevel mixed methods analysis of different aspects in learning as an adult in Europe – LLL2010 Integrated report. Tallinn.*

Key results of the research project are collected in the following two edited volumes:

- Riddell, Sheila, Markowitsch, Jörg & Weedon, Elisabet (Eds.) (2012) *Lifelong Learning in Europe: Equity and Efficiency in the Balance*, Bristol, Policy Press.

- Saar, Ellu, Ure, Odd Bjorn & Holford, John (Eds.) (2012, forthcoming) *Lifelong Learning in Europe: National Patterns and Challenges*, Cheltenham Edward Elgar.

The following section provides a short introduction of the project's five subprojects and selected outcomes; it also highlights publications based on the subprojects. The final project report (Saar & Roosalu 2011) provides an exhaustive list of publications based on the project's results. Subproject 4 and its methods (for which I was responsible) is described in more detail, as the book is mainly built on its results.

Subproject 1 – Review of recent LLL policies in thirteen countries

Based on literature surveys and document analysis, the current LLL policy context in thirteen countries had been revised and analysed in country reports. The synthesis of these reports is – beyond a project report – available as *Holford, John, Riddell, Sheila, Weedon, Elisabet, Litjens, Judith & Hannan, Guy (2008) Patterns of Lifelong Learning – Policy & Practice in an Expanding Europe, Vienna, Münster, LIT.*

Subproject 2 – Cross-country comparative analysis of European micro-data sets on formal adult education

Two micro-data sets – the Ad hoc module of the Labour Force Survey on Lifelong Learning 2003 and the first Adult Education Survey 2005–2007 – have been analysed for participation in formal adult education for all countries, covered by the data sets. (Due to delayed data availability, the subproject had been postponed to the final phase of the project). Methods used include descriptive statistics and regression models. Results are available in a synthesis report: *Hefler, Günter, Róbert, Péter, Ringler, Paul, Sági, Matild, Rammel, Stephanie, Balogh, Anikó & Markowitsch, Jörg (2011) Formal adult education in Context – The view of European Statistics – SP 2 – Synthesis Report – LLL2010 project. Krems, Danube University Krems – TARKI.*

Subproject 3 – Survey on participants in formal adult education

A large-scale, quantitative survey – based mainly on a written questionnaire, yet including some groups of learners with semi-structured, face-to-face interviews – was implemented in all participating countries, aiming at including at least 1000 participants per country, covering all ISCED levels relevant for formal adult education in the various countries. The questionnaire covered – beyond information on social statistics – items on attitudes towards lifelong learning and the assessment of the current formal programmes. An additional survey collected information on the educational organisations offering formal adult education. Each country drafted a report. A comparative report is available: *Boeren, Ellen, Roosmaa, Eve-Liis, Saar, Ellu and & Nicaise, Ides (2011) Adult Learners in formal adult education – Experience and Perceptions – Subproject 3 Comparative Report. Sixth FP Integrated Project no.: 513321 Towards a Lifelong Learning Society in Europe: The Contribution of the Education System (LLL2010). Leuven & Tallinn.*

Subproject 4 – Company case studies on the use of formal adult education within small and medium enterprises

Partners' teams implemented in twelve out of the thirteen countries (except for the Czech Republic), six to eight qualitative case studies on the use of formal adult education in small and medium enterprises. They followed a common methodological approach, developed by the Austrian team, accessible in three working papers on the project's homepage (Markowitsch & Hefler 2008b, c and d).

For case studies, small and medium enterprises (with less than 250 employees and not owned by larger corporations) belonging to two broad groups of sectors (selected fields of manufacturing; selected fields of business-to-business services, for details see Markowitsch & Hefler 2008b) had been contacted, where at least one (preferably more than one) employee participates in formal adult education. For the case studies, one to two members of the management and one or two – occasionally even more – participants in formal adult education had been interviewed, based on a commonly agreed, semi-structured interview guideline, translated in local language. All interviews had been fully transcribed. National teams provided case studies (in English) on the interviews and analysis of available documentation as well as a national report, discussing case studies in context. Based on case studies and country report, I have written a synthesis report: Hefler, Günter (2010) The qualification-supporting company – The Significance of Formal Adult Education in Small and Medium Organisations – Comparative Report – Subproject 4 – LLL2010 Status: Version 2.0, Krems: Danube University Krems, which has become the nucleus of the current book. All material is available at the project homepage.

The public has access to case studies, based on 243 interviews, for 86 enterprises, covering 126 individual participants in formal adult education. The length of the case studies varies between 6–15 pages. Overview 23 is taken from a concise summary of the empirical work available in the final project report (Saar & Rossalu, Section 3.2.3).

Overview 23: Number of case studies and interviews per country

	Total of country case studies	10–19	20–49	50–99	100–249	250–499	Number of interviews total	Number of interviewed participants
Austria	8	1	1	1	4	1	19	10
Belgium	8	2	1	2	1	2	23	10
Bulgaria	7	2	0	1	4	0	24	9
England	6	0	2	3	1	0	16	7
Estonia	7	3	2	1	1	0	22	12
Hungary	6	1	2	2	1	0	14	6
Ireland	6	1	3	0	2	0	12	6
Lithuania	12	7	0	0	5	0	24	18
Norway	6	0	3	0	1	2	21	11
Russia	6	1	2	1	2	0	16	9
Scotland	6	1	2	2	0	1	24	12
Slovenia	8	1	0	3	4	0	28	16
total	86	20	18	16	26	6	243	126

Source: Saar & Roosalu 2011

The selection of enterprises aimed at achieving the greatest variety of meaningful cases: participants engaged in education on different ISCED levels; they represented a wide range of backgrounds (age, migration background, minority status, language, etc.). Enterprises selected and participants included are by no means representative for all enterprises or participants in formal adult education in one country or in general. Self-selection of enterprises ready to participate clearly contributes to selection bias. We clearly over-sampled for our case studies the enterprises with management quite interested in the topic of formal adult education.

On the information available in the case studies, participation events (see Section 4.4), company's training cultures (see Section 5.3) and support patterns (see Section 5.4) has been classified independently by two researchers (Daniel Bacher, Günter Hefler). When classifications done by the two researchers differ, we reassessed cases. Where types could not be developed because of too little information, the case was excluded from the analysis.

In 89 case studies, we have sufficient information on 113 participants (41 % are women and 59 % are men). Nearly a quarter (24 %) of participants interviewed were younger than 25 at the time of interview. Another quarter (27 %) of them were between 25–29 and one third (32 %) between 30–39. Only 18 % of participants were older than 40, while none of our interviewees was older than 55. Age structure of men and women are quite identical, only the proportion of women older than 40 is slightly lower that than of men.

Ten percent of the participants interviewed start from a low educational background and have no qualification above ISCED 2 level. The largest group of participants (50 %) holds a qualification on ISCED 3 level or ISCED 4 (men: 61 %; women: 33 %). 40 % have already acquired a qualification on a higher education level (ISCED 5 or 6) before starting another round in formal adult education (men: 32 %, women: 54 %). Female participants among interviewees clearly start more often on the basis of a higher education degree than male participants.

Of the 17 % of all participants engaged in programmes offering qualifications on up to ISCED Level 3, 15 of participants are engaged in studies leading to ISCED 4. Two third of participants (67 %) enters programmes on higher education level, respectively on postgraduate level. Reflecting their higher starting position, female participants are more often engaged in postgraduate programmes than men (men: 7 %, women: 22 %).

All interviewees were employed. Their employer organisations belong either to selected sectors in manufacturing (46 % of participants) or selected sectors in services (54 % of participants). However, among female interviewees, a majority work in the service sector (72 % of women compared to 42 % of men). Employing organisations belong (mainly) to small and medium enterprises, however, the survey has voluntarily excluded micro-enterprises with less than 10 employees. About 22 % of participants work for organisations with 10–19 employees, 17 % for organisations with 20–49, 24 % for such with 50–99 and 28 % for organisation with 100–249 enterprises. 9 %

of employees work for enterprises with 250–499 employees. The size structure of the enterprises is quite similar for both sexes.

Subproject 5 – Perceptions of school officials and policy makers on access to formal adult education

196 semi-structured qualitative interviews, representing 83 educational institutions, with head teachers, school managers, policy makers and members of the educational bureaucracies had been implemented in 12 partner countries and analysed. Interviews focussed on the perceptions of access opportunities for adults to formal education. A summary report on the results is available: *Downes, Paul (2011) A Systems Level Focus on Access to Education for Traditionally Marginalised Groups in Europe: Comparing Strategies, Policy and Practice in Twelve European Countries – LLL2010 Project Report 5 – Subproject 5. Tallinn.*

8.2 References

Abbott, Andrew (1988) *The system of professions – An Essay on the division of expert labor*, University of Chicago Press, Chicago.

Acemoglu, Daron & Pischke, Jorn-Steffen (1999) Beyond Becker: Training in Imperfect Labour Markets. *The Economic Journal*, 109, F112–42.

Ahlgren, Linda, Riddell, Sheila and Weedon, Elisabet (2008a) LLL2010 – Subproject 4 – Case Study 57 – Scotland: Manufacturing Company B – Extensive in-house Work Training within a Traditionally Low-skilled Enterprise, Edinburgh: University of Edinburgh (UEDIN).

Ahlgren, Linda, Riddell, Sheila and Weedon, Elisabet (2008b) LLL2010 – Subproject 4 – Case Study 58 – Scotland: Production Company C (Business to Business) – Expansive Education but Limited Lifelong Learning in a Knowledge Intensive Organization, Edinburgh: University of Edinburgh (UEDIN).

Ahlgren, Linda, Riddell, Sheila and Weedon, Elisabet (2009) LLL2010 – Subproject 4 – Country Report Scotland: The Role of Formal Education in Workforce Development in Scotland, Edinburgh: University of Edinburgh (UEDIN).

Albrecht-Heide, Astrid (1974) *Entfremdung statt Emanzipation: Sozialisationsbedingungen des zweiten Bildungsweges*, Frankfurt/M., Athenäum-Verl.

Antikainen, Ari (1996) *Living in a learning society: life-histories, identities, and education*, London, Falmer Press.

Appelbaum, Eileen, Bailey, Thomas, Berg, Peter & Kalleberg, Arne L. (2000) *Manufacturing advantage: why high-performance work systems pay off*, Ithaca; London, IRL Press.

Arundel, Anthony, Lorenz, Edward, Lundvall, Bengt-Ake & Valeyre, Antoine (2007) How Europe's economies learn: a comparison of work organization and innovation mode for the EU-15, *Industrial and Corporate Change*, 16, 1175–1210.

Ariès, Philippe (1962) *Centuries of childhood*, London, Pimlico, 1996.

Arthur, Michael B., Hall, Douglas T. & Lawrence, Barbara S. (Eds.) (1989) *Handbook of career theory*, New York, Cambridge University Press.

Arthur, Michael B., Hall, Douglas T. & Lawrence, Barbara S. (1989) Generating new directions in career theory: the case for a transdisciplinary approach. in Arthur, Michael B., Hall, Douglas T. & Lawrence, Barbara S. (Eds.) *Handbook of career theory*. New York, Cambridge University Press, 7–25.

Ashton, David N. & Green, Francis (1996) *Education, training and the global economy*, Cheltenham, Edward Elgar.

Aslanian, Carol B. & Brickell, Henry M. (1980) *Americans in Transition – Life Changes as reasons for adult learning*, New York, College Entrance Examination Board.

Aspin, David (Ed.) (2001) *International handbook on lifelong learning*, Dordrecht [Netherlands]; London, Kluwer Academic Publishers.

Asselmeyer, Herbert (1996) *Einmal Schule – immer Schule? Eine empirische Studie zum Lernverständnis Erwachsener*, Frankfurt am Main, Peter Lang.

Attewell, Paul (1990) What is Skill? *Work and Occupations*, 17, 422–448.

Attewell, Paul A. & Lavin, David E. (2007) *Passing the torch: does higher education for the disadvantaged pay off across the generations?*, New York, Russell Sage Foundation.

Backes-Gellner, Uschi & Mure, Johannes (2005) The Skill-Weights Approach on Firm Specific Human Capital: Empirical Results for Germany – Working Paper.

Baker, David P. (2011) Forward and backward, horizontal and vertical: Transformation of occupational credentialing in the schooled society. *Research in Social Stratification and Mobility*, 29, 5–29.

Barney, Jay B. & Hesterly, William (1999) Organizational Economics: Understanding the Relation between Organizations and Economic Analysis. in Clegg, Stewart & Hardy, Cynthia (Eds.) *Studying organization: theory & method*. London, SAGE, 109–141.

Barney, Jay (1991) Firm Resources and Sustained Competitive Advantage. *Journal of Management* 17, 99–120.

Baron, James M. & Bielby, William T. (1980) Bringing the Firms Back in: Stratification, Segmentation and the Organization of Work. *American Sociological Review*, 45, 737–65.

Baron, James N. (1984) Organizational perspectives on stratification. *Annual Review of Sociology*, 10, 37–69.

Baron, James N., Dobbin, Frank R. & Jennings, P. Devereaux (1986) War and Peace: The Evolution of Modern Personnel Administration in U.S. Industry. *The American Journal of Sociology*, 92, 350–383.

Baron, James N. & Hannan, Michael T. (1994) The Impact of Economics on Contemporary Sociology. *Journal of Economic Literature*, 32, 1111–1146.

Battilana, Julie, Leca, Bernard & Boxenbaum, Eva (2009) How Actors Change Institutions: Towards a Theory of Institutional Entrepreneurship. *The Academy of Management Annals,* 3 (1), 65–107.

Baum, Joel A. C. (1999) Organizational Ecology. in Clegg, Stewart & Hardy, Cynthia (Eds.) *Studying organization: theory & method.* London, Sage, 71–108.

Baum, Joel A. C. & Shipilov, Andrew V. (2006) Ecological Approaches to Organizations. in Clegg, Stewart R., Hardy, Cynthia, Lawrence, Thomas B. & Nord, Walter R. (Eds.) *The Sage handbook of organization studies – 2nd Edition.* 2nd ed. ed. London, Sage, 55–110

Beck, Ulrich (2000) *The brave new world of work,* Cambridge, Polity Press.

Becker, Gary Stanley (1975) *Human capital – a theoretical and empirical analysis, with special reference to education,* New York, National Bureau of Economic Research.

Benavot, Aaron (1983) The Rise and Decline of Vocational Education. *Sociology of Education,* 56, 63–76.

Berg, Ivar & Govelick, Sherry (1973) *Education and jobs: the great training robbery,* Harmondsworth, Penguin Education.

Berger, Peter L. & Luckmann, Thomas (1967) *The social construction of reality. A treatise in the sociology of knowledge,* New York, Anchor books.

Bernardi, Fabrizio, Blossfeld, Hans-Peter & Mills, Melinda (Eds.) (2006) *Globalization, uncertainty and men's careers: an international comparison,* Cheltenham, Edward Elgar.

Bielby, William T. & Baron, James N. (1986) Men and Women at Work: Sex Segregation and Statistical Discrimination. *The American Journal of Sociology,* 91, 759–799.

Bishop, John H. (1988) Do Empoyers Share the Costs and Benefits of General Training? CAHRS Working Paper Series – Paper 429. Ithaca, Center for Advanced Human Resource Studies (CAHRS) – Cornell University.

Bishop, John H. & Kang, Suk (1996) Do Some Employers Share the Costs and Benefits of General Training? CAHRS Working Paper Series – Paper 188. Ithaca, Center for Advanced Human Resource Studies (CAHRS) – Cornell University.

Biesta, Gert J., Field, John, Hodkinson, Phil, Macleod, Flora J. & Goodson, Ivor F. (2011) *Improving learning through the lifecourse: learning lives,* London, Routledge.

Blossfeld, Hans-Peter & Hofmeister, Heather A. (2006) *Globalization, uncertainty and women's careers: an international comparison,* Cheltenham, Edward Elgar.

Blyton, Paul, Bacon, Nick A., Heery, Edmund & Fiorito, Jack (Eds.) (2008) *The SAGE handbook of industrial relations,* Los Angeles; London, Sage.

Bock, John C. (1976) The Institutionalization of Nonformal Education: A Response to Conflicting Needs. *Comparative Education Review,* 20, 346–367.

Boli, John & Thomas, George M. (Eds.) (1999) *Constructing World Culture – International nongovernmental organizations since 1875,* Standford, Standford University Press.

Boshier, Roger (1971) Motivational Orientations of Adult Education Participants: a Factor Analytic Exploration of Houle's Typology, *Adult Education Quarterly*, 21, 3–26.

Boshier, Roger (1976) Factor Analysts At Large: a Critical Review of the Motivational Orientation Literature. *Adult Education Quarterly*, 27, 24–47.

Boshier, Roger & Collins, John B. (1985) The Houle Typology After Twenty-Two Years: A Large-Scale Empirical Test. *Adult Education Quarterly*, 35, 113–130.

Boshier, Roger (1991) Psychometric Properties of the Alternative Form of the Education Participation Scale. *Adult Education Quarterly*, 41, 150–167.

Boshier, Roger, Huang, Yan, Song, Qihui & Song, Lei (2006) Market Socialism Meets the Lost Generation: Motivational Orientations of Adult Learners in Shanghai. *Adult Education Quarterly*, 56, 201–226.

Bound, John & Turner, Sarah (2002). Going to war and going to college: Did World War II and the G.I. Bill increase educational attainment for returning veterans? *Journal of Labor Economics*, 20:784–815.

Bourdieu, Pierre (1984) *Distinction: a social critique of the judgement of taste,* London Routledge.

Bourdieu, Pierre (1990) *The logic of practice*, Cambridge, Polity.

Bourdieu, Pierre (1995) *The Rules of Art – Genesis and Structure of the Literary Field*, Stanford, California, Stanford University Press.

Bourdieu, Pierre & Passeron, Jean-Claude (1996) *Reproduction in education, society and culture*, London, Sage.

Bourgeois, Etienne, Duke, Chris, Guyot, Jean-Luc & Merrill, Barbara (1999) *The adult university*, Buckingham, SRHE and Open University Press.

Bowles, Samuel & Gintis, Herbert (1976) *Schooling in capitalist America: educational reform and the contradictions of economic life*, London, Routledge and Kegan Paul.

Brint, Steven (1998) *Schools and societies*, Thousand Oaks; London, Pine Forge Press.

Bremer, Helmut (2007) *Soziale Milieus, Habitus und Lernen – Zur sozialen Selektivität des Bildungswesens am Beispiel der Weiterbildung*, Weinheim und München, Juventa Verlag.

Brinton, Mary C. (2005) Education and the Economy. in Smelser, Neil J. & Swedberg, Richard (Eds.) The *Handbook of economic sociology*. Second Edition, Princeton, Oxford, Princeton University Press, 575–601.

Brinton, Mary C. (2011) *Lost in Transition – Youth, Work, and Instability in Postindustrial Japan,* Cambridge, Cambridge University Press.

Broek, Simon, Buiskool, Bert-Jan & Hake, Barry (2010) Impact of ongoing reforms in education and training on the adult learning sector (2nd phase) – Final report; Study financed by the European Commission DG EAC (EAC/15/2009). Zoetermeer.

Brown, Phillip & Hesketh, Anthony (2004) *The mismanagement of talent – employability and jobs in the knowledge economy*, Oxford, Oxford University Press.

Brown, Philip, Green, Andy & Lauder, Hugh (Eds.) (2001) *High Skills: Globalization, Competitiveness, and Skill Formation*, Oxford.

Bruce, Steve & Yearley, Steven (2006) *The Sage dictionary of sociology*, London, SAGE.

Brunello, Girogio, Garibaldi, Pietro & Wasmer, Etienne (Eds.) (2007) *Education and Training in Europe*, Oxford, Oxford University Press.

Bunch, Kay J. (2007) Training Failure as a Consequence of Organizational Culture. *Human Resource Development Review*, 6, 142–167.

Busemeyer, Marius R. & Iversen, Torben (2012) The Comparative Political Economy of Collective Skill Formation. in Busemeyer, Marius R. & Trampusch, Christine (Eds.) *The Political Economy of Collective Skill Formation*. Oxford, Oxford University Press, 205–233.

Chabbott, Colette (2003) *Constructing Education for Development – International Organizations and Education for All*, London: RoutledgeFalmer.

Chase, Ivan D. (1991) Vacancy Chains. *Annual Review of Sociology*, 17, 133–54.

Campbell, John L. & Pedersen, Ove Kaj (2001) Introduction – The rise of neoliberalism and institutional analysis. in Campbell, John L. & Pedersen, Ove Kaj (Eds.) *The rise of neoliberalism and institutional analysis*. Princeton [u.a.], Princeton Univ. Press, 1–23.

Carron, Gabriel & Carr-Hill, Roy A. (1991) Non-formal education: information and Planning issues. in Planning, International Institute for Educational (Ed.) *IIEP Research Report No. 90*.

CEDEFOP (2004) Terminology of vocational training policy – A multilingual glossary for an enlarged Europe. Office for Official Publications of the European Communities (Ed.) Luxembourg.

CEDEFOP (2009) Using tax incentives to promote education and training. in European Centre for the Development of Vocational Training (Ed.) CEDEFOP panorama series; 165. Luxembourg, Office for Official Publ. of the Europ. Communities.

CEDEFOP (2010) Employer-provided vocational training in Europe – Evaluation and interpretation of the third continuing vocational training survey. Luxembourg, Publications Office of the European Union.

Chu, Shui-Kee (1996) Statistics of Adult and Nonformal education, in Tuijnman, A. C. (Ed.) *The International Encyclopedia of Adult Education and Training*. Oxford, Pergamon Press, 878–883.

Clausen, John A. (1986) *The life course: a sociological perspective*, Englewood Cliffs, N.J., Prentice-Hall.

Colletta, Nat J. (1996) Formal, Informal and Nonformal Education. in Tuijnman, A. C. (Ed.) *The International Encyclopedia of Adult Education and Training*. Oxford, Pergamon Press, 22–27.

Colley, Helen, Hodkinson, Phil & Malcom, Janice (2003) Informality and formality in learning: a report for the Learning and Skills Research Centre. Leeds, Lifelong Learning Institute – University of Leeds.

Collins, Randall (1971) Functional and Conflict Theories of Educational Stratification. *American Sociological Review*, 36, 1002–1019.

Collins, Randall (1979) *The credential society: an historical sociology of education and stratification,* New York; London, Academic Press.

Coombs, Philip H. (1968) *The world educational crisis: a systems analysis*, Oxford University Press.

Coombs, Philip H. & Ahmed, Manzoor (1974) *Attacking rural poverty: how nonformal education can help,* Baltimore, Johns Hopkins University Press.

Coombs, Philip H., Prosser, Roy C. & Ahmed, Manzoor (1973) New Paths to Learning for Rural Children and Youth. International Council for Educational Development.

Courtney, Sean (1992) *Why adults learn – towards a Theory of Participation in Adult Education*, London, Routledge.

Cristini, Annalisa, Gaj, Alessandro & Leoni, Riccardo (2003) The gains from investing in workplace organisation. Department of Economics "Hyman Minsky", University of Bergamo.

Cristini, Annalisa , Gaj, Alessandro, & Leoni, Riccardo. (2008). Direct and Indirect Complementarity between Workplace Reorganization and New Technology. *Rivista di Politica Economica* (March-April), 87–117.

Cross, Patricia K. ([2]1992) *Adults as Learners: Increasing Participation and Facilitating Learning*, San Francisco, Jossey-Bass.

Crossan, Beth, Field, John, Gallacher, Jim & Merrill, Barbara (2003) Understanding participation in learning for non-traditional adult learners: learning careers and the construction of learning identities. *British Journal of Sociology of Education,* 24, 55–67.

Crouch, Colin (2002) Skill formation systems. *International Encyclopedia of Business and Management.* London, Thomson, 5879–5886.

Crouch, Colin (2006) Skill Formation Systems. in Ackroyd, Stephen, Batt, Rosemary, Thompson, Paul & Tolbert, Pamela S. (Eds.) *The Oxford Handbook of Work and Organization.* Oxford, Oxford University Press, 95–114.

Crouch, Colin, Finegold, David and Sako, Mari (1998) *Are Skills the Answer? – The Political Economy of Skill Creation in Advanced Industrial Countries,* New York: Oxford University Press.

Culpepper, Pepper D. & Finegold, David (1999) *The German skills machine: sustaining comparative advantage in a global economy,* New York; Oxford, Berghahn.

Cytrynbaum, Solomon, & Crites, John O. (1989) The utility of adult development theory in understanding career adjustment process, in Arthur, Michael B., Hall, Douglas T. & Lawrence, Barbara S. (Eds.), *Handbook of career theory*, New York: Cambridge University Press, 66–88.

Dalton, Gene W. 1989. Developmental views of careers in organizations. In M. B. Arthur, D. T. Hall & B. S. Lawrence (Eds.), *Handbook of career theory*, New York: Cambridge University Press, 89–109.

Daft, Richard L., Willmott, Johnathan & Willmott, Hugh (2010) *Organization: theory and design*, Andover Cengage Learning.

Deal, Terrence E. & Kennedy, Allan (1999) *The new corporate cultures: revitalizing the workplace after downsizing, mergers, and reengineering*, London, Texere.

DiMaggio, Paul (1988) Interest and agency in institutional theory. in Zucker, Lynne G. (Ed.) *Institutional patterns and organizations: culture and environment* – Conference on institutional theory: Papers. Cambridge, MA, Ballinger, 3–21.

DiMaggio, Paul (1991) Constructing an Organizational Field as a Professional Project: U.S. Art Museums, 1920–1940. in Powell, Walter W. & DiMaggio, Paul J. (Eds.) *The New institutionalism in organizational analysis*. Chicago, London, University of Chicago Press, 267–292.

DiMaggio, Paul J. & Powell, Walter W. (1983) The Iron Cage Revisited: Institutional Isomorphism and Collective Rationality in Organizational Fields. *American Sociological Review*, 48, 147–160.

DiTomaso, Nancy, Post, Corinne & Parks-Yancy, Rochelle (2007) Workforce Diversity and Inequality: Power, Status, and Numbers. *Annual Review of Sociology*, 33, 473–501.

Djelic, Marie-Laure & Sahlin-Andersson, Kerstin (2006) *Transnational governance: institutional dynamics of regulation*, Cambridge, Cambridge University Press.

Dobbin, Frank (2009) *Inventing Equal Opportunity*, Princeton, Princeton University Press.

Dobbin, Frank & Boychuk, Terry (1999) National Employment Systems and Job Autonomy: Why Job Autonomy is High in the Nordic Countries and Low in the United States, Canada, and Australia. *Organization Studies*, 20, 257–291.

Dobbin, Frank & Sutton, Frank R. (1998) The Strength of a Weak State: The Rights Revolution and the Rise of Human Resources Management Divisions. *The American Journal of Sociology*, 104, 441–476.

Dobbin, Frank, Simmons, Beth & Garrett, Geoffrey (2007) The Global Diffusion of Public Policies: Social Construction, Coercion, Competition, or Learning? *Annual Review of Sociology*, 33, 449–72.

Dobbin, Frank, Sutton, John R., Meyer, John W. & Scott, Richard W. (1994) Equal Opportunity Law and the Construction of Internal Labor Markets. in Scott, Richard W. & Meyer, W. John (Eds.) *Institutional environments and organizations – Structural complexity and individualism*. Thousand Oaks (California), Sage, 272–300.

Dore, Ronald Ph. (1976) *The diploma disease: education, qualification and development.* London: Allen and Unwin.

Downes, Paul (2011) A Systems Level Focus on Access to Education for Traditionally Marginalised Groups in Europe: Comparing Strategies, Policy and Practice in Twelve European Countries – LLL2010 Project Report 5 – Subproject 5. Tallinn.

Dreeben, Robert (1968) *On what is learned in school*, Addison-Wesley.

Dreyfus, Hubert L., Dreyfus, Stuart E. & Athanasiou, Tom (1986) *Mind over machine: the power of human intuition and expertise in the era of the computer*, Oxford, Basil Blackwell.

Drori, Gili S., Meyer, John W. & Hwang, Hokyu (2006a) Introduction. in Drori, Gili S., Meyer, John W. & Hwang, Hokyu (Eds.) *Globalization and organization: world society and organizational change.* Oxford; New York, Oxford University Press, 1–22.

Drori, Gili S., Meyer, John W. & Hwang, Hokyu (2006b) World Society and the Proliferation of Formal Organisation. in Drori, Gili S., Meyer, John W. & Hwang, Hokyu (Eds.) *Globalization and organization: world* society and organizational change. Oxford; New York, Oxford University Press, 25–49.

Ebbinghaus, Bernhard & Kittel, Bernhard (2006) Europäische Sozialmodelle à la carte: Gibt es institutionelle Wahlverwandtschaften zwischen Wohlfahrtsstaat und Arbeitsbeziehungen? in Beckert, Jens & Streeck, Wolfgang (Eds.) *Transformationen des Kapitalismus: Festschrift für Wolfgang Streeck zum sechzigsten Geburtstag.* Frankfurt/Main [u.a.], Campus-Verl., 233–247.

EDC/CSHD SP4 Project Team (2008) LLL2010 – Subproject 4 – Case Study 48 – Ireland: SP4 – Case Study 4. Print and Packaging., St. Patrick's College (EDC/CSHD).

Edwards, P. K. & Wajcman, Judy (2005) *The politics of working life*, Oxford, Oxford University Press.

Elder, Glen H. (1998) *Children of the Great Depression: social change life experience*, Boulder, Colo.; Oxford, Westview.

Elder, Glen H. & Shanahan, Michael J. (2006) The Life Course and Human Development. in Lerner, R. E. (Ed.) *Handbook of Child Psychology* (6th edition, volume 1). Hoboken, Wiley, 665–717.

Elman, Cheryl & O'Rand, Angela M. (2004) The Race Is to the Swift: Socioeconomic Origins, Adult Education, and Wage Attainment. *American Journal of Sociology,* 110, 123–60.

Elman, Cheryl & O'Rand, Angela M. (2007) The effects of social origins, life events, and institutional sorting on adults' school transitions. *Social Science Research,* 36 1276–1299.

Ely, Robin J. & Meyerson, Debra E. (2000) Theories of gender in organizations: A new approach to organizational analysis and change. *Research in Organizational Behaviour,* 22, 103–151.

Ely, Robin J. & Meyerson, Debra E. (2010) An organizational approach to undoing gender: The unlikely case of offshore oil platforms. *Research in Organizational Behavior,* 30, 3–34.

Ericsson, K. Anders (Ed.) (2009) *Development of professional expertise: toward measurement of expert performance and design of optimal learning environments,* New York, Cambridge, Cambridge University Press.

Ericsson, K. Anders, Krampe, Ralf Th. & Tesch-Römer, Clemens (1993) The role of deliberate practice in the acquisition of expert performance. *Psychological Review,* 100, 363–406.

Estevez-Abe, Margarita, Iversen, Torben & Soskice, David W. (2001) Social protection and the formation of skills: a reinterpretation of the welfare state. in Soskice, David W. & Hall, Peter A. (Eds.) *Varieties of capitalism: the institutional foundations of comparative advantage.* Oxford, Oxford University Press, 145–183.

European Commission (2001) Communication: Making a European Area of Lifelong Learning a Reality. Brussels.

European Commission (2007) Communication of the Commission to the Council, the European Parliament, the European Economic and Social Comittee, the Committee of the Regions – Action Plan on Adult Learning: It is always a good time to learn – COM (2007) 558 final.

European Council (2009) Council conclusions of 12 May 2009 on a strategic framework for European cooperation in education and training ('ET 2020') – Official Journal of the European Union – Official Journal of the European Union – (2009/C 119/02).

EUROSTAT (2006) Classification of learning activities – Manual. Luxembourg, Office for Official Publications of the European Communities.

EURYDICE (2011) *Adults in Formal Education – Policies and Practices in Europe,* Brussels: Education, Audiovisual and Culture Executive Agency.

Eyraud, Francois, Marsden, David & Silvestre, Jean-Jacques (1990) Occupational and internal markets in Britain and France. *International Labour Review,* 129, 501–517.

Fenwick, Tara J. (2000) Expanding Conceptions of Experiential Learning: A Review of the Five Contemporary Perspectives on Cognition. *Adult Education Quarterly,* 50, 243–272.

Fenwick, Tara (2011) Learning 'social responsibility' in the workplace: conjuring, unsettling, and folding boundaries. *Pedagogy, Culture & Society,* 19, 41–60.

Field, John (2005) *Social capital and lifelong learning,* Bristol, Policy Press.

Field, John (2006) *Lifelong Learning and the New Educational Order,* Stroke-on-Trent, Trentham.

Finegold, David & Soskice, David (1988) The Failure of British Training: Analysis and Prescription. *Oxford Review of Economic Policy*, 4, 21–53.

Finegold, David (2006) The Role of Education and Training Systems in Innovation. in Hage, Jerald & Meeus, Marius T. H. (Eds.) *Innovation, science, and institutional change.* Oxford, Oxford University Press,391–412.

Fleischer, Viktor, Hefler, Günter & Markowitsch, Jörg (2010) Wissensempowerment – Förderung der beruflichen Weiterbildungskompetenz und Weiterbildungsmotivation von bildungsfernen Personengruppen in Wien – Studie im Auftrage der MA 27 (EU-Strategie und Wirtschaftsentwicklung) der Stadt Wien Langfassung und Projektdokumentation. Wien, 3s research laboratory.

Fligstein, Neil (2001) *The architecture of markets: an economic sociology of twenty-first century capitalist societies,* Princeton, N.J.; Chichester, Princeton University Press.

Fligstein, Neil & Byrkjeflot, Haldor (1996) The Logic of Employment Systems. in Pock, John, Baron, James N., Grusky, David B. & Treiman, Donald J. (Eds.) *Social differentiation and social inequality: essays in honor of John Pock.* Boulder, Westview Press, 11–35.

Fligstein, Neil & Dauter, Luke (2007) The Sociology of Markets. *Annual Review of Sociology,* 33, 105–28.

Fordham, Paul, Poulton, Geoff & Randle, Lawrence (1983) Non-formal Work: A new kind of provision. in Tight, Malcolm (Ed.) *Education for adults. Vol 2, Educational opportunities for adults.* London, Croom Helm, 243–254.

Fourcade, Marion (2006) The Construction of a Global Profession: The Transnationalization of Economics. *American Journal of Sociology,* 112, 145–94.

Franklin, Kenneth (1997) National vocational qualifications, Scottish vocational qualifications and competence-based education and training: from De Ville to Beaumont. *Journal of Vocational Education & Training*, 49, 511–530.

Freidson, Eliot (2001) *Professionalism – The Third Logic*, Cambridge: Polity Press.

Freire, Paulo (1971) *Pedagogy of the oppressed,* [N. Y.], Herder.

Freud, Sigmund ([1899] 2008) *The interpretation of dreams*, Oxford, Oxford University Press.

Friedland, Roger & Alford, Robert R. (1991) Bringing Society Back In: Symbols, Practices, and Institutional Contradictions. in Powell, Walter W. & DiMaggio, Paul J. (Eds.) *The New institutionalism in organizational analysis.* Chicago; London, University of Chicago Press, 232–263.

Fuller, Alison & Unwin, Lorna (2003) Creating a 'Modern Apprenticeship': A critique of the UK's multi-sector, social inclusion approach. *Journal of Education and Work,* 16, 5–25.

Fuller, Bruce & Rubinson, Richard (1992) Does the State Expand Schooling? Review of the Evidence. in Fuller, Bruce & Rubinson, Richard (Eds.) *The political construction of education: the state, school expansion, and economic change.* New York, London, Praeger, 1–28.

Furlong, Andy (2008) The Japanese hikikomori phenomenon: acute social withdrawal among young people. *The Sociological Review,* 56, 309–325.

Fuwa, Kazuhiko (2001) Lifelong education in Japan, a highly school-centred society: educational opportunities and practical educational activities for adults. *International Journal of Lifelong Education,* 20, 127–136.

Gorard, Stephen & Rees, Gareth (2002) *Creating a learning society? Learning careers and policies for lifelong learning,* Bristol, The Policy Press.

Graf, Anita (2002) *Lebenszyklusorientierte Personalentwicklung – Ein Ansatz für die Erhaltung und Förderung von Leistungsfähigkeit und -bereitschaft während des gesamten betrieblichen Lebenszyklus,* Bern Stuttgart Wien, Verlag Paul Haupt.

Greenwood, Royston, Oliver, Christine, Sahlin, Kerstine & Suddaby, Roy (Eds.) (2008) *The SAGE handbook of organizational institutionalism,* Los Angeles, Calif. [u.a.], Sage Publ.

Grubb, W. Norton & Lazerson, Marvin (2004) *The education gospel: the economic power of schooling.* Cambridge, Mass.; London: Harvard University Press.

Guest, David E. & Sturges, Jane (2007) Living to Work- Working to Live: Conceptualizations of Careers Among Contemporary Workers. in Gunz, Hugh & Peiperl, Maury (Eds.) *Handbook of Career Studies.* Thousand Oaks, California, Sage, 310–326.

Hage, Jerald & Garnier, Maurice (1992) Strong States and Educational Expansion: France versus Italy. in Fuller, Bruce & Rubinson, Richard (Eds.) *The political construction of education: the state, school expansion, and economic change.* New York, London, Praeger, 155–171.

Hall, Peter A. (2010) Historical Institutionalism in Rationalist and Sociologcal Perspective. in Mahoney, James & Thelen, Kathleen (Eds.) *Explaining institutional change: ambiguity, agency, and power in historical institutionalism.* New York, Cambridge University Press, 204–224.

Hall, Peter A. & Taylor, Rosemarcy R. (1996) Political Science and the Three New Institutionalisms. *Political Studies,* XLIV, 936–957.

Harney, Klaus & Koch, Sascha (2010) Steuerungsprobleme im Zweiten Bildungsweg. Eine empirische und organisationstheoretische Analyse des Phänomens der bildungssystemischen Funktionsüberlappung. in Dollhausen, Karin, Feld, Timm C. & Seitter, Wolfgang (Eds.) *Erwachsenenpädagogische Organisationsforschung.* Wiesbaden, VS Verlag, 197–218.

Hartz, Stefanie (2009) Diffusionsprozesse in der Weiterbildung – eine Analyse aus der Perspektive des Neo-Institutionalismus. in Koch, Sascha & Schemmann, Michael (Eds.) *Neo-Institutionalismus in der Erziehungswissenschaft – Grundlegende Texte und empirische Studien.* Wiesbaden, VS Verlag, 133–159.

Havighurst, Robert James (1972) *Developmental tasks and education,* [S.l.], McKay.

Hefler, Günter (2010a) The qualification-supporting company – The Significance of Formal Adult Education in Small and Medium Organizations – Comparative Report – Subproject 4 – LLL2010 Status: Version 2.0, Krems: Danube University Krems.

Hefler, Günter (2010b) Zwischen Steuerung und Ritual – Möglichkeiten und Grenzen betrieblicher Nutzung von Weiterbildungsindikatoren aus neoinstitutionalistischer Sicht. *BWP – Berufsbildung in Wissenschaft und Praxis*, 39, 31–34.

Hefler, Günter & Markowitsch, Jörg (2008) To Train or Not to Train – Explaining differences in average enterprise training performance in Europe – a framework approach. in Markowitsch, Jörg & Hefler, Günter (Eds.) *Enterprise Training in Europe – Comparative Studies on Cultures, Markets and Public Support Initiatives* Vienna, LIT, 23–60.

Hefler, Günter & Markowitsch, Jörg (2009) Maß nehmen? Zur (Un-) Möglichkeit des Benchmarking betrieblicher Weiterbildungspolitik auf Basis der CVTS Daten. in Behringer, Friederike, Käpplinger, Bernd & Pätzold, Günter (Eds.) *Betriebliche Weiterbildung – der Continuing Vocational Training Survey (CVTS) im Spiegel nationaler und europäischer Perspektiven*. Stuttgart, Franz Steiner Verlag, 169–183.

Hefler, Günter & Markowitsch, Jörg (2010) Formal adult learning and working in Europe: a new typology of participation patterns. *Journal for workplace learning*, 22, 79–93.

Hefler, Günter & Markowitsch, Jörg (2012a) Bridging Institutional Divides: Linking education, careers and work in 'organizational space' and 'skill space' dominated employment systems. in Brooks, Rachel, Fuller, Alison & Waters, Johanna (Eds.) *Changing Spaces of Education – New Perspectives on the Nature of Learning*. London, Routledge, 160–181.

Hefler, Günter & Markowitsch, Jörg (2012b forthcoming) Seven types of formal adult education and their organisational fields: Towards a comparative framework. in Saar, Ellu, Ure, Odd Bjorn & Roosalu, Triin (Eds.) *Lifelong Learning in Europe: National Patterns and Challenges*. Cheltenham, Edward Elgar.

Hefler, Günter & Markowitsch, Jörg (2012c) The qualification providing enterprise? – Support for formal adult education in small and medium enterprises. in Riddell, Sheila, Markowitsch, Jörg & Weedon, Elisabet (Eds.) *Lifelong Learning in Europe: Equity and Efficiency in the Balance*. Bristol, Policy Press.

Hefler, Günter & Bacher, Daniel (2008a) LLL2010 – Subproject 4 – Case Study 18 – Austria: XY Chemicals Austria – Formal Adult Education as a Strategic Resource for Growth, Sector Family 1 – 50–249 Employees, Krems: Danube University Krems.

Hefler, Günter & Bacher, Daniel (2008b) LLL2010 – Subproject 4 – Case Study 22 – Austria: XY Plastic: A Well-established Training Culture and Experimental Use of Formal Education to Foster Innovation and Internationalisation. Sector Family 1 – 250–499 Employees, Krems: Danube University Krems.

Hefler, Günter & Bacher, Daniel (2008c) LLL2010 – Subproject 4 – Case Study 16 – Austria: XY media: Initiating a formal education course to manage growth processes. Sector Family 2 – 20–49 employees. Danube University Krems.

Hefler, Günter, Markowitsch, Jörg & Bacher, Daniel (2008) LLL2010 – Subproject 4 – Country Report Austria: SMEs and the participation of Workers in Formal Learning. Internal Working Document, Krems: Danube University Krems.

Hefler, Günter, Róbert, Péter, Ringler, Paul, Sági, Matild, Rammel, Stephanie, Balogh, Anikó & Markowitsch, Jörg (2011) Formal adult education in Context – The view of European Statistics – SP 2 – Synthesis Report – LLL2010 project. Krems, Danube University Krems – TARKI.

Hillmert, Steffen & Jacob, Marita (2003) Bildungsprozesse zwischen Diskontinuität und Karriere: Das Phänomen der Mehrfachausbildungen. *Zeitschrift für Soziologie,* 32, 325–345.

Hillmert, Steffen & Jacob, Marita (2008) Zweite Chance im Schulsystem? – Zur sozialen Selektivität bei 'späteren' Bildungsentscheidungen. in Berger, Peter A. & Kahlert, Heike (Ed.) *Institutionalisierte Ungleichheit – Wie das Bildungswesen Chancen blockiert,* 2nd Edition. Weinheim und München: Juventa, 155–176.

Hodson, Randy (2001) *Dignity at work,* Cambridge, Cambridge University Press.

Hoffman, Andrew J. (2001) Linking Organizational and Field-Level Analyses: The Diffusion of Corporate Environmental Practice. *Organization Environment,* 14, 133–156.

Hofstede, Geert & Hofstede, Gert Jan (2005) *Cultures and Organizations – Software of the Mind: Intercultural Cooperation and Its Importance for Survival,* New York, McGraw-Hill.

Holford, John, Engel, Laura C. & Wilson, Helena L. (2008a) LLL2010 – Subproject 4 – Case Study 36 – England: Copper Products Incorporated. Sector Family A, 50–99 employees, University of Nottingham, UK.

Holford, John, Engel, Laura C. & Wilson, Helena L. (2008b) LLL2010 – Subproject 4 – Case Study 36 – England: Copper Products Incorporated. Sector Family A, 50–99 employees, University of Nottingham, UK.

Hollister, Matissa (2011) Employment Stability in the U.S. Labor Market: Rhetoric versus Reality. The *Annual Review of Sociology,* 37, 15.1–15.20.

Hoppers, Wim (2006) Non-formal education and basic education reform: a conceptual review. UNESCO International Institute for Educational Planning.

Hostetler, Andrew J., Sweet, Stephen & Moen, Phyllis (2007) Gendered Career Paths: A Life Course Perspective on Returning to School. *Sex Roles,* 56, 85–103.

Houle, Cyril O. (1961) *The Inquiring Mind,* Madison, University of Wisconsin Press.

Ilieva, Kornelia (2008) LLL2010 – Subproject 4 – Case Study 10 – Bulgaria: SP 4 – Case Study 2. ME: Formal education – the difficult road from the individual initiative to the institutional strategy. Sector Family 1 – 50 – 249 employees; D-DG., Institute of Sociology at Bulgarian Academy of Sciences.

Inbar, Dan E. (Ed.) (1990) *Second chance in education: an interdisciplinary and international perspective,* London, Falmer.

Inbar, Dan & Sever, Rita (1989) The Importance of Making Promises: An Analysis of Second-Chance Policies. *Comparative Education Review,* 33, 232–242.

Illich, Ivan (1971) *Deschooling society,* Harmondsworth, Penguin Education.

Jacob, Marita & Weiss, Felix (2011) Class origin and young adults' re-enrollment, *Research in Social Stratification and Mobility,* 29, 4, 415–426.

Jacoby, Sanford M. (1984) The Development of Internal Labor Markets in American Manufacturing Firms. in Osterman, Paul (Ed.) *Internal labor markets.* Cambridge, Mass. [u.a.], MIT Press, 23–69.

Jakobi, Anja P. (2009) *International organizations and lifelong learning: from global agendas to policy diffusion,* Basingstoke [u.a.], Palgrave Macmillan.

Jarvis, Peter (Ed.) (2009) *The Routledge international handbook of lifelong learning,* London, Routledge.

Jones, Candace & Dunn, Mary (2007) Careers and Institutions: The Centrality of Careers to Organizational Studies. in Gunz, Hugh & Peiperl, Maury (Eds.) *Handbook of Career Studies.* Thousand Oaks, California, Sage, 437–450.

Józan, Anna (2008) LLL2010 – Subproject 4 – Case Study 79 – Hungary: XY Industrial Wholesale Ltd. Hungary (Sector 'g51', 10–49 employees). Tárki.

Kamens, David H. (1977) Legitimating Myths and Educational Organization: The Relationship Between Organizational Ideology and Formal Structure. *American Sociological Review,* 42, 208–219.

Kamens, David H. (1985) Youth and the State: A Cross-National Analysis of the Changing Status of Adolescence. *Comparative Political Studies,* 18, 3–36.

Kamens, David H. & Mcneely, Connie L. (2010) Globalization and the Growth of International Educational Testing and National Assessment. *Comparative Education Review,* 54, 5–25.

Kasworm, Carol E., Rose, Amy D. & Ross-Gordon, Jovita M. (Eds.) (2010) *Handbook of adult and continuing education,* Los Angeles, SAGE.

King, Kenneth (ed.) (1976) *Education and Community in Africa.* (Centre of African Studies, University of Edinburgh).

Kish-Gephart, Jennifer J., Detert, James R., Trevino, Linda Klebe & Edmondson, Amy C. (2009) Silenced by fear: The nature, sources, and consequences of fear at work. *Research in Organizational Behavior,* 29 163–193.

Knowles, Malcom S., Holton, Elwood F. III & Swanson, Richard A. (2005) *The adult learner – the definitive classic in adult education and human resource development,* Amsterdam, Elsevier.

Koch, Sascha & Schemmann, Michael (Eds.) (2009) *Neo-Institutionalismus in der Erziehungswissenschaft – Grundlegende Texte und empirische Studien,* Wiesbaden, VS Verlag.

Koike, Kazuo & Inoki, Takenori (Eds.) (1990) *Skill formation in Japan and Southeast Asia*, University of Tokyo Press.

Koike, Kazuo (1994) Learning and incentive system in Japanese industries. in Aoki, Masahiko & Dore, Ronald Philip (Eds.) *The Japanese firm: the sources of competitive strength*. Oxford [u.a.], Oxford Univ. Press, 41–65.

Khokhlova, Anisya (2008) LLL2010 – Subproject 4 – Case Study 82 – Russia: Research-and-production firm 'A+'. Formal Education as an Adaptation Strategy & Development Resource (Family A; 50–249 employees). St. Petersburg State University (SPSU).

Krüger, Helga (1999) Gender and Skills. Distributive Ramifications of the German Skill System. in Culpepper, Pepper D. & Finegold, David (Eds.) *The German skills machine: sustaining comparative advantage in a global economy*. New York; Oxford, Berghahn, 189–227.

Laplanche, Jean & Pontalis, Jean-Bertrand (1973) *The language of psycho-analysis*, London, Karnac and the Institute of Psycho-Analysis.

Larson, Magali Sarfatti (1977) *The rise of professionalism – A Sociological Analysis*, Berkeley University of California Press.

Lawrence, Barbara S. & Tolbert, Pamela S. (2007) Organizational Demography and Individual Careers: Structure, Norms, and Outcomes. in Gunz, Hugh & Peiperl, Maury (Eds.) *Handbook of Career Studies*. Thousand Oaks, California, Sage, 399–421.

Lawrence, Thomas B. (2008) Power, Institutions and Organizations. in Greenwood, Royston, Oliver, Christine, Sahlin, Kerstine & Suddaby, Roy (Eds.) *The SAGE handbook of organizational institutionalism*. Los Angeles, Calif. [u.a.], Sage Publ., 170–197.

Lazonick, William (2006) Corporate Restructuring. in Ackroyd, Stephen, Batt, Rosemary, Thompson, Paul & Tolbert, Pamela S. (Eds.) *The Oxford Handbook of Work and Organization*. Oxford, Oxford University Press, 577–601.

Lebaron, Frédéric (2000) *La croyance économique: les économistes entre science et politique*, Paris, Ed. du Seuil.

Leicht, Kevin T. & Fennell, Mary L. (1997) The Changing Organizational Context of Professional Work. *Annual Review of Sociology*, 23, 215–231.

Leoni, Riccardo, Cristini, Annalisa, Labory, Sandrine & Gaj, Alessandro (2001) New Work Practices in Italy. Adoption and Performance Effects. in "Hyman P. Minsky" Economics Department University of Bergamo (Ed.).

Leoni, Riccardo & Gaj, Alessandro (2009) Education, Informal Learning and Development of Key Competencies in Workplaces. The Importance of Organizational Design – Working Paper.

Levinson, Daniel J. (1980) Toward a Conception of the Adult Life course. in Smelser, Neil J. & Erikson, Erik H. (Eds.) *Themes of work and love in adulthood*. Cambridge, Mass., Harvard University Press, 265–290.

Levinson, Daniel J. & Levinson, Judy (1996) *The seasons of a woman's life – A fascinating exploration of the events, thoughts, and life experiences that all women share,* New York, Ballantine Books.

Levinson, Daniel, Darrow, Charlotte N., Klein, Edward B., Levinson, Maria H. & McKee, Braxton (1978) *The Seasons of a Man's Life*, New York, Alfred A. Knopf.

Lewin, Kurt (1997) *Resolving social conflicts; Field theory in social science,* Washington, DC, American Psychological Association.

Loewenstein, Mark A. & Spletzer, James R. (1997) Delayed formal on-the-job training. *Industrial and Labor Relations Review,* 51, 82–99.

Lounsbury, Michael & Ventresca, Marc J. (2002) Social Structure and Organizations revisited. *Social Structure and Organizations Revisited*, 19, 3–36.

Lounsbury, Michael (2008) Institutional rationality and practice variation: New directions in the institutional analysis of practice. *Accounting, Organizations and Society,* 33 349–361.

Luo, Xiaowei (2002) From technical skills to personal development: employee training in U.S. organizations in the twentieth century. in Sahlin-Andersson, Kerstin & Engwall, Lars (Eds.) *The expansion of management knowledge: carriers, flows, and sources.* Stanford, Calif.; [Great Britain], Stanford Business Books, 195–211.

Luo, Xiaowei (2006) The Spread of a "Human Resource" Culture: Institutional Individualism and the Rise of Personal Development Training. in Drori, Gili S., Meyer, John W. & Hwang, Hokyu (Eds.) *Globalization and organization: world society and organizational change.* Oxford; New York, Oxford University Press, 225–240.

Luo, Xiaowei (2007) Continuous Learning: The Influence of National Institutional Logics on Training Attitudes. *Organization Science,* 18, 280–296.

MacKeracher, Dorothy, Suart, Theresa & Potter, Judith (2006) Barriers to Participation in Adult Learning – State of the field report. University of New Brunswick.

Mahoney, James & Thelen, Kathleen (2009) A Theory of Gradual Institutional Change. in Mahoney, James & Thelen, Kathleen (Eds.) *Explaining institutional change: ambiguity, agency, and power in historical institutionalism.* New York, Cambridge University Press, 1–37.

Marsden, David (1999) *A Theory of Employment Systems: Micro-Foundations of Societal Diversity*, Oxford: Oxford University Press.

Markowitsch, Jörg & Hefler, Günter (2008a) LLL2010 – Subproject 4 – Guidelines for case studies in SP 4 Version 3.0 – (25 February 2008) – Internal working document, Danube University Krems.

Markowitsch, Jörg & Hefler, Günter (2008b) LLL2010 – Subproject 4 – Guidelines for interviews for case studies in SP 4 – Version 2.0 – (21 January 2008) – Internal working document, Danube University Krems.

Markowitsch, Jörg & Hefler, Günter (2008c) LLL2010 – Subproject 4 – Theoretical, methodological and statistical background for SP 4 – Version 2.0 – (24 January 2008c) – Internal working document.

Markowitsch, Jörg, Hefler, Günter, Rammel, Stephanie & Ringler, Paul (2012, forthcoming) Nobody's darling – Dynamics and inertia of formal adult education in Austria. in Saar, Ellu, Ure, Odd Bjorn & Roosalu, Triin (Eds.) *Lifelong Learning in Europe: National Patterns and Challenges.* Cheltenham, Edward Elgar.

Markowitsch, Jörg & Jonach, Michaela (2006) Anerkennung und Zertifizierung betrieblicher Aus- und Weiterbildungsleistungen im Kontext nationaler und internationaler Entwicklungen. Eine Überblicksexpertise. in BMWA(Ed.) Wien.

Marrs, Kira (2009) Herrschaft und Kontrolle in der Arbeit. in Böhle, Fritz, Voß, Günter G. & Wachtler, Günther (Eds.) *Handbuch Arbeitssoziologie.* Münster, VS Verlag für Sozialwissenschaften, 331–356.

Martin, Joanne (2002) *Organizational culture: mapping the terrain.* Thousand Oaks, Calif.; London, Sage.

Martin, John Levi (2003) What Is Field Theory? *The American Journal of Sociology,* 109, 1–49.

Maurice, Marc (1995) The social foundations of technical innovation: engineers and the division of labour in France and Japan, in Littek, W. and Charles, T. (eds) *The New Dimension of Labour – Emerging forms of Work Organization in International Perspective,* Berlin: Walter de Gruyter, 317–347.

Maurice, M. (2000) The paradoxes of societal analysis – a review of the past and prospects of the future, in Maurice, M. and Sorge, A. (eds) *Embedding Organizations – Societal Analysis of Actors, Organizations and Socio-economic Context,* Amsterdam: John Benjamins, 13–36.

Maurice, M. and Sorge, A. (eds) (2000) *Embedding Organizations – Societal Analysis of Actors, Organizations and Socio-economic Context,* Amsterdam: John Benjamins.

Maurice, Marc, Sorge, Arndt & Warner, Malcolm (1980) Societal Differences in Organizing Manufacturing Units: A Comparison of France, West Germany, and Great Britain. *Organization Studies,* 1, 59–86.

Maurice, Marc, Sellier, Francois & Silvestre, Jean-Jacques (1986) *The Social Foundations of Industrial Power – A comparison of France and Germany,* Cambridge, Mass., MIT Press.

Maurission-Barrère, Marie-Agnès (2000) Explaining changes in institutional frameworks – Societal patterns of business coordination. in Maurice, Marc & Sorge, Arndt (Eds.) *Embedding organizations: societal analysis of actors, organizations and socio-economic context.* Amsterdam, John Benjamins, 357–371.

Mayer, Karl Ulrich (2009) New Directions in Life Course Research. *Annual Review of Sociology,* 35, 413–33.

Mayer, Karl Ulrich, Grunow, Daniela & Nitsche, Natalie (2010) Mythos Flexibilisierung? – Wie instabil sind Berufsbiografien wirklich und als wie instabil werden sie wahrgenommen? *Kölner Zeitschrift für Soziologie und Sozialpsychologie,* 62, 369–402.

Mazza, Carmelo, Sahlin-Andersson, Kerstin & Pedersen, Jesper Strandgaard (2005) European Constructions of an American Model – Developments of Four MBA Programmes. *Management Learning,* 36, 471–491.

Merriam, Sharan B. & Brockett, Ralph G. (2007) *The profession and practice of adult education: an introduction,* San Francisco, Calif., Jossey-Bass Publishers.

Merriam, Sharan B., Caffarella, Rosemary S. & Baumgartner, Lisa M. (2007) *Learning in adulthood – a comprehensive guide,* San Francisco, John Wiley & Sons, Inc.

Meyer, Heinz-Dieter & Rowan, Brian (Eds.) (2006) *The new institutionalism in education,* New York, State University of New York Press.

Meyer, John W. (1970) The Charter: Conditions of Diffuse Socialization in Schools. in Scott, William Richard (Ed.) *Social processes and social structures: an introduction to sociology.* New York, London, Holt, Rinehart and Winston, 564–578

Meyer, John W. (1977) The effects of education as an institution. *The American Journal of Sociology,* 83: 55–77.

Meyer, John W. & Rowan, Brian (1977) Institutionalized Organizations: Formal structures as myth and ceremony. *American Journal of Sociology,* 83, 340–363.

Meyer, John W. (1992) The Social Construction of Motives for Educational Expansion, in Fuller, Bruce & Rubinson, Richard (Eds.) *The political construction of education: the state, school expansion, and economic change.* New York, London, Praeger, 225–238.

Meyer, John W. & Rowan, Brian (1978) The Structure of Educational Organizations. in Meyer, Marshall W. (Ed.) *Environments and organizations.* San Francisco Jossey-Bass, 78–109.

Meyer, John W. & Jepperson, Roland L. (2000) The 'Actors' of Modern Society: The Cultural Construction of Social Agency. *Sociological Theory,* 18, 100–120.

Meyer, John W., Ramirez, Francisco O., Frank, David John & Schofer, Evan (2007) Higher Education as an Institution. in Gumport, Patricia J. (Ed.) *Sociology of higher education: contributions and their contexts.* Baltimore, Md.; London, Johns Hopkins University Press, 187–221.

Meyer, John W., Scott, Richard W. & Deal, Terrence E. (1981) Institutional and Technical Sources of Organizational Structure: Explaining the Structure of Educational Organizations. in Stein, Herman D. (Ed.) *Organization and the human services: cross-disciplinary reflections.* Philadelphia, Temple U.P., 151–179.

Mills, Melinda & Blossfeld, Hans-Peter (2006) Globalization, patchwork careers and the individualization of inequality? A 12-country comparison of men's mid-career job mobility. in Bernardi, Fabrizio, Blossfeld, Hans-Peter & Mills, Melinda (Eds.) *Globalization, uncertainty and men's careers: an international comparison.* Cheltenham, Edward Elgar, 457–482.

Mills, Melinda, Blossfeld, Hans-Peter, Buchholz, Sandra, Hofäcker, Dirk, Bernardi, Fabrizio & Hofmeister, Heather A. (2008) Converging Divergences? – An international comparison of the impact of globalization on industrial relations and employment careers. *International sociology*, 23, 561–595.

Mintzberg, Henry (1979) *The structuring of organizations: a synthesis of the research,* Englewood Cliffs; London, Prentice-Hall.

Mirčeva, Jasmina (2008) LLL2010 – Subproject 4 – Case Study 2 – Slovenia: SP 4 – Case Study B. Improving the effectiveness of the company's performance through stimulating the employees participation in formal education. NACE: C 25.930; DJ 28.730, Sector Family 1 – 50 – 250 employees., Slovenian Institute for adult education (SIAE).

Monahan, C. Susanne, Meyer, W. John & Scott, Richard W. (1994) Employee Training – the expansion of organizational citizenship. in Scott, Richard W. & Meyer, W. John (Eds.) *Institutional environments and organizations – Structural complexity and individualism.* Thousand Oaks (California), Sage, 255–271.

Morgan, Glenn, Campbell, John, Crouch, Colin Ove, Pedersen, Kaj & Whitley, Richard (Eds.) (2010) *The Oxford handbook of comparative institutional analysis*, Oxford, Oxford University Press.

Müller, Detlef K., Ringer, Fritz K. & Simon, Brian (1987) *The Rise of the modern educational system: structural change and social reproduction 1870–1920,* Cambridge, Cambridge University Press.

Müller, Walter & Gangl, Markus (Eds.) (2003) *Transitions from education to work in Europe the integration of youth into EU labour markets*, Oxford [u.a.], Oxford Univ. Press.

National Center for Education Statistics (2006) National Household Education Surveys Program of 2005 – Adult Education Participation in 2004–05. Washington.

Nielsen, Klaus (2007) The 'institutional turn' in the social sciences: a review of approaches and a future research agenda. in Ioannides, Stavros & Nielsen, Klaus (Eds.) *Economics and the social sciences: boundaries, interaction and integration.* Cheltenham, Edward Elgar, 91–111.

Nonaka, Ikujirō & Takeuchi, Hirotaka (1995) *The knowledge-creating company: how Japanese companies create the dynamics of innovation,* New York, Oxford Univ. Press.

Nonaka, Ikujirō & Toyama, Ryoko (2007) Why do Firms Differ? The Theory of the Knowledge-Creating Firm. in Ichijo, Kazuo & Nonaka, Ikujirō (Eds.) *Knowledge Creation and management – New challenges for managers.* New York, Oxford University Press, 13–31.

OECD (1973) Recurrent Education: A Strategy for Lifelong Learning.OECD (1999) Classifying Educational Programmes Manual for ISCED-97 – Implementation in OECD Countries. 1999 Edition, Paris.

OECD (2004) *OECD handbook for internationally comparative education statistics – concepts, standards, definitions and classifications,* Paris, OECD.

OECD (2007) *Qualifications Systems – Bridges To Lifelong Learning,* Paris.

Oliver, Christine (1991) Strategic responses to institutional processes, *Academy of Management Review,* 16, 145–179.

O'Reilly, Jacqueline (2000) Is it time to gender the societal effect? in Maurice, Marc & Sorge, Arndt (Eds.) *Embedding organizations: societal analysis of actors, organizations and socio-economic context.* Amsterdam, John Benjamins, 343–356.

Osterman, Paul & Burton, Diane M. (2006) Ports and Ladders: The Nature and Relevance of Internal Labor Markets in a Changing World. in Ackroyd, Stephen, Batt, Rosemary, Thompson, Paul & Tolbert, Pamela S. (Eds.) *The Oxford Handbook of Work and Organization.* Oxford, Oxford University Press, 425–445.

Ouchi, William G. & Wilkins, Alan L. (1985) Organizational Culture. *Annual Review of Sociology,* 11, 457–83.

Pedersen, Jesper Strandgaard & Dobbin, Frank (2006) In Search of Identity and Legitimation: Bridging Organizational Culture and Neoinstitutionalism. *American Behavioral Scientist,* 49, 897–907.

Perlowa, Leslie A. & Repenning, Nelson P. (2009) The dynamics of silencing conflict. *Research in Organizational Behavior,* 29, 195–223.

Pernicka, Susanne & Stefan, Lücking (2012 forthcoming) How knowledge shapes collective action: professionalism, market closure and bureaucracy in the fields of university and non-university research. *Journal of Industrial Relations*, Vol. 54.

Powell, Justin J.W., Coutrot, Laurence, Graf, Lukas, Bernhard, Nadine, Kieffer, Annick & Solga, Heike (2009) Comparing the Relationship between Vocational and Higher Education in Germany and France. Social Science Research Center Berlin (WZB). Berlin.

Powell, Walter W. & DiMaggio, Paul J. (1991a) Introduction. in Powell, Walter W. & DiMaggio, Paul J. (Eds.) *The New institutionalism in organizational analysis.* Chicago; London, University of Chicago Press, 1–40.

Rao, Hayagreeva, Monin, Philippe & Durand, Rodolphe (2003) Institutional Change in Toque Ville: Nouvelle Cuisine as an Identity Movement in French Gastronomy. *American Journal of Sociology,* 108, 795–843.

Reisz, Robert D. & Stock, Manfred (2006) Zwischen Expansion und Kontraktion – Zur Entwicklung der Hochschulbildung in Osteuropa 1950–2000. *Berliner Journal für Soziologie,* 77–93.

Resnik, Julia (2007) The Democratisation of the Education System in France after the Second World War: A Neo-Weberian Glocal Approach to Education Reforms. *British Journal of Educational Studies,* 55, 155–181.

Riddell, Sheila, Ahlgren, Linda & Weedon, Elisabet (2009) Equity and lifelong learning: lessons from workplace learning in Scottish SMEs. *International Journal of Lifelong Education*, 28, 777–795.

Riddell, Sheila, Markowitsch, Jörg & Weedon, Elisabet (Eds.) (2012, forthcoming) *Lifelong Learning in Europe: Equity and Efficiency in the Balance*, Bristol, Policy Press.

Ringer, Fritz K. (1979) *Education and society in modern Europe*, Bloomington; London, Indiana University Press.

Rivera, Lauren A. (2011) Ivies, extracurriculars, and exclusion: Elite employers' use of educational credentials. *Research in Social Stratification and Mobility*, 29, 71–90.

Rogers, Alan (2004) *Non-formal education: flexible schooling or participatory education? CERC Studies in comparative education no 15*, Hong Kong Comparative Education Research Centre (CERC), Faculty of Education, Hong Kong University.

Rubenson, Kjell (1976) Recruitment in adult education – a research strategy. Stockholm.

Rubenson, Kjell (2009) Lifelong learning – Between humanism and global capitalism. in Jarvis, Peter (Ed.) *The Routledge international handbook of lifelong learning*. London, Routledge, 411–422.

Rubenson, Kjell (Ed.) (2011) *Adult learning and education*, London, Academic.

Rubenson, Kjell & Desjardins, Richard (2009) The Impact of Welfare State Regimes on Barriers to Participation in Adult Education: A Bounded Agency Model. *Adult Education Quarterly*, 59, 187–207.

Rubinson, Richard & Browne, Irene (1994) Education and the Economy. in Smelser, Neil J. & Swedberg, Richard (Eds.) *The handbook of economic sociology*. Princeton; Chichester, Princeton University Press; New York: Russell Sage Foundation, 581–599.

Russell, Willy (1981) *Educating Rita: a comedy*, London, French.

Saar, Ellu & Roosalu, Triin (2011) Towards a Lifelong Learning Society in Europe: The Role of Education Systems – Results from multilevel mixed methods analysis of different aspects in learning as an adult in Europe – LLL2010 Integrated report. Tallinn.

Saar, Ellu & Ure, Odd Bjorn (2012, forthcoming) Lifelong learning systems: overview and extension of different typologies. in Saar, Ellu, Ure, Odd Bjorn & Roosalu, Triin (Eds.) *Lifelong Learning in Europe: National Patterns and Challenges*. Cheltenham, Edward Elgar.

Saar, Ellu, Ure, Odd Bjorn & Holford, John (Eds.) (2012, forthcoming) *Lifelong Learning in Europe: National Patterns and Challenges*, Cheltenham Edward Elgar.

Schein, Edgar H. (1978) *Career Dynamics: Matching Individual and Organizational Needs.* Reading, Massachusetts, Addison-Wesley Publishing Company.

Schleicher, Klaus (1990) Second Chance – Emancipation and/or Alienation: The German Experience. in Inbar, Dan E. (Ed.) *Second Chance in Education*. London, Falmer, 167–191.

Schlossberg, Nancy K. (1984) *Counselling adults in transition – Linking practice with theory,* New York, Springer.

Schneider, Silke L. (Ed.) (2008) *The International Standard Classification of Education (ISCED-97) – An Evaluation of Content and Criterion Validity for 15 European Countries,* Mannheim, Mannheimer Zentrum für Europäische Sozialforschung.

Schoonhoven, Claudia Bird & Dobbin, Frank (2010) *Stanford's organization theory renaissance, 1970–2000,* Bingley, Emerald.

Scott, Richard W. & Meyer, W. John (1994) The rise of training programs in firms and agencies: an institutional perspective. in Scott, Richard W. & Meyer, W. John (Eds.) *Institutional environments and organizations – Structural complexity and individualism.* Thousand Oaks (California), Sage, 228–254

Scott, W. Richard (2008a) Approaching adulthood: the maturing of institutional theory. *Theory and Society,* 37, 427–442.

Scott, W. Richard (³2008b) *Institutions and organizations: ideas and interests,* London, SAGE.

Scott, W. Richard (2008c) Lords of the Dance: Professionals as Institutional Agents. *Organization Studies,* 29, 219–238.

Scott, W. Richard & Davis, Gerald F. (2007) *Organizations and organizing: rational, natural and open systems perspectives,* Upper Saddle River, N.J., Pearson Prentice Hall.

Scott, W. Richard & Meyer, John W. (1991) The Organization of Societal Sectors: Propositions and Early Evidence. in Powell, Walter W. & DiMaggio, Paul J. (Eds.) *The New institutionalism in organizational analysis.* Chicago; London, University of Chicago Press, 108–140.

Senge, Konstanze (2011) *Das Neue am Neo-Institutionalismus – Der Neo-Institutionalismus im Kontext der Organisationswissenschaft*, Wiesbaden, VS Verlag für Sozialwissenschaft.

Setftersten, Richard A. Jr. & Lovegreen, Loren D. (1998) Educational Experiences Throughout Adult Life: New Hopes or No Hope for Life-Course Flexibility? *Research on Aging,* 20, 506–538.

Shavit, Yossi & Müller, Walter (1998) *From school to work: a comparative study of educational qualifications and occupational destinations*, Oxford, Clarendon Press.

Shavit, Yossi & Müller, Walter (2000) Vocational secondary education – Where diversion and where safety net?, *European Societies*, 2, 29–50.

Siara, Christian (1986) *Untypische Statuspassagen: Bildungs- und Berufsfindungsprozesse im 2. Bildungsweg,* Frankfurt/Main [u.a.], Campus-Verl.

Simkins, Tim (1977) *Non-formal education and development: Some critical issues,* [S.l.], University of Manchester.

Solga, Heike (2008) Lack of training – Employment opportunities for low-skilled persons from a sociological and microeconomic perspective in Mayer, Karl Ulrich & Solga, Heike (Eds.) *Skill Formation – Interdisciplinary and cross-national perspectives.* Cambridge, Cambridge University Press, 173–204.

Soskice, David W. & Hall, Peter A. (2001) *Varieties of capitalism: the institutional foundations of comparative advantage,* Oxford, Oxford University Press.

Stainback, Kevin, Tomaskovic-Devey, Donald & Skaggs, Sheryl (2010) Organizational Approaches to Inequality: Inertia, Relative Power, and Environments. *Annual Review of Sociology,* 36, 225–247.

Stichweh, Rudolf (1994) *Wissenschaft, Universität, Professionen: soziologische Analysen,* Frankfurt am Main, Suhrkamp.

Strauß, Bernhard & Kohl, Steffi (2009) Entwicklung der Psychotherapie und der Psychotherapieausbildung in europäischen Ländern. *Psychotherapeut,* 54, 457–463.

Streeck, Wolfgang (1997) Beneficial Constraints: On the Economic Limits of Rational Voluntarism. in (Eds.) Hollingsworth, J. Rogers & Boyer, Robert *Contemporary Capitalism: The Embeddedness of Institutions.* Cambridge: Cambridge University Press, 197–219.

Streeck, Wolfgang (2011) Skills and Politics – General and Specific. *MPIfG Discussion Paper 11/ 1.* Cologne, Max Planck Institute for the Study of Societies.

Streeck, Wolfgang & Thelen, Kathleen Ann (2005) Introduction: Institutional Change in Advanced Political Economies. in Streeck, Wolfgang & Thelen, Kathleen Ann (Eds.) *Beyond continuity: institutional change in advanced political economies.* Oxford, Oxford University Press, 1–39.

Sugarman, Léonie (2001) *Life-span development: frameworks, accounts, and strategies,* London, Routledge.

Sullivan, Sherry E. & Baruch, Yehuda (2009) Advances in Career Theory and Research: A Critical Review and Agenda for Future Exploration. *Journal of Management,* 35, 1542–1571.

Sung, Johnny, Turbin, Jill & Ashton, David (2000) Towards a Framework for the Comparative Analysis of National Systems of Skill Formation. *International Journal of Training and Development,* 4, 8–25.

Tamm, Auni (2008a) LLL2010 – Subproject 4 – Case Study 43 – Estonia: Formal adult education as a part of HRM. Production Company, Institute for international and social studies, Tallinn University.

Tamm, Auni (2008b) LLL2010 – Subproject 4 – Case Study 38 – Estonia: Formal adult education as a strategic resource for growth. Business to business., Institute for international and social studies, Tallinn University.

Taniguchi, Hiromi & Kaufman, Gayle (2007) Belated entry: Gender differences and similarities in the pattern of nontraditional college enrolment. *Social Science Research,* 36 550–568.

EDC/CSHD SP4 PROJECT TEAM (2008) LLL2010 – Subproject 4 – Case Study 48 – Ireland: SP4 – Case Study 4. Print and Packaging, St. Patrick's College (EDC/CSHD).

Thelen, Kathleen (2004) *How Institutions Evolve – The Political Economy of Skills in Germany, Britain, the United States, and Japan*, Cambridge: Cambridge University Press.

Thornton, Patricia H. & Ocasio, William (1999) Institutional Logics and the Historical Contingency of Power in Organizations: Executive Succession in the Higher Education Publishing Industry. *The American Journal of Sociology,* 105, 801–843.

Tippelt, Rudolf & Barz, Heiner (Eds.) (2004) *Weiterbildung und soziale Milieus in Deutschland – Band 2: Adressaten- und Milieuforschung zu Weiterbildungsverhalten und -interessen*, Bielefeld, Bertelsmann Verlag.

Tippelt, Rudolf, Reich, Jutta, Hippel, Aiga von, Barz, Heiner & Baum, Dajana (2008) *Weiterbildung und soziale Milieus in Deutschland – Band 3: Milieumarketing implementieren*, Bielefeld, Bertelsmann Verlag.

Trow, Martin (1973) Problems in the Transition from Elite to Mass Higher Education. Carnegie Commission on Higher Education.

Trow, Martin (2005) Reflections on the Transition from Elite to Mass to Universal Access: Forms and Phases of Higher Education in Modern Societies since WWII. Berkeley, Institute of Governmental Studies, UC Berkeley.

Tuijnman, Albert C. (1996) Recurrent Education. in Tuijnman, Albert C. (Ed.) *International encyclopedia of adult education and training.* Oxford [u.a.], Pergamon Press, 99–106.

Tuijnman, Albert & Boström, Ann-Kristin (2002) Changing notions of lifelong education and lifelong learning. *International Review of Education*, 48, 93–110.

Turner, Ralph H. (1960) Sponsored and contest mobility and the school system. *American Sociological Review,* 25, 855–867.

UNESCO, International Commission on the Development of Education, Faure, Edgar, Herrera, Felipe, Kaddoura, Abdul-Razzak, Lopes, Henri, Petrovsky, Arthur V., Rahnema, Majid & Ward, Frederick Champion (1972) *Learning to be. The world of education today and tomorrow*, Paris, UNESCO – London: Harrap.

UNESCO (1975) Manual for the Collection of Adult Education Statistics. Office of Statistics.

UNESCO (1979) Terminology of adult education, Paris.

UNESCO, United Nations Educational Scientific and Cultural Organization (1997 [Reedition 2006]) International Standard Classification of Education (ISCED 1997).

[UOE] UNESCO, OECD & EUROSTAT (2010a) UOE data collection on education systems – Volume 1 – Manual Concepts, definitions and classifications. Montreal, Paris, Luxembourg.

[UOE] UNESCO, OECD & EUROSTAT (2010b) UOE data collection on education systems – Volume 2 – Manual Concepts, definitions and classifications. Montreal, Paris, Luxembourg.

[UOE] UNESCO, OECD & EUROSTAT (2010c) UOE data collection on education systems – Volume 3 – Manual Concepts, definitions and classifications. Montreal, Paris, Luxembourg.

University of Florence, Deutsches Institut für Erwachsenenbildung (DIE) & Institutul Român De Educatie a Adultilor (IREA) (2010) Enabling the low skilled to take their qualifications 'one step up' – Implementation of the Action plan on adult learning: Final Report: Key Factors Analysis and Final Recommendations – Report on behalf of the European Commission. Florence.

Ure, Odd Bjørn & Bjørg, Eva Aaslid (2008) LLL2010 – Subproject 4 – Case Study 52 – Norway: In-company training is important to secure the quality of the employees. A case study of XY Metals Norway., Fafo, Institute for Labour and Social Research.

Van Den Berg, Peter T. & Wilderom, Celeste P.M. (2004) Defining, Measuring, and Comparing Organisational Cultures. *Applied Psychology: An International Review,* 53, 570 –582.

Vermeersch, Lode & De Rick, Katleen (2008a) LLL2010 – Subproject 4 – Case Study 28 – Belgium: Case study – SME 5, HIVA – Higher Institute of Labour Studies.

Vermeersch, Lode & De Rick, Katleen (2008b) LLL2010 – Subproject 4 – Case Study 25 – Belgium: Case study – SME 2, HIVA – Higher Institute of Labour Studies.

Vroom, Victor Harold (1964) *Work and Motivation*, New York, John Wiley & Sons.

Wakeford, Nina (1993) Beyond Educating Rita: mature students and access courses. *Oxford Review of Education*, 19, 217 – 230.

Walgenbach, Peter & Meyer, Renate E. (2008) *Neoinstitutionalistische Organisationstheorie*, Stuttgart, Kohlhammer.

Werner, Emmy E. (1990) Protective Factors and Individual Resilience. in Meisels, Samuel J. & Shonkoff, Jack P. (Eds.) *Handbook of early childhood intervention.* Cambridge, Cambridge University Press, 97–116.

Werner, Heinz, König, Ingeborg, Bennet, Roger & Scott-Leuteritz, Karen (2004) *IAB Glossar English*, Nürnberg, IAB.

West, Linden (1996) *Beyond fragments: adults, motivation, and higher education: a biographical analysis*, London, Taylor & Francis.

White, Harrison Colyar (1970) *Chains of opportunity: system models of mobility in organizations*, Cambridge (Mass.), Harvard University Press.

Whitley, Richard (2007) *Business systems and organizational capabilities: the institutional structuring of competitive competences,* Oxford, Oxford University Press.

Wiseman, Alexander W. (2010) The Uses of Evidence for Educational Policymaking: Global Contexts and International Trends. *Review of research in education*, 34, 1–24.

Wittchen, Hans-Ulrich & Jacobi, Frank (2005) Size and burden of mental disorders in Europe – a critical review and appraisal of 27 studies. *European Neuropsychopharmacology,* 15, 357–376.

Wolfe, Donald, O'Connor, Dennis & Crary, Marcy (1990) Transformations of Life Structure and Personal Paradigm During the Midlife Transition. *Human Relations,* 43, 957–973.

Woodward, Joan (1965) *Industrial Organization: Theory and Practice*, Oxford: Oxford University Press.

Wooten, Melissa & Hoffman, Andrew J. (2008) Organizational Fields: Past, Present and Future. in Greenwood, Royston, Oliver, Christine, Sahlin, Kerstine & Suddaby, Roy (Eds.) *The SAGE handbook of organizational institutionalism.* Los Angeles, Calif. [u.a.], Sage Publ., 130–147.